On-Line Profits

ON-LINE PROFITS

A MANAGER'S GUIDE TO ELECTRONIC COMMERCE

PETER G.W. KEEN AND CRAIGG BALLANCE

Harvard Business School Press
Boston, Massachusetts

01 00 99 98 97   5 4 3 2 1

Library of Congress Cataloging-in-Publication Data

Keen, Peter G. W.
   On-line profits : a manager's guide to electronic commerce /
Peter G.W. Keen and Craigg Ballance.
      p.   cm.
   Includes index.
   ISBN 0-87584-790-0 (hc : alk. paper). —ISBN 0-87584-821-4
(pb :   alk. paper)
   1. Electronic commerce.   I. Ballance, Craigg, 1954–   .
II. Title.
HF5548.32.K43   1997
658.8′00285—DC21   97-11882
                                                    CIP

The paper used in this publication meets the requirements of the
American National Standard for Permanence of Paper for Printed
Library Materials Z39.49-1984.

As always, my thanks and appreciation to my family, and my gratitude to Tracy Torregrossa for masterminding the turning of these words into a real book.
—*Peter Keen*

Many thanks to all those who helped in the writing of this book, particularly my wife and family for their unending support and John McNeil for his insights into ERS.
—*Craigg Ballance*

Contents

Introduction

Electronic Commerce: How Fast, How Soon?

Electronic commerce is the use of computers and telecommunications in the routine business transactions that most affect the basics of an organization's operations: everyday relationships with suppliers, customers, banks, insurers, distributors, and other trading partners. Already nearly as common and essential to the business mainstream as the telephone, electronic commerce is no longer considered the domain of high-tech "computer people." Use of the most established components of electronic commerce—electronic data interchange and electronic corporate payments—has been growing for over a decade at rates of around 20 percent a year and is rapidly becoming the norm in business.

Once electronic commerce becomes the norm, it will be a competitive necessity, not an option. Technological improvements have accelerated and extended the proven and steady applications of electronic commerce in the 1990s. The combination of low-cost, high-performance telecommunications and personal computers led to the astonishing emergence of the Internet as a marketing channel for business. A telecommunications infrastructure that is opening electronic commerce to small firms as well as large, the Internet is a vehicle for companies to rapidly develop both internal and external information and communication systems. It seems, from the recent growth in use of the World Wide Web, that the "Net" will eventually be a massive market for almost every type of business. The big question is whether over-loaded communications lines, which are already causing current Internet users delays and frustration, will curtail Internet use. Will the users who persist be limited to the narrow electronic commerce community of mainly professional males, with well above average incomes, who use the Internet largely for electronic mail and who are currently the demographic core of Internet users? It is more likely that telecommunications companies will find ways to ease the traffic jam on the information highway so that growth can continue.

Electronic commerce is the most efficient way to do business in an era when telecommunications allows more and more options for customer contact. The main benefit is savings in the costs of doing business. Computer-to-computer processing of transactions between customers and suppliers and, to a far lesser extent as yet, between companies and customers, eliminates documents and the overhead and administration associated with them. If it's the most efficient—the best—way to do business, then it's obviously something every manager needs to make part of his or her thinking. That's what this book is about: providing business managers with a nonhype, nontechnical, reliable, and interesting guide to this new business territory.

Today's managers need this guide. The value of electronic commerce can be difficult to measure, and even more challenging to explain, for several reasons.

First, electronic commerce, or EC, is not just a single technology or tool: it is a combination of technologies, applications, processes, and business strategies. Managers savvy about both business processes and strategy may not know much about, and may even be intimidated by, EC technology and put off by its jargon. The best EC technical professionals have enough to do just to keep up with the technology and may not appreciate the realities of process and organization that business managers face and may thus be unable to offer much guidance.

EC cannot be accomplished by any single enterprise working alone, regardless of the quality of its technologies or business strategies. Like any other means of commerce, EC is fundamentally about business relationships. Managing the relationship is the starting point for managing electronic commerce, the first priority. Then comes managing processes and technology.

A third important fact to understand when getting started in electronic commerce is that EC systems and procedures must be consistent with each industry's practices, relationships, and power structures. Because EC concerns relationships between enterprises, its progress depends heavily on industry associations and working groups to define the *standards*—the formats and procedures—for electronic relationships. In the automotive industry, for example, electronic commerce got in gear when competitors collaborated through what is now the Automotive Industry Advisory Group. By contrast, progress in using electronic data interchange (EDI) in healthcare was long blocked by the fragmentation of the healthcare industry: hospitals, insurers, government agencies such as Medicaid, pharmacists, and others were using different forms for recording information and different formats for exchanging information. Much of the impetus in EDI in various industries came because power players in an industry required their suppliers to adopt the new way of doing business. When a Wal-Mart or a Toyota invests in electronic commerce, it inevitably changes its suppliers' role in the supply chain, necessitating *their* investment in EC. The power player thus strengthens ties with its main electronic partners, eliminates trade with suppliers that lack the EC capability, and reduces the total number of companies it works with. Power players that have switched to electronic commerce have changed the very nature of the supply process, eliminating invoices, allowing suppliers to monitor and replenish inventory without purchase orders, and scheduling payment for goods when they are used rather than when they are delivered. These changes have introduced terms to the vocabulary of electronic commerce that may mystify the uninitiated business manager, such as "evaluated receipts settlements," "vendor-managed inventory," and "paid on production."

The goals of this Manager's Guide are to demystify electronic commerce, establish its value, orient managers to the key technical issues, and help them make EC part of their own planning.

The value of EC is HUGE! Electronic commerce has already provided three major benefits to enterprise. We use the past tense because we are not making any of the wild predictions that litter books and articles about the promised wonders of information technology. Electronic commerce is proven, not potential. The potential is even bigger, but as you read this guide, you won't need to think, "Yeah, sounds great, but where's the evidence?" We offer plenty of evidence and examples that electronic commerce:

- Reduces the *cost* of creating, moving, managing, and processing individual documents, transactions, and other forms of information exchange between enterprises. The savings per transaction are often well over 80 percent, an opportunity no organization can afford to neglect. We could fill an entire book with figures showing how companies cut the cost of processing purchase orders, invoices, and payments from $50 to $5 or $5 to 50 cents.

- Transforms *relationships* between trading organizations to their mutual benefit, because the information flows are more timely, coordinated, and accurate when sent and processed electronically—thus improving the quality of decisions made by management.

- Opens up additional *channels* through which to market and sell products and services. The Internet is the most obviously alluring channel, but in business-to-business commerce electronic links have opened up many opportunities to reach out to customers through new levels of convenience, location-independent service, and the lean structures often termed "the virtual organization." The lower price of electronic channels can also reduce costs and increase profitability. Many of the best examples of the value of EC are in the manufacturing, transportation, and retail industries, because these were the first industries to implement electronic data interchange more than 10 years ago.

- Simplifies and streamlines business *processes,* removing administration, delays, errors, and overhead.

- Directly and fairly immediately contributes to *shareholder value,* through reductions in working capital that has a direct carrying cost: inventories, accounts receivable, and in-transit goods.

Electronic commerce is a means to a business end. Improvement of costs, relationships, channels, processes, and shareholder value is the goal. Technology is the enabler. The main technology-based tools of EC are (1) *electronic data interchange,* the elimination of all the paper, steps, delays, and errors that burden companies with their cost and impede service, flexibility, and responsiveness; (2) *electronic money management;* and (3) *electronic logistics* that integrate the firm's supply chain. EC also uses electronic tools in the relationship between consumers and business. The most familiar example is the automated teller machine, or ATM, which has changed the basics of banking. Its less mature cousins, the debit card, which debits the customer's checking account at point of sale, and the "smart card," such as the prepaid phone card, are gaining momentum. Meanwhile, the Internet and the World Wide Web enlarge the electronic commerce matrix. Among the tools rapidly emerging are secure payment mechanisms for on-line purchasing; electronic catalogs, store fronts, and malls; electronic cash, an application that is as yet unproven; extensions of credit cards; on-line banking services; and on-line business-to-business information sharing.

Most of the applications of electronic commerce are undramatic, and businesses typically delegate the functions they address to administrative units. It is easy for executives to consider processing and issuing purchase orders and collecting accounts receivable, for instance, as just part of the background activities of the firm—administrative operations that are obviously important but in no way "strategic." Electronic commerce makes such operations truly strategic for the simple reason that it entirely changes the nature of business relationships and the profitability of a firm in relation to its competitors. The three types of relationship affected are person to person, person to computer, and computer to computer. These three categories define the general interactions that are driving the practical applications of EC technology and processes today.

Person-to-Person Interactions

Most often person-to-person contact is by electronic mail, fax, or 1-800 telephone numbers. The driving application is obviously communication between people, those who send a request or order and those who receive and interpret it. The electronic part of this interaction is the network that conveys messages. Person-to-person commerce has been growing rapidly because of the availability of the Internet and subscription services for using it, such as America Online and CompuServe. The combination of competition and technology innovation has also produced low-cost fax machines for transmitting documents virtually instantaneously, as well as fax features built into personal computers. The same combination has led to a rapid drop in telecommunications prices. The result is the growth of person-to-person commerce. The primary advantage of this type of relationship is its flexibility. The other types of electronic commerce—person-to-computer and computer-to-computer—require structuring procedures and ensuring that there are no ambiguities of terms. The disadvantage of person-to-person electronic communication is the administration, facilities, and time required for simple transactions. Such transactions can be handled more conveniently through a person-to-computer relationship, since the computer stays awake all day and night, and transactions cost just cents and seconds to process. Getting your credit card balance by pushbutton phone and computerized voice response is a good example.

Person-to-Computer Interactions

This is the area of electronic commerce where there has been the most widespread and visible activity over the past several decades, ranging from the automated teller machine to electronic cash management services and most recently to electronic purchases via the Internet. Person-to-computer commerce delivers services by means of a *template*—a script the computer follows in its questions and responses to the customer—or preformatted menus of options, controlled by a computer program. The fixed scripts can lead to inflexible and irritating dialog structures; there's no human common sense to correct obvious errors, say to recognize names (as when the person on the phone gives her name as Jean Grogan, while the computer software must have it as Grogan, Jean), or to accept shorthand inputs such as "Philly" or extended ones such as "Philadelphia, Pennsylvania," and so on. Designing the dialog for phone access to computers or for transactions on the World Wide Web is an art. A lot of potential users bail out after the fifth "Press 1 to . . ., Press 2 to . . ."

Computer-to-Computer Interactions

Corporate applications of electronic commerce have focused on computer-to-computer interactions. The output of one computer program becomes the input to another. The system that used to generate a printed purchase order and mail it to the supplier now sends the purchase order as an electronic data interchange message to a computer at the supplier's facility. The order is automatically, electronically received and input by the supplier's own order-processing software and does not have to be keyed in. Payments are similarly automatic, with electronic funds

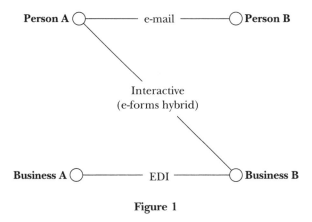

Figure 1

transfers (EFT) replacing checks. It makes no sense to spend $50 on paper and people when two computers can structure the transaction for a few cents. As a result, more and more large firms that already had comprehensive computer systems and data communication networks handling all their outgoing commercial documents started to adopt EDI and EFT in the early 1980s. That meant requiring trading partners to adopt their "proprietary" systems, which used company-, software-, or hardware-specific formats and protocols. The dependence on firm-specific, proprietary systems was as inconvenient as if person-to-person electronic commerce relationships depended entirely on which make of fax machine each party used. The entire evolution in computer-to-computer EC has been to remove as many restrictions as possible on *which* computers could be used.

Figure 1 is a simple representation of the matrix of electronic commerce interactions, each of which has its role and value for every business.

Electronic Commerce as Competitive Necessity

Imagine trying to run a company today without telephones and fax machines, telling your customers and suppliers that you only do business by mail. How about trying to run a company in the year 2000 without the basic tools of electronic commerce? Without electronic data interchange for handling purchase orders and invoicing, without electronic payments, and without electronic links between your own logistical processes and those of your key trading partners that streamline the entire supply chain? We all take phones and fax for granted today. On the rare occasions the phone system is "down" for a few hours—or even a few minutes— business comes to a halt. The phoneless company is the businessless company. How soon will it be before we take electronic commerce just as much for granted and the EC-deficient company becomes the business-deficient company? How soon will firms be as dependent on their EC base as they are on phones in the everyday operations that determine their quality of service, financial strength, efficiency, and speed?

The answer is "not long"—if not now, then certainly within the next three to five years, based on the compounded 20 percent annual growth over the past decade in just about every established area of electronic commerce. You don't need any wild hype about Information Supersomethings—Highways, Society, Age, or the like—to be sure that electronic commerce will at least double in the next four years. Doubling would merely continue the historical trend. Although it is harder to predict the growth rate for newer components, especially those that use the Internet to replace traditional buying and payment mechanisms, they are likely to spread at least as fast as the earlier ones. So, the minimal growth in EC is a doubling in four years; tripling is not unlikely.

It's not the raw numbers that matter, though. What matters is the priority of EC in business, the transition from a relatively minor element of largely administrative functions to an integral component of business basics. What matters most is the acceptance of electronic commerce as the basic way to conduct business. The more competitive the industry and the greater the pressures to improve service, cut costs, and speed up operations, the more quickly electronic commerce becomes a business priority.

The tie between competitiveness and electronic capability has been apparent in the automotive industry and in retailing. About

20 years ago, North American automobile manufacturers were challenged by foreign imports and were being beaten at their own game. Many commentators saw American car makers as an endangered species, as Chrysler, Ford, and General Motors went through crisis after crisis. Today, they are in good shape, having moved aggressively, if belatedly, to improve quality, following the path of Toyota; to speed up time to market, again following Toyota; and to exploit electronic commerce, way in advance of Toyota. Many of the key innovations in EDI came from the North American auto industry, including evaluated receipts settlement (payment on receipt of goods, with no invoice) as well as the concept called advance shipment notice and "paid on production." The Automotive Industry Advisory Group, originally named the Transportation Data Coordinating Committee, pioneered in bringing together competitors to cooperate so that they could all benefit from common procedures and formats necessary for practical electronic transactions. Today, if you were to ask any of the "Big Three" automakers what business without EC would be like, the only reasonable answer would be that there would *be* no business, for without EC and EDI they would have ceased to be competitive: they would no longer exist. These giant firms cannot even contemplate using paper and people today the way they did just a decade ago. And the evolution continues.

That evolution is built on electronic data interchange, the core or innermost circle of electronic commerce. EDI streamlines business processes. Electronic money management, the next circle or ring of the electronic commerce wheel, leverages the financial capital that is the fuel of profits. Electronic logistics, the outermost circle, which encompasses just about all the business relationships of a company, provide the support for the streamlined, process-smart organization that makes the most of every practical opportunity to simplify the basics of its business and to improve its speed, responsiveness, and reliability. Individually, these improvements typically improve the productivity of target processes by 20 to 40 percent. The processes are 20 to 40 percent faster and cheaper than beforehand, and have 20 to 40 percent fewer errors. *Together,* they make electronic commerce the base for running a firm well in the era of just-in-time everything—just-in-time production, distribution, service, and communication. The EC-less company of 2002—five years from the publication of this Manager's Guide—faces the following problems:

- Most large companies simply won't use the EC-less firm as a supplier. Already, many elite customers demand suppliers use EDI in their relationships with them.

- A company without EC will not be able to pay its taxes in a timely manner. Almost every state tax agency as well as the IRS is moving to require electronic filing and payment of taxes by medium to large firms.

- The EC-less firm will be unable to bid on many commercial contracts since those will be posted on the Internet and processed electronically. Government agencies and such large companies as General Electric are publishing most of their requests for bids onto the World Wide Web.

- The cost of operating without EC will be an administrative and overhead burden that is like a tax on the firm's operations, a tax that its competitors who engage in EC do not have to pay. Nearly every study of EDI shows that it slashes transaction costs by a factor of 5 to 10, so it's crazy for any firm not to exploit this proven opportunity.

- The EC-less firm will waste money on every financial transaction it makes; this is like sticking a check in a drawer for a few months instead of cashing it. Electronic payment systems, funds transfers, automated clearing houses, and Financial EDI (FEDI) are the money equivalent of just-in-time inventory and lean production—they are just-in-time and on-time cash management.

- It will be unable to match the streamlining of core processes that the leaders in its industry have already made.

- Finally, without electronic commerce, the firm will be just a little slower than its competition every year, just a little more expensive, just a little less reliable, and in the end just a lot less successful. The process-smart leaders in retailing, manufacturing, financial services, distribution, and transportation are 50 percent more productive in terms of revenues per employee and profits per employee than the *median* for their industry. (To verify these figures, glance at *Business Week*'s and *Fortune*'s quarterly reports on corporate performance.)

None of these are radical predictions. As the 1990s draw to a close, managers can no longer afford the equivalent of St. Augustine's famous prayer, "Oh Lord, make me chaste—but not yet.": Oh Lord, let's implement electronic commerce—but not till next year. As the many examples scattered throughout the glossary of this Manager's Guide clearly indicate, it's time to move. Electronic commerce is the opportunity of the 1990s, but it will be the necessity of 2002.

The Components of Electronic Commerce

Electronic Data Interchange:
A Foundation Block for the Sound Business

Electronic data interchange is one of the two foundation blocks of EC; the other is electronic payments. EDI is computer-to-computer communication of business messages in agreed-on standard codes and formats. These codes allow direct, automatic, instantaneous input of messages to transaction-processing systems without requiring human handling or rekeying on the receiver's end. The most obvious applications are in order entry, payments, and distribution. It's a simple concept that requires relatively simple technology. The complexity lies in the organizational changes needed to exploit the technical opportunity and in the vital need to build cooperation, collaboration, and trust among all parties involved: business, suppliers, and customers. Trust is the currency of EDI.

The proven benefits of EDI are so substantial that it's hard to see why so many firms in industry after industry have not followed the lead of the pioneers, many of whom implemented it in the early 1980s. Here are some instances that were newsworthy just a few years ago but now are almost ho-hum:

- *Automotive manufacturers* cut processing and administrative costs from an average of $61 to $6 per truck shipment by eliminating invoices and other paper documents, using EDI to match order to delivery.

- *Digital Equipment Corporation* cut procurement lead times by 30% and inventory levels by 90% between 1987 and 1993 by using EDI for over $4 billion worth of procurement of materials, supplies, and services a year.

- *Thermo King,* a firm with $65 million sales, cut order costs from $50 to $10 for each of 20,000 spare parts items; with "hard" savings of $3.4 million in inventory-stocking costs and the release of $4.9 million of cash from reduced inventory.

- *General Electric* cut materials inventory from 7 weeks' supply to 2.5 and reduced suppliers' inventory by half. Material lead times dropped from 60 to 10 days and the cost of a purchase order from $52 to $12.

- *Pacific Bell* cut purchase cycle time by 13 days through the use of basic EDI, another 17 days by adding advanced shipment electronic notices and bar coding, and yet another 13 days by adding electronic funds transfers.

- *Grocery industry surveys* show that before EDI, almost 30% of supplier invoices were "in dispute" because of some processing error; with EDI, the figure is close to zero.
- *Texas Instruments* linked EDI to bar coding for tracking office supplies. The corporation also was able to free up 40,000 square feet of warehouse space, worth close to $1 million a year, cut inventory by $2 million, and reduce cycle time from 3 days to 1. Error rates at TI are now 1 in 10,000 orders where they once were 1 in 25.
- *IBM* in Fishkill, New York, reduced the number of purchase orders per year from 7,700 to 970 for the same volume of goods and reduced the number of suppliers from 718 to 8, with an average of 9% price cut in return for volumes. IBM also used EDI to cut a 6% error rate for incoming shipments to close to zero and to achieve a 65% savings in inventory carrying costs.
- *1,560 EDI users* surveyed in the United States in 1994 reported error rates cut from 10% to 4% and cycle time reduced by 40% on average.
- *One hundred car dealers* surveyed reported that they were able to cut the time needed to process paper-based car loan applications from 1 to 2 weeks to as short as 1 minute, with 25% of the applications requiring no human intervention.

The examples listed could be multiplied by, quite literally, a thousand. They range from straightforward and substantial savings in time and cost to more basic changes in the nature of customer–supplier relationships and transformation of logistical and supply chain processes. Any firm, large or small, can gain these benefits. The technical risks are minimal, and provided issues of training, incentives, communication, and project management are handled carefully and explicitly, implementation is increasingly straightforward. So, it makes little sense for a firm *not* to adopt a way of doing business that is well-proven, increasingly inexpensive in terms of both capital investment and operating costs, and ever more convenient and simple in terms of technology, especially with the Internet and value-added network providers offering the telecommunications facilities that previously demanded strong in-house technical expertise.

So far, though, relatively few firms have seized this opportunity for profit. Most estimates are that fewer than 20 percent of large firms have embedded EDI in the core of their business operations. An executive of one of the largest providers of EDI software commented in mid-1996 that he knew of around 40,000 companies using EDI—a small proportion of the 2 million firms in the United States. There are plenty of reasons for the slow adoption of EDI, despite its proven payoff. They are the same reasons that apply to all innovations in the application of information technology that change organization, process, and skill needs: (1) initial overselling and false expectations followed by disillusion and dismissal of the concept; (2) underestimation of the challenges of meshing technical change with organizational change; (3) lack of interest, commitment, and policy guidance on the part of senior business management; (4) a bewildering proliferation of hardware, software, telecommunications, and information components that too often were "incompatible"; and (5) the lack of precise, agreed-on, consistent, and widely available EDI "standards" for message formats and contents.

Most of these excuses for postponing the switch to electronic commerce represented very tough problems in the 1980s, when the pioneers in EDI, mostly in the automotive and retailing industries, had no base of experience to guide them, lacked cheap and efficient technology, and had to start from scratch in setting standards. As a result, what may be termed First Wave EDI was dominated by proprietary systems defined by companies with sufficient clout in the marketplace both to fund their deployment, often giving free software to suppliers, and to force suppliers to adopt them. Ford, General Motors, Sears, and RJ Reynolds are just a few examples of pacesetters. Each of these corporations announced to suppliers in the 1980s that within a given period they would no longer accept paper invoices and that purchase orders would be processed via electronic links. The supplier had to adopt the powerful customer's systems and formats, meaning that in order to serve different customers, the supplier would have to handle multiple software systems. An extreme of this situation has been in healthcare, where each hospital would have had to comply with literally several hundred different document formats in order to process insurance claims and payments. This obviously blocked the development of EDI in some industries and made transactions administratively costly, complex, and prone to errors and delays.

Historically, the relationship between large customers and their suppliers prior to the emergence of EDI was largely adversarial rather than cooperative (and so it remains in some instances). Companies carefully guarded information, in order to gain an advantage in negotiations. They often played suppliers off against each other, looking for an ever better deal in price and terms of payment. They would exploit the opportunity of slow payments to smaller suppliers who needed their business, while insisting that smaller customers pay more quickly. EDI began and continues a shift toward far more trusting and cooperative arrangements, which eventually is likely to be the most far-reaching consequence of electronic commerce. In the First Wave, though, some companies continued to exploit their power advantage, not sharing the benefits they themselves gained from the introduction of EDI. Gradually, however, more and more of them recognized that they would gain by, first, encouraging cooperative long-term relationships with a smaller number of suppliers and, second, sharing information with suppliers in order to optimize the entire supply chain and improve every partner's costs and processes.

Old habits die slowly, though. One of the authors of this book remembers working in 1991 with a major food company that was being forced by a leading supermarket chain to adopt its EDI system. The head of production literally thumped the table at a meeting and expressed his opposition by saying "XYZ [the firm's largest competitor] isn't the enemy. [The supermarket] is." Imagine. The customer as the enemy! He argued cogently, though, that the supermarket chain would squeeze the company, demanding ever speedier delivery at increasingly short notice, which it did. He saw immense costs in introducing new computer systems, disliked the idea that the customer would demand access to the firm's inventory data bases, and all in all preferred the old days when both parties jostled each other in competitive cooperation.

Second Wave EDI, today's standard practice and the imminent competitive necessity for the well-run firm, is far different. Collaboration drives innovation now. First, the standard-setting process, the key to extending EDI across types of transaction and across industries, has become quite literally routine. Instead of proprietary standards, there are now two related families of standards, ANSI X12 and EDIFACT. The American National Standards Institute, known by the acronym ANSI, is a huge cooperative organization that provides a forum where interested parties can work together to define, vote on, and publish standards. It has become the home for electronic data interchange, its Accredited Standards Committee, known as X12, producing EDI transaction sets in many different areas, including the following examples:

- *Air transportation.* Air freight details (X12 110), shipment status message (114), rate update (129)

- *General.* Invoice (810), credit/debit adjustment (812), tax information reporting (826), contract award (836), request for quotation (840), purchase order (850), shipping schedule (862), report of test results (863), notice of employment status (540)

- *Warehousing.* Shipping order (940), stock-transfer shipment notice (943)

- *Healthcare.* Claims/payment advice (835), patient information request (274), eligibility inquiry (270)

- *Phone service.* Bills (811)

- *Retailing and wholesaling.* Price sales catalog transaction (832)

- *Government.* An electronic equivalent of a levy or garnishment order that can be sent to such agencies as Health and Human Services, Treasury, and Social Security by an agency charged with collecting delinquent child support payments (521); electronic tax filing (813)

- *Mortgage applications.* Appraisal request (261)

This list gives just a flavor of the wide range of X12 standards. To these may be added more technical standards developed by computer and telecommunications providers. There's also a whole alphabet soup of industry association standards (many spelled out in the glossary of this book), such as ACH (bank payments), AIAG (automotive), ASN (advance shipment notice), EDIFACT (international trade), TFX (tax payments), VICS (retailing), and WINS (warehousing). Cooperation is thus the core of EDI, far more than technology, as numerous ANSI subcommittees continually work on EDI transaction sets for mortgage applications, payment of utility bills, processing of health insurance claims, and electronic catalogs of prices and products for drug wholesalers, among hundreds of applications.

The automotive industry became the leader in EDI when the major manufacturers abandoned their efforts to impose their own firms' systems and standards and set up the Automotive Industry Action Group (AIAG), whose rationale, and indeed that of EDI in general, was summarized by its executive director in late 1996:

> In today's industry, communication and interaction throughout the supply chain is critical. More than 60 percent of the cost of a new vehicle comes from the supply chain. . . . and the way to minimize that cost while protecting profits is to work together as an industry on precompetitive issues, eliminating waste and streamlining processes. . . . that is why AIAG was created (*EDI Insider,* November 10, 1996).

Retailing and banking have their own cooperative associations. Internationally, EDIFACT, a cooperative forum analogous to ANSI's X12 Accredited Standards Committee was set up under the aegis of the United Nations to focus on international EDI, producing transaction sets for trade documentation, insurance, customs, and the like. ANSI and EDIFACT work harmoniously together.

Standardization, the shift from proprietary to "open" standards in electronic commerce, has meant that more and more EDI transaction sets are being added by the year, and that the costs of implementing the software get lower and lower. The wide ANSI/EDIFACT base means that general-purpose software facilitates straightforward additions to existing EDI capabilities, just as the Microsoft Windows operating system enables users to add applications to their personal computers without needing someone to write additional programs. A growing support industry translates firms' transaction data to and from relevant transaction sets, handles issues of technical conversion between different types of computer, provides technical expertise, and in many instances takes over all the functions needed for EDI operations. These *value added networks* (VANs) and EDI "hubs" are, again, part of the cooperative drive of electronic commerce. Insurance Value Added Network Services (IVANS), for instance, is a VAN set up in 1983 to handle everything from telecommunications transmission to consulting in electronic commerce for the insurance industry. It offers what it calls an electronic pathway for more than 500 firms and a total of 1 million users. Many of the firms on this network are competitors, but they use the pathway to gain economies everywhere, receiving telecommunications discounts of 25 to 50 percent through IVANS' massive buying power, as well as the benefits of IVANS' technological expertise, centralized network management, and software support.

This style of coordination and resource-sharing is spreading to previously fragmented industries. For example, the healthcare industry's hundreds of different formats, codes, forms, and procedures now necessary for handling the same relatively simple process of authorizing and paying insurance claims are being transformed to an industry standard through ANSI X12 835, a transaction set established by the Working Group on EDI. The Group, which includes representatives from all parties in healthcare responded to its first challenge by defeating an effort by the U.S. Health Care Management Administration (HCMA) to impose its own preferred standard on the industry (that agency has a lot of clout as it funds half of Medicare). It took executive action by the White House to warn HCMA off and let the ethos of collaboration move the industry ahead. Once the Working Group on EDI had agreed on its new X12 standards, its members voted to choose a single provider to operate a shared healthcare VAN. They chose Baxter Travenol, one of the longest-established players in customer–supplier electronic links for hospital and pharmacy supplies.

Second Wave EDI has benefited from the accelerating improvement in almost every area of telecommunications, the technology key to collaboration, coordination, and communication. Deregulation, which took place only in 1984 and affected only long-distance telephone carriers, rapidly lowered telecom costs, improved service, and brought new providers into national and international markets. Many of the new providers focused on services for business-to-business data communication (i.e., non-voice communication) in general and for EDI in particular. Deregulation of the U.S. telecommunications industry having been completed in 1996, both cost and services are expected to expand and improve even further.

In the First Wave of EDI, trading partners—the electronic commerce term for companies routinely involved with each other in buying, selling, moving, and paying for goods and services—had to link to slow and expensive "private" networks, which large firms leased to them on a monthly basis. A number of value-added networks were in effect privately run facilities operated by industry associations or third parties to be used for EDI transactions.

All in all, the telecommunications part of EDI was complex and expensive.

Now, it is neither. The established value-added networks of the 1980s have evolved into EDI utilities that serve as hubs through which large and small companies can quickly start up their EDI operations, add new trading partners, or incorporate new transaction sets. Rapidly dropping prices for computers have also shifted EDI from a software application run on midsized and large mainframe computers to a network application distributed across many low-cost, high-speed desktop devices. Personal computers in doctors' offices, car dealerships, stores, or anywhere else can handle the "front end" of the EDI transactions. Servers which are more powerful PCs with sophisticated telecommunications and large data storage capabilities, coordinate the flow of message traffic and information into and out of the hub and translate data from one standard format and transaction set to others. Within the hub, larger computers coordinate the overall processing. The use of PCs at the front end, on the user's desktop, made EDI available to small as well as large firms. It also enabled the rapid diffusion of EDI software.

Together, cooperation and technology extended EDI to more and more companies within a community of trading partners. The EDI Group provides reliable and comprehensive surveys of EDI growth, use, and cost. Its figures for 1995 show not only that EDI is highly affordable but also that it is no longer the luxury of the large firm. The Group estimates that it costs only about $2,000 to add to a hub a trading partner that is new to EDI, and under $3,000 to add a new transaction set. The time an inexperienced new trading partner needs to begin using EDI is only about three weeks; an experienced partner needs only half that time. A transaction set can be implemented in just two weeks. And whereas as recently as 1993, companies using EDI had an average of 1,200 staff, in 1995 the number had dropped to just under 200. EDI is now in the mainstream of small as well as large business. Much of the reason for this, of course, is that small businesses are suppliers to large ones. Surveys continue to show that most companies state that the primary factor in their decision to adopt EDI is that a key supplier demanded they do so.

The Third Wave of EDI is gathering speed and height. The new driving force is most obviously the Internet, but that's really just the cresting of the Second Wave. The Net augments rather than changes the mainstream of EDI, simply providing access from and to anyone in the world who has a PC and an Internet address. It extends the reach of telecommunications and dramatically cuts costs for small-volume users. That opens up EDI for more and more trading relationships, including business-to-consumer electronic commerce. One of the developments well underway is the use of the Internet for electronic billing by utilities, using new ANSI transaction sets, for instance.

All this is valuable and innovative, but it's mainly a continuation of today's mainstream, which was in itself an augmentation of the First Wave. The next wave will surely be bigger, too. Some commentators expect a tsunami, a massive tidal wave that crashes on the shore and wrecks the physical structures of existing businesses—the Internet Electronic Commerce Powerwave. Instead of just "surfing the Web," we'll all then be trying to stay afloat and not drown. The wave could indeed drown us but probably won't. The wilder visions of a Wired Future may well come to pass in time, but over the next 10 years, we expect the same gradual evolution as over the past 10: continued progress in standards, ever-improving technology, frequent hype and overselling, rapidly dropping costs, and EDI increasingly taking over earlier practices.

What will make the Third Wave the biggest wave to date is the convergence of EDI and electronic payments and the emergence of EDI as the base for integrated logistics not just electronic administration. The impetus is simply the demands of business in a very competitive environment, pressures on margins and prices, the demand for quality as a basic rather than a premium to be charged extra for (except on airlines!), service as the differentiator, and the vital need to eliminate waste everywhere. The human costs of this kind of change are often high, and it has to be admitted from the outset that one of the consequences of electronic commerce is the elimination of many jobs, mostly administrative links in the process chain. But it is the price firms must pay in order to survive. The best firms are streamlining, reengineering, or downsizing, to ensure their own survival and are ready to commit to and invest in people in order to empower them to operate in the new electronic commerce. The evidence that firms can at the same time use electronic commerce to eliminate jobs and create jobs is that the most noted leaders in electronic logistics—Federal Express and Wal-Mart, for instance—are still pretty good places to work. The laggards may still have the paper bureaucracies but they are being forced to downsize too.

Electronic Money Management: From Seashells to Gold to Bits

Electronic payments, the second fundamental building block of electronic commerce, are being extended toward the management of all aspects of money rather than just what is often termed Financial EDI (FEDI). It is electronic payments that have transformed the nature and scale of international foreign exchange trading, the movement of funds by banks and businesses worldwide, and cash management for firms' short-term investment. The figures are mind-numbingly large. For instance, while the physical exports of the two largest trading nations, the United States and Germany (Japan is only number 3), amount to around $800 billion a year, international foreign exchange trading is double that per *day*. New York City financial institutions process $1.5 trillion a day in electronic payments and trading transactions. London banks handle 40 percent of the world's foreign exchange trades; their weekly volumes are larger than the United Kingdom's gross domestic production. Two trillion dollars of funds transfers a day travel through a single international network, SWIFT, the Society for Worldwide Interbank Financial Telecommunications.

Electronic payment systems have been around for nearly 20 years. They have been almost entirely the province of banking, which provides them as a service mainly to large firms. The SWIFT network is owned by over 2,000 banks and handles transactions among almost 4,000 financial institutions in 88 countries. In the United States, the 30 regional automated clearing houses owned by associations of banks serve as the workhouse for corporate payments. The United Kingdom has its CHAPS (Clearing House for Automated Payments Systems), the United States its CHIPS (Clearing House Interbank Payments System).

The banks' systems have been the electronic support to the physical operations of companies. They are a somewhat old-fashioned and even unglamorous base first, for FEDI, which integrates payments into the business processes they are part of and, more recently, for the much more radical extension from corporate financial transactions to consumer–business interaction and the invention of new modes of service and new products. For many people in the information technology field, "electronic commerce" means electronic buying and selling, with the Internet as the key to the future. The Internet is a largely unproven element for which it may be many years before proven applications and tools emerge. It includes entirely new forms of electronic money, such as credit card payments and even new currencies. A few examples follow.

First Virtual Holdings. Customers sign up for the service by providing credit card information, which First Virtual Holdings stores offline, so that it cannot be tapped into over the Internet. Customers receive an ID number to use for transactions over the Net. The merchant does not know the identity of the purchaser except by this ID. Transactions are handled by a private telecommunications network, which updates the credit card account information. To confirm transactions, the system sends an electronic mail message (e-mail) a second or so after the purchase is made, to which the buyer must reply before the transaction can be completed. The merchant pays 29 cents per transaction plus 2 percent of the price of the goods sold. Since there is no transfer of funds over the Net, this is a simple and safe system, built on well-established infrastructures and processes. First Virtual had signed up close to 150,000 customers and 2,000 merchants by early 1997.

Bayshore Trust of Canada. One of the first banks to handle loans completely over the Internet, Bayshore Trust processes loans in around two minutes, offering a rate one-eighth percent lower than loans originated through its 16 branches, at one-tenth the overhead cost.

CyberCash. Customers set up bank accounts with funds specifically for spending on the Net. When they make purchases, money is directly transferred from the buyer's to the seller's CyberCash account. Each of the two parties pays a fee of 30 cents per transaction.

DigiCash. In the most radical approach to electronic payment, customers purchase "digital cash" ("Think of digital cash as the serial number on a dollar bill that has shed its paper body and entered the ether," *Wired,* August 1996) via their credit cards or bank accounts. Purchases are secure and anonymous since the serial numbers on the DigiCash are maintained by the merchant and bank and the merchant has no idea whatsoever of the buyer's identity. The transaction cost is kept low, about one-tenth of a cent. Unlike credit cards, which provide convenience but not privacy, DigiCash combines privacy, convenience, low transaction cost, and security over the Net.

Millicent. A system is being developed to handle very small purchases at very low cost. Today, the cost of processing a fee, say, a one cent fee for downloading a short piece of information from the Internet is many times more than the fee itself. Advocates of the World Wide Web anticipate that the ability to handle microcents or even nanocents (billionths of a cent) will be key in the longer term if the Web is to become a major base for electronic commerce. *Wired* comments: "Would-be barons of digital microeconomics say there is a potential annual market of several hundred billion dollars" (August 1996). Not if the transactions cost several hundreds of billions to process. *Wired* adds, "the only thing missing is the technology to really make it fly." Millicent offers an early approach to getting the new market off the ground. It involves "scrip"—fake money, like two-for-one coupons, food stamps, or gift certificates. In the proposed system, merchants create their own scrip—McDonald dollars, for example—which they sell to small brokers, who are well-established and well-trusted banks. Buyers buy currency from these brokers, who have the scale of operations to spread their own costs over a wide customer base. Anyone could tap into the requests for and transfer of the scrip, but the scrip is so small in value that the cost of transfer will be more than it's worth. The targeted transactions are as low as a cent, and the fee one-tenth of a cent.

Some of these proposals are pretty wild. In the meantime, firms require reliable and practical methods of handling the basics of money via electronic commerce as they now handle the basics of logistics via electronic data interchange. From a business (rather than technology) viewpoint, electronic payment systems are, first, an essential operating tool, and second, part of the move toward an entirely new but increasingly practical integration of paper, process, and payment. The vision for the future is like that of the Internet visionaries, with electronic money as the norm and cash and checks the occasional exception.

EDI began in the purchasing departments of manufacturing companies, whereas electronic payments began in banks, with electronic funds transfers in the early 1970s and electronic cash management taking off in the early 1980s. Telegraphing cash to stranded motorists or errant offspring via Western Union was one of the earliest consumer applications of this technology, but the main use has been to speed up the movement of money by large firms, first domestically and now globally.

Until recently, electronic payments and EDI were separate organizational functions that moved at a very different pace. Electronic payment systems focused on efficient and reliable movement of funds, with the banks in control. EDI control was in the hands of the most aggressive and innovative manufacturers and retailers, who forced the pace, extending its reach from purchasing and along the entire supply chain. For users of EDI, electronic payments mean more than funds transfers and cash management, the forte of banks. Rather, such payments are an integral part of just-in-time business logistics, an area where most banks have little expertise or even interest.

Now the action—as well as the risk and uncertainty—is in the financial side of electronic commerce. In order for the Internet to become a mass market shopping mall (1) credit card payments not only must be secure, which they already largely are, but also must be perceived by consumers to be secure, which they largely are not; (2) very small payments must be processed at an acceptably low transaction cost; and (3) all the many electronic transactions have to link easily and automatically into established systems for electronic banking payment.

It's hard to forecast how and when electronic payments will move from FEDI to electronic money. With FEDI, the money remains the same as before; bank balances, debits, and credits. It's basically a form of an electronic check plus an electronic letter providing instructions on where to deposit the money. The new mechanisms and media are very different. Consider, for instance, one current candidate for substituting bits for cash. Mondex, a company headquartered in Brussels, has run a pilot program on a large scale in several countries involving an "electronic purse" into which cash can be stored in different currencies and authorized for use for different purposes. The "purse" is a card the size of a credit card, with a computer chip in it. It can be used for low-cost transactions such as buying a newspaper or a candy bar. Because the cash is preloaded in the card, there is no need for the seller to link to a central computer for authorization as is necessary with a credit card. Mondex purses, sometimes called smart wallets, can be linked together, so that, for instance, a parent could transfer money to a son or daughter, loading it into separate parts of the wallet; one part of the cash might be stored so that it can only be used for medical transactions. The wallet can store cash in multiple currencies, simplifying international travel.

Banks love the idea of the electronic purse, which is why the European Mondex was set up and funded by a banking consortium. The "smart card" is cheaper to operate than a debit card, which requires a link from the store to the bank's systems. Credit card firms see it as a natural and inevitable evolution of their own product. That's why MasterCard bid to own 51 percent of Mondex in November 1996. Most retailers like the idea of not having to handle cash, which has to be sorted and attracts robbers and dishonest store staff.

But many commentators believe MasterCard made its bid for Mondex because MasterCard's trials of its own electronic purse had produced disappointing results. Visa has its own version, Visa Cash, which it piloted fairly successfully at the 1996 Summer Olympic Games, with adequate but unexciting results. Europay has its own rival to Mondex, called Clip. The most widely used system, the only one to date that is a clear commercial success, is Portugal's DMB card, which has 170,000 active users and close to 50,000 terminals installed in stores, gas stations, and taxis. Disposable purse systems are in use in Denmark, ATM cards with reloadable chips in Austria, and pilot projects everywhere. The results have been mixed, with acceptance highest among consumers in Australia and Hong Kong. No one system has emerged as the standard and, until it does, retailers will not commit to installing expensive equipment in stores. Governments and tax authorities are concerned that the anonymity of the electronic purse and the ability to transfer money between purses will inevitably lead to nefarious uses, most obviously for avoiding taxes.

Mondex aims to be the world standard. It may succeed. But

in the meantime, the risks and uncertainties are high. Even the president of MasterCard International admits: "The reason for all of these pilots is that no one has proven the business case. I'll be really interested to see if anyone makes money out of this" (*Financial Times,* November 13, 1996).

In the long term, electronic money management is surely inevitable. In the meantime, the most likely developments are in the extended use of credit cards for on-line transactions on the Internet, with new bank mechanisms emerging to handle processing, merchant information, and payments.

Integrated Business Logistics

Electronic commerce ultimately is about putting all the pieces together—electronic data interchange, electronic money management, and the supporting telecommunications, information management, and other technical tools. The goal—what electronic commerce really means for business—is the integration of processes that span companies, geography, and business functions. This integration is the target of the virtual organization: Quick Response in retailing, agile production, so-called time-based competition, and the many efforts to create organizational responsiveness and flexibility. Some firms are well on the way to creating the information- and communication-driven business by means of electronic commerce—for example:

- *First Line* in the United Kingdom is a start-up provider of insurance services entirely by phone, with no branches. First Line captured 10 percent of Britain's automobile insurance market in its first two years. Fidelity Investments similarly preempted traditional security brokerage and mutual funds firms in the United States via phones and technology.

- *Benneton* has implemented backward integration for the entire chain of clothing manufacture and sale. Point-of-sale information triggers production decisions. All sweaters are white when manufactured in Taiwan. They are not dyed until the last practical moment before they are sent to the stores. Data from each store dictates what colors to dye the sweaters and in what numbers for that store.

- *Nike* is famous for being a shoe "manufacturer" that makes no shoes and retains only R&D and marketing as its core activities, outsourcing everything else.

- *Verifone,* the maker of most of the credit card authorization and processing devices in stores, is a company that has no offices. It lives by electronic mail; even requests for hiring secretaries are handled electronically.

From a business perspective, these examples point to the growing strategic importance of electronic commerce. These companies began with the older tools of First Wave EDI, electronic mail, electronic payments, and electronic point-of-sale transactions. Look at how much they all achieved well before the mid-1990s. They represent what the now much debased term "reengineering" originally aimed to achieve: process-driven organizations that streamline and coordinate processes in sequence, instead of breaking them up into departmental and functional steps with fiefdoms, paper everywhere, and unnecessary administration along a chain of "hand-offs" from one department to another. The examples above show just how much electronic commerce is already practical. Add in new and ever-improving technology, more and more proven EDI tools, stable electronic money-management mechanisms, and growing experience in process transformation, and it seems clear that they are the blueprint for the company of tomorrow.

There are several ways of viewing electronic commerce in terms of business logistics. Each of the following offers substantial payoffs.

Workflow Coordination

At the most tactical level, electronic commerce is part of the general move in organizations to streamline processes, reduce waste and cost, and increase speed and communication among all the organizational units and people involved. The focus is on the firm's internal processes and on handling routine, simple transactions with trading partners, including customers, suppliers, and such third parties as banks and distributors. EDI and FEDI are the obvious starting points.

Trading Partner Relationships

The focus shifts from transactions with trading partners to relationships with them. As in the automotive industry, EC can change the nature of the relationship from "us vs. them" to mutual cooperation based on sharing of information, collaboration, and trust. The result is improved efficiency and the narrowing of suppliers from a large pool who compete on price and delivery to a smaller group who tailor output to the buyer's needs.

The key issue is contracting. The old style customer–supplier relationship relied heavily on the *ex post* contract. Such a contract spells out in detail all terms and conditions and addresses legal responsibilities and liabilities. *Ex post* contracts are designed to deal with someone or something going wrong after the contract is signed; lawyers then comb the contract to determine who's at fault. With EDI, the goal of collaboration shifts to mutual trust rather than law as the base for contracting. The *ex ante* contract and the *trading partner agreement* (TPA) lay out how the parties are going to work together. If things go wrong, which they inevitably will at times, the TPA lays out the steps to repair the problem. The TPA is the blueprint for establishing mutual understanding and responsibilities, since without trust, there can be no collaboration.

Zero Working Capital

One way to evaluate your company's electronic commerce capabilities is to look at its balance sheet. The asset side shows its working capital: cash, receivables, materials, work in process, and finished goods inventory. For centuries, bankers treated these as assets, viewing them as collateral for loans. Analysts tracked working capital ratios of assets to liabilities (payables and short-term debt).

In the world of electronic commerce, most working capital is a business liability, not a financial asset. If your firm has excess cash, it's not using the tools of electronic trading and investment. Large accounts receivable are evidence of inadequate use of electronic payments, electronic data interchange, netting, and related systems. High materials inventories mean poor customer–supplier electronic links and poor trading partner agreements. Large finished goods inventory means a neglect of the many tools of just-in-time production and distribution. Many firms have recognized this shift in the status of working capital—from accounting statement asset to business liability. Their goal is zero working capital. Several even aim at *negative* working capital. They aim to collect promptly the money owed to them, but to stretch out payments to the firms to whom they owe money. The resulting balance sheet will thus show just a few days in receivables and months in payables.

Logistics Integration

Electronic commerce is an integral part of the logistics revolution that marks more and more industries. Integrating logistics involves organizing the firm's planning, operations, organization, and information around processes, not around functions and departments. It includes managing the supply chain, concurrent engineering, Quick Response (in retailing), and such blueprints for the organization of tomorrow as the virtual company and networked enterprise. Day-to-day transactions are the core of logistics and of electronic commerce.

Organizational Agility

Electronic commerce is essential for the agile organization that combines flexibility in processes and structures with leveraging of skills through technology, training and career opportunities and rewards, and just-in-time everything—production, distribution, replenishment, payments, scheduling, customer service, and the like. Electronic commerce contributes to agility in every aspect of everyday transactions. It can prevent first-rate products from being undermined by tenth-rate management of product inventory. It can also prevent the undermining of superb customer service by misprocessing of payments or delays in insurance claims.

It's not news to any manager that just about every force in business advances the demand for more flexibility, responsiveness, use of teams, customer service, speed, and removal of the constraints of organizational structure on strategy. Let's call this organizational agility. Electronic commerce doesn't in itself create it, but is a catalyst and support. Indeed, it's hard to see how any firm committed to flexibility as its strategic priority can progress without electronic commerce.

The Internet and Intranets

As recently as 1994, electronic commerce meant EDI, corporate cash management, and banking funds transfer systems. Now it also means the Internet and *intranets,* which are networks that employ Internet technology but restrict access to information and services to employees and privileged trading partners. For some commentators, electronic commerce and the Internet are synonymous. Extrapolating from the recent 100 percent (or greater) growth per year in the number of users and providers of services on the World Wide Web, they see the Internet as the base for a massive consumer market for on-line retailing, selling of new information services, and handling of payments. Forecasts of the size of the Internet market vary widely, even wildly—from *Electronic Marketing*'s claim that "the on-line market is expected to reach over $1.4 billion by the year 2000" (Margo Komenan, *Electronic Marketing,* p. xxiii), to Forrester Research's estimate that the Internet will be a $6 billion market by 2000, to the IDC

Research's prediction that the market will be $150 billion annually.

If the market turns out to be in the range of hundreds of billions of dollars rather than tens of billions, then Internet and electronic commerce will indeed be synonymous. Keep in mind that $1 billion dollars is just 4 dollars per household. The sales of Barbie dolls is more than $1 billion a year; electronic commerce on the Internet in 1996 was around half that.

Nonetheless, even if, as some experts predict, the Internet growth surge slows, due to the Web's slowness and unreliability for the home user, the mainstream of electronic commerce will still continue along its established path for business-to-business relationships. EC's growth rate of roughly 20 percent a year has been sustained for a decade without dependence on the Internet. Obviously, the more the Internet is used in general, the more it will be used for electronic commerce. The Internet extends the reach of value-added telecommunications networks that are the main vehicles for EDI, making it simple and economical for small firms to implement most though not yet all the components of electronic commerce that large ones routinely employ. Perhaps most important for the evolution of electronic commerce is that the Internet's technology is the base for intranets.

Our own view is that the Internet will *not* reach the hundreds of billions of dollars level in person-to-computer electronic commerce for many years. Its growth will be blocked in the short term because it has well-known problems of reliability and capacity; its predominant users are affluent technical professional males, not representative of the general populace; and people are generally content with fax for communication, paper catalogs for mail order, 1-800 numbers for ordering, and printed newspapers and magazines. There *have* been a number of striking successes in Internet retailing and plenty of activity in financial services, especially in ensuring secure use of credit cards, but the successes are largely confined to niche selling of books (Amazon), wines (Virtual Vineyards), computer hardware and software (many companies), and travel. The payment systems are still largely in the pilot stage and no industry leader has emerged. Of course it is possible that in the next few years users of personal computers who browse the Internet for information and entertainment will make it the home equivalent of the ATM machine, thus opening a mass market for person-to-computer electronic commerce, but whatever the optimists predict, their forecasts have no realistic empirical base as yet. The promised mass consumer market has not yet appeared, and there is no evidence that it will do so soon.

The more immediate impact of the Internet on business will be in business-to-business electronic commerce via *intranets*. Intranets use Internet technology to solve several of the oldest and most difficult problems in corporate use of computers and telecommunications.

- *Reach:* Who can access the firm's on-line services and information resources?

- *Range:* What information and services can be automatically and immediately cross-linked?

- *Ease of use:* How natural do users find it to access the system and navigate its menus and options, and how much training do they need?

The Internet is in many ways a clumsy, insecure, and unreliable tool, but its weaknesses count little compared to its strengths in these three areas.

Reach: TCP/IP Ending Communication Problems

Throughout the more than 40-year history of computing and data communications, a central problem has been that any computer system trying to link to another one has had to know what type of device it is. The main reason is the technology evolved by companies such as IBM, AT&T, Digital Equipment, Wang, Microsoft, Apple, and the other pacesetters of their era was proprietary (vendor-specific), as were the "standards" (rules for formats and connections) and "protocols" the systems used. Protocols are the definitions of procedures, signals, and information coding needed for a sender and receiver to be in sync with each other. For instance, an IBM personal computer could interconnect to computers that used Apple's software and to local area networks (LANs). (A LAN connects PCs within one office or company and allows them to share the same software and information.) Little by little, first IBM's and then Microsoft's systems achieved such dominance in the marketplace that other vendors either incorporated them or added facilities for interconnecting to them. Committees from the international telecommunications phone service monopolies took the lead in defining a massive blueprint for interconnecting everything to everything, called the Open Systems Interconnection (OSI) reference model, which provided a blueprint for "open" versus proprietary systems but did not offer specific products. But open systems were slow to emerge and, as the pace of technology innovation accelerated, new personal computers, multimedia, and new modes of telecommunications transmission made the OSI model obsolete. New technologies accelerated the standard-setting process, exacerbating the problem of incompatibilities among systems.

Once telecommunications became cheap to install and operate, the Transmission Control Protocol/Internet Protocol (TCP/IP) entirely changed all this. Bedrock of the Internet, this communications protocol allows any computer of any type anywhere in the world to link to another computer of any type anywhere in the world. (TCP/IP is still a clumsy and inefficient protocol and lacks many features essential to businesses.) Previously, firms like IBM and AT&T built their services with security, cost, and efficiency as priorities; they developed even the simplest of telecommunications applications, electronic mail, as proprietary systems. Before TCP/IP, to send a message by, say, MCI Mail, to a computer using IBM's Profs or Digital Equipment's Decnet was impossible without expensive computer hardware and software designed to translate message formats and communications protocols.

The community of technical professionals, mainly in universities, who worked on or near the U.S. Defense Department's ARPANET and the National Science Foundation's NSFNET, which eventually became the Internet, took a pragmatic view of telecommunications: Connect and communicate and don't worry about efficiency, security, and network management controls. They invented or enabled many innovations in telecommunications in order to make this possible and then practical. For example, *packet-switching* breaks telecommunications messages into small units, called packets, that can be pumped through a network like units on a conveyor belt in an assembly line instead of tying up the communication channel in the way a phone call does. *Routers* are devices that manage telecommunications traffic across dissimilar networks. And the *World Wide Web* is the key to transforming the Internet from a network that only people with sophisticated understanding of information technology could use into something almost as easy as a VCR.

The transition took time. For several decades, TCP/IP and the software operating system called UNIX remained an exotic niche. Anyone other than computer experts found ARPANET, Bitnet, and NSFNET, the forerunners of the Internet, horribly difficult. The mainstream of IBM and Apple personal computers did not employ the TCP/IP protocol until the early 1990s. With the invention of the World Wide Web in 1992 and the rapid development of easy-to-use Web-browser software, the strengths of TCP/IP came to the fore. The transmission protocol made the Internet a worldwide service to which any personal computer software and hardware vendor could tailor its products without having to invest in complex new software. The Web is easy for personal computer users to access either as providers or as users of services, information, and goods. Companies can transfer information from their transaction-processing IBM systems and other proprietary systems. On-line information services like America Online were driven by the exploding growth of the World Wide Web to add "gateways"—computers that link to the Internet—so there is no longer any real boundary between them and the Net.

TCP/IP is now *the* protocol of electronic commerce. EC providers can now communicate with any computer thanks to TCP/IP. Computers can now link to each other as easily as telephones and postal services do. Trading partners have relied on phones and mail for most of this century in their person-to-person interactions. TCP/IP is the phone/mail/fax of the late 1990s.

Range: The Genius of Web Browsers

Without the World Wide Web, TCP/IP might have remained the way "nerds" and academics communicated with one another. Until 1992, the Internet was a network that could be used only if you knew how to type a complex set of commands to invoke its services. The Web defined a subset of the Net that uses what is called hypertext (Web addresses routinely begin with "http" for *hypertext transfer protocol*) to connect information items—Web pages—to each other. Hypertext, a concept invented in the 1970s, views information as a dynamic set of pointers inside computer memory rather than the tidy sequence of books and structures of data bases.

The Web provided an entirely new way of interacting with information on-line. Any Web page can highlight a link to another page so that, starting from a simple screen display of a Web site's "home page," users of personal computers can explore a universe of hypertext links. The Hypertext Markup Language (HTML) for creating Web pages and hypertext links can be learned quickly and makes it cheap to build basic Web sites.

It was the Web browser, though, that went beyond just displaying Web sites. The term is now somewhat misleading, in that the leading browsers, Netscape's Navigator, Microsoft's Internet Explorer and those offered by on-line services like America Online, are powerful tools for handling just about any Internet application, including file transfers and electronic mail, for building Internet applications, and for ensuring security. While the initial purpose of the Web browser was simply to make the Internet easy to access and use, they solved the biggest single problem firms have faced in their use of information technology, one that we term *range*. (For a detailed discussion of reach and range, see Peter Keen's *Shaping the Future: Business Design Through Information Technology*, Harvard Business School Press, 1990.)

Whereas *reach* defines who can access the firm's information and on-line services, *range* is the extent to which these services are "integrated" instead of being separate systems that cannot be combined. The basic information systems and transaction-processing systems in most organizations were built as separate applications, so that, for instance, banks used different systems and customer identification codes for handling checking accounts, mortgages, credit cards, and savings. In pharmaceutical firms, clinical trial data in individual countries were built on different software, hardware, telecommunications, and data base platforms. Most manufacturers had to keep engineering, accounting, inventory, and financial data in separate departments, systems, and technology bases.

Integration of information and systems was unintentionally prevented by many forces, among them limitations of the available technology; hurried, ad hoc implementation of urgently needed basic transaction systems case-by-case; competition between software and hardware providers that offered very different features based on very different standards and technology foundations; and the dominance of the departmental structure of organizations in the 1960s through 1980s. During the eighties, the thrust of information technology supply and demand was toward open systems, interconnection, and common standards. Electronic commerce benefited from this, and electronic data interchange was one of the strongest catalysts for it, since EC would be impossible without standards for companies' systems to link to one another and share information.

Even with EDI standards, though, an almost intractable problem was that the information in far too many old transaction-processing systems could not be accessed or shared easily. In many areas of business, firms did not have the technical staff resources, business justification, management commitment, or available tools to develop accessible information resources. This was especially true in human resources, in customer service departments of organizations where systems had evolved as "islands" of automation, in research and development, and in public relations. All of these functions fell outside the mainstream of information and transaction systems.

Personal computers had, if anything, led to less, not more, information being accessible as a shared resource. They encouraged the development of even more local and departmental systems, with little coordination and in many instances with an explicit resistance to oversight from central corporate information services groups, who were seen, sometimes accurately, as bureaucratic control freaks who disliked the intrusion of "amateurs" with "toy" computers. Apple Computer deliberately made its telecommunications and software incompatible with IBM's mainstream systems, a move that meant that its products could not become the front-end "client" that accessed information and communication "servers" and ultimately lost Apple the big business marketplace.

Integration became the watchword of business use of information technology in the 1990s: integrated financial software, integrated customer data bases, and integrated logistics were developed. The growing focus on business processes, teams, and customer service as the building blocks of new organizational forms demanded integration of systems. "Legacy" systems inherited from an earlier era of information processing blocked that and still do in many instances. The tools of the Internet brought a solution. Web-browser software plus the toolkit of the Internet programmer/Webmaster/developer offered a way to make information look integrated and a vehicle so simple to use that for the first time in the history of information technology there is no need for training.

The key trick of the trade here is hypertext. The challenge for systems developers in integrating information across older systems is that they have to write complex software links, using what are termed client/server systems, application program interfaces, distributed relational data bases, agents, applets, and other tools. Most of these would work only for given types of information using given vendors' software and data base management systems. TCP/IP solved the problem of how to move the information; it extends *reach* but does not in itself provide *range*. A browser like Netscape lets any type of information in any application or any data base be linked like just another Web page. This solution to the problem of incompatible systems is inefficient and can involve some complicated technical minutiae, but it works. Here are two examples of what this means in practice:

Modernization via Intranet. One of us is working with a phone company in Latin America that has recently lost its monopoly and faces aggressive competition. A priority of this company is to improve its billing and customer service information capabilities. Large business customers want consolidated billing, fast response to queries, and a single point of contact for problems. The phone company has multiple systems that are hard to access and completely without links between them; the systems cannot be accessed by customers on-line. The company is participating in a massive project involving a number of European and other phone companies to develop a system that will cost it around $50 million. The project is lagging behind schedule and won't be in place for several years. Meanwhile, the firm has been losing market share as national and U.S. companies target its best corporate clients.

The phone company has now solved many of the problems described, however. Using Netscape Navigator and software development tools designed for building on-line applications quickly, the firm was able to build in a matter of months an intranet system that offers consolidated billing and customer relationship data. It still can't meet the requirements of on-line transaction processing, and the system is a little slow—but it works. The intranet system is easy to access and use and it cost just thousands, not millions, of dollars to build. Most important, it provides the basis for the firm to develop simple systems to respond to business needs as they arise.

Integrating Systems via the World Wide Web. One of the world's three largest pharmaceutical firms spent several years trying to find a way to integrate worldwide information on clinical trials of new drugs without having to spend the GNP of a small country to do so. For decades, the U.S. Food and Drug Administration would not accept data from other countries. There was thus no incentive to integrate the systems that processed data in the 160 countries where the firm operates. Now, however, the FDA allows and even encourages the submission of data from anywhere, in its concern to speed up time-to-market for life-saving drugs, especially for treatment of AIDS. The pharmaceutical firm's head of information systems revealed that the lowest price the top systems-integration firms like EDS and Andersen Consulting estimated for building a worldwide clinical trials system was $200 million. But just one year later, the firm has an integrated system, built in about three months by two people. Again, the system is slow, incomplete, and can't handle transaction processing. It works, though, and is easy to access and use. It serves as the front end that allows the firm access to previously incompatible systems throughout the world. In this case, Netscape Navigator is the window into what looks like an integrated system. The Web is the access vehicle, and TCP/IP the electronic messenger service.

Ease of Use: Hypertext as Point and Go

Navigator, like Internet Explorer, Spyglass, Mosaic, and other Web browsers, offers a deceptively simple feature that is as radical in its impact on the use of computers as spreadsheets were for personal computers: we term it *mundaneness.* "Mundane" means ordinary, everyday, taken for granted. Think of renting a car at an airport. You don't need to look up directions in a manual to get the car started. You probably can't even recall exactly where the instruments were on the last car you rented, yet you started it up without thinking and drove to your business destination.

Computers have not been mundane. The euphemism "user-friendly" was thrown around in ads touting new pieces of software for a full decade—it really meant "less user-hostile than last year." Computers are still difficult to use. The genius of the combination of browsers, the Web, and hypertext is that they make intranets simpler to use than any other information-retrieval system. To our knowledge, there's no "Learning to Use the Web" training industry. That is because no special training is needed. Navigator, for example, offers a commonsense, natural—mundane—way to use computers to find information, ask questions, and make transactions. Its users don't need to know anything about the type or location of the many computers that store the information that can be accessed from a single Web page; TCP/IP handles that. Nor do they need to know or understand the nature of the information, since hypertext links make numbers, pictures, and videos just "objects" to be transferred. And it is unnecessary for users to worry about software procedures for obtaining information, since the Web browser disguises the links in the same way that the telephone disguises the complexities of voltages, cycles, "hand shakes," error detection, call accounting, latency, and hundreds of other technical issues; you just pick up the phone, dial the number, and say "Hello." Internet browsers aren't quite as mundane as the telephone, but they are still by far the most natural and easy-to-use software available on personal computers—and the most enjoyable.

Summary: Internet-Enabled Electronic Commerce

Clearly, no firm can ignore the Internet in its planning for electronic commerce. No one can predict with any assurance the future of the Net and its impact on big business, small business, politics, education, government, entertainment, law, banking, . . .—that is, its impact on life on this planet as we know it or can imagine it. Both of the writers of this guide are enthusiastic skeptics about the Internet. We distrust hype. We have both worked in the field of electronic commerce for well over 10 years. We've been enthusiasts for years and our enthusiasm predates the Internet. Nothing about the Internet changes the fundamentals of electronic commerce and its evolution, although the Internet certainly enables every element of electronic commerce. The single belief underlying our guide is that electronic commerce is close to becoming the mainstream of business and a requirement for the firm that aspires to be (or remain) a well-run business in the early 2000s. That will be so regardless of the Internet, but the Internet opens up new opportunities, and intranets are close to being a necessity for every firm.

The Business Management Agenda

The aim of this book is to help business managers take an active, not reactive, role in their firms' planning for electronic commerce, to give them a straightforward, sensible, reliable, and interesting briefing on its technical, business, and organizational essentials, and to demystify the vocabulary. Forget the hype that pops up in so many discussions—the Information Age, Internet, wired society, and the like. If electronic commerce just continues its 1990–1996 pace of a 15 to 20 percent per year increase, it will be used in the purchasing of $300–400 billion of goods in the United States alone by the year 2000. Every large manufacturing company and retailer will require its suppliers to link to it electronically. Many already do. Firms that have not yet achieved that level of electronic commerce have a lot of catching up to do. The present level goes beyond the basic installation of EC, extending both its scale and its likely impacts. The future opens up many practical new opportunities, among which will inevitably be some that will be overpromised and overhyped; business multimedia, the Internet, and new forms of electronic cash will drive many of these.

The focus of this guide for business managers is the present and the immediate future. Trading partner relationships, money management, and logistics are the areas of the business where every single day the well-run company carries out the activities that are the essential background for its customer service, quality management, revenues, and profits, and does so just a little bit better than competitors and a little bit better every year. Other companies may have distinctive products, marketing strategies, and the like, but neglect the basics. At some point, that neglect catches up with them. They have to downsize, outsource, reengineer, reorganize, restructure, or apply some other of the "re-" words that dominate management thought and practice today. "Re-" means try again.

Electronic commerce makes it unnecessary to have to try again. Adopt the best proven tools for running the basics of the business well. Join this new mainstream. Evolve your firm's electronic commerce strategy and base carefully and continuously. Take a good look at your processes and trading partner relationships and be willing to act sensibly but quickly. It's a good time to move now and a pretty safe one, too. Until the early 1990s, although plenty of tools were in the proving stage, the organizational, technical, and economic risks of electronic commerce warned managers off. They had seen too many promises from technology crash and burn in disappointment and disaster. There was thus little momentum to sustain commitment in many companies to electronic payments, electronic data interchange, electronic customer–supplier links, point-of-sale logistics, and the like.

Now, the basic tools of electronic commerce are fully proven and new technology is opening up more and more cost effective opportunities. Electronic commerce is no longer about information technology, any more than 1-800 numbers are about telephone technology. It's about business basics. That makes electronic commerce part of management basics. This book is a guide to those basics. No business manager can afford not to be conversant with and comfortable in making decisions about electronic commerce. Our aim is to help you do this.

The Glossary of Terms

Electronic business has two main elements: (1) the technical infrastructures and delivery platforms that make it practical, and (2) the business configuration that exploits those platforms. Our guide mainly addresses the business configuration, addressing only the technical issues and terms that a business manager will find helpful to understand in making business choices. (A companion book to this one, *Every Manager's Guide to Information Technology,* by Peter Keen, covers the technology in detail. Another, *Every Manager's Guide to Business Processes,* by Peter Keen and Ellen Knapp, covers the details of process change.)

We've designed this Manager's Guide to provide business managers with a reliable, simple, and interesting overview of the key terms and concepts they need to understand in order to take the lead in exploiting the opportunities of electronic commerce. The terms include the fundamentals of electronic data interchange, electronic banking, and money management; the many legal and security issues that increasingly determine the practicality of using technology in intercompany business activities; the growing range of electronic logistical processes; key standards; the Internet as a business resource; and international trading.

The Glossary of Terms, which constitutes the main part of this book, is intended for browsing, reference, or for reading straight through. For each term it presents a short definition followed by a discussion of the term's relevance to business. We include plenty of illustrative examples from companies and cross-references to other relevant glossary terms. We avoid hype, taking a conservative position regarding the trends and impacts of electronic commerce. What is happening in electronic commerce *today* is in itself exciting and often radical, so we try to present an accurate and comprehensive overview of current activity and solid trends. We have no ideology, methodology, or theory to sell. This is a book about business common sense, presented in as commonsense a way as we can.

Foundation Terms

The Glossary of Terms in this book contains nearly 150 entries and cross-references. A subset of the entries constitutes a basic management vocabulary for electronic commerce. Readers seeking a quick orientation to electronic commerce can read the entries for the twenty-six terms listed here. Together with the overview provided in the preceding introduction, they form the foundation for building management understanding of electronic commerce. These foundation term entries are in italic type to distinguish them from the rest of the glossary.

ANSI X12

Authentication

Data Encryption Standard (DES)

Digital Cash

Digital Signature

EDI Translation Software

Electronic Cash

Electronic Commerce Standard-Setting

Electronic Data Interchange (EDI)

Electronic Mail

Electronic Purse/Wallet

Expenditures on Electronic Commerce

Financial EDI

Firewall

Internet Electronic Commerce

Intranets

Legal Issues Concerning Electronic Commerce

Nonrepudiation

Payment Systems

Public Key Cryptography

Security

Smart Card

Store and Forward

Stored-Value Card

Trading Partner Agreement

Transaction Set

Many of the nearly 150 terms in this manager's glossary will be as unfamiliar to business managers and information systems professionals as were those of the nascent personal computer industry in the mid-1980s. But they will soon be as much a part of everyone's vocabulary as terms like Windows, Pentium, local area network, and Internet are now. Personal computers put computer power on the desk and in the briefcase, moving computers out of the data center and into the business. Telecommunications moved from phones and telex to the very basics of customer service and organizational coordination. Electronic commerce moves information technology into the center of intercompany business, customer–supplier relationships, banking, and payments. That makes it part of everyday management thinking, planning, and decision making—the core of business management.

Glossary of Terms

ACH See **Automated Clearing Houses.**

Advance Notification of Payment In advance notification of payment, the payer/sender provides payment details to the receiver in advance of actual funds transfer. The main purpose is to optimize the management of bank balances throughout the sender's operations, so that disposition of the funds and cash management can be planned and handled in advance of the actual transfer of funds. Obviously the receiving organization benefits as well, since it can use the notification to do the same for itself.

General Electric's Corporate Electronic Payment System (COEPS) employs this approach as a value-added component of GE's payments processing service. Detractors of the concept say that a prudent corporate treasurer would not apply funds to a particular activity until the actual value transfer has been confirmed. At the same time, the ability to forecast incoming payments and identify problems or issues that may be associated with those payments has proven to be a strategic advantage for companies that use such a scheme. They think of advance notification in terms of ways to manage the financial logistics of the firm rather than just in terms of payments. In a sense, they use it as

By providing companies with full information about a forthcoming payment before it is made, General Electric has increased productivity in credits and collections, as measured by accounts per collector, by 30 percent.

the equivalent of just-in-time (JIT) production in manufacturing—as just-in-time money management.

Advance Shipment Notice (ASN)   The advance shipment notice, more commonly referred to as the ASN, is an electronic document developed to reduce the time, errors, and costs associated with the transfer of goods. Whether the product is groceries, auto parts, retail merchandise, or hospital supplies, the transfer of goods between trading partners is often tedious and expensive. It's a process in which labor costs are high, not only to physically move the goods, but also to reconcile the shipment information with the originating order.

The ASN is not just the electronic equivalent of today's paper-based shipping documents. Rather, it can be used as the basis for making trade processes more efficient. The ASN is structured in four sections, technically termed Hierarchical Levels: Shipment, Order, Pack, and Item.

- The *Shipment* level has all the information regarding the shipment. Such information includes the transport company, type of vehicle being used, vehicle number, and address information including the origin and destination of shipments.

- The *Order* level contains all of the specific order information, such as the purchase order number. An ASN may have multiple Order level sections, referred to as "loops."

- The *Pack* level lists the type and number of container. This hierarchical level can be divided into sublevels if the type of containerization requires it. For example, if the ordered items are packaged in cartons and then placed on skids, the skids are referenced by unique numbers. The second sublevel references the cartons on the skids.

- The *Item* level contains all item-specific information, such as part number and quantity.

"Much of the move toward using EDI in the automotive world is due to one word—Japan. In meeting the Japanese challenge, EDI was one of the applications used by the U.S. automotive industry to improve the quality, efficiency, and competitiveness traditionally found in automotive factories." (David Mackay, EDI in the Australian Automotive Industry, 1996, 154)

Ted Annis, CEO of Supply Tech Inc. comments, "We're using EDI because we are trying to become more efficient through just-in-time manufacturing methods. Now we've achieved fast turnaround and reduced inventory. But if suppliers don't send the

In the (old) world of paper processing, with documents processed manually, a buyer sends out a purchase order (PO). The PO specifies to the seller exactly what the buyer wishes to acquire, where, when, and how much. It is the seller's responsibility to fulfill the order and deliver the goods to the buyer, meeting the precise terms of the order. The seller packs and ships the goods and includes a packing slip and bill of lading detailing to the buyer what was shipped and how. Once the goods have been shipped, the seller generates an invoice for the buyer in order to receive payment. This invoice explains exactly what is being billed, at what price, and at what quantity. Before paying for the delivered goods, the buyer examines the shipment and matches it to the original PO in order to validate the shipment's accuracy. Only after completing a comparison between the shipped goods and PO does the buyer begin the payment process. In the manual/paper world of business this process is very time-consuming and costly.

right parts or send something that isn't what they said it is, they've defeated the purpose. By scanning bar code labels into the ASN, what is going on the truck to be shipped is what is included in the ASN. There is no intermediate human step. So, the benefit is a reduction in shipping errors."

The ASN is an electronic, paperless document that replaces the packing slip. It can also be the base for eliminating or simplifying several steps in the aforementioned paper/manual chain of trade. When used as just a glorified packing slip, the ASN contains all of the information that would have been printed on paper, such as the shipping address, number of containers, and a description of the contents. It is then transmitted in advance of the goods to the receiver to keep on file in anticipation of arrival of the goods. Now that the buyer/receiver has the ASN, that firm knows exactly what is being shipped and when and can thus schedule its operations accordingly. In addition to maximizing the efficiency of the receiver's time, an advanced matching of the ASN to the PO informs the buyer beforehand of any discrepancies.

The ASN closes the order-to-delivery loop. Bar coding in conjunction with EDI means that even less human intervention is needed and makes data collection rapid and accurate. Creating an ASN with a bar code scanner is easy. The shipper uses labeled, bar coded shipping containers (whether carton, skid, or barrel is

"Logistics touches just about everyone in a corporation. It's the cracks between the traditional organization that need to be managed, hence the term 'supply chain management.'. . . Unclogging the information pipeline cleans out the inventory pipeline. The more manufacturers know about the movement of products, the less inventory they need. . . . Companies are spending about 10% of revenue on logistics. Better management can cut that in half."
(Information Week, 20 November, 1995)

irrelevant). Then at loading time, before placing items in a container, the shipper first scans the container's label. Each individual item's bar coded part number is scanned as the part is placed in the container. Scanning the part numbers allows additional item level information to be retrieved subsequently from corporate data bases, eliminating the need for hand keying large volumes of data. This process is repeated until the shipment is ready to be loaded for transport. The scanner now holds the information on *exactly* which items are in which containers and at what quantities. The containers are then loaded onto their respective vehicles for transport, at which time the *vehicle*'s bar code ID is also scanned or recorded. Order information can also be added to the ASN as it is pulled from the inbound PO, which was received sometime earlier. The scanned data is then downloaded to the EDI system and an ASN created and transmitted. The efficiency of packers and shippers is greatly increased because the task of scanning bar codes is easier and a great deal quicker than manually recording and inputting all of the required data.

At the receiving facility, the ASN is received and staff are scheduled according to the inbound volumes. Once the goods have arrived, the containers are scanned and matched to the ASN. Not only does this scanning provide an electronically stored receipt confirmation that can be printed out at any time as needed, but it tells the receiver what is in the box should the receiver later wish to verify the shipment at the item level.

Order discrepancies such as incorrect items and overshipments can be anticipated with the ASN. The problems can be resolved prior to the arrival of the goods. In addition to cross-referencing the inbound ASN to the original outbound PO, the inbound invoice, which usually follows the ASN, can be eliminated. The receiver already knows what was shipped, and once the receiver has verified delivery against what was ordered, he can pay the seller using the quantities specified in the ASN. The process of electronically sending a PO, receiving an ASN, and validating and paying the ASN is known as evaluated receipt settlement (ERS). Of course, successful ERS depends on a close relationship of mutual trust and technical competence between trading partners. This relationship must include provisions for handling incorrect shipments and for terms of payment.

The retail industry has been highly successful in implementing ERS. The bulk of the major players in the marketplace rely on ERS in their efforts to streamline procurement and see it as a cornerstone of competitive positioning. In manufacturing, ERS is the base for both supplier relationships and production planning. The goal is to minimize inventory levels through just-in-time inventory management and at the same time to maximize information about inventory arrivals. With JIT, firms don't have the buffer stocks of on-hand materials and parts to offset late or incomplete deliveries, so they must have up-to-the-minute information. For example, an auto manufacturer will forward its production schedule to a supplier, say a steel processor that builds chassis. With the production schedule in hand, the processor/supplier knows how many chassis the auto manufacturer will need and when. The purchase release dates inform the processor/supplier when to ship the chassis. Once the shipment is ready, the steel processor will send the auto manufacturer an ASN revealing exactly what is being shipped and when. The auto manufacturer in turn can match this ASN to the production schedule to ensure that enough chassis will be available for production. In the event that a shortage may occur, the ASN warns the auto manufacturer to look elsewhere to find the parts (in this case, the chassis) required to keep production on schedule. Thus, the auto manufacturer eliminates the necessity for millions of dollars worth of bulky inventory and relies heavily on the supplier to keep the production line rolling. The supplier in turn is happy with this continuous replenishment system because it keeps the supplier's operations functioning at a consistent level throughout the year.

Our discussions with companies that are leaders in using electronic commerce to streamline their logistical processes indicate that they see ASN as one of the most important single tools

The logic of electronic business logistics is to improve the productivity of all the parties in the supply chain. By sending information through ASN prior to delivery of goods, the time needed to unload the shipment at the retailer's docking station is reduced. The retailer can optimize its own procedures and the sender can be sure that the goods will move quickly from station to shelf.

for their firms' competitive positioning. That is why we discuss the ASN in more detail than most of the entries in this Glossary of Terms. The ASN is not a substitution of electronic messages for paper documents but the very basis for integrating the entire supply chain.

See also **Evaluated Receipt Settlement.**

AIAG   See **Automotive Industry Action Group.**

American National Standards Institute (ANSI) The American National Standards Institute was founded in 1918 and is now central to the development of standards for U.S. industry. Its 1,300 members include business companies, government agencies, and trade associations. ANSI has become the central U.S. forum for setting EDI standards, with its X12 Accredited Standards Committee, known as X12, the focal point for the evolution of ever-more comprehensive and consistent X12 "transaction sets." A transaction set defines trade terms and message formats completely and precisely for such basic transactions as purchase orders. There are also X12 transaction sets for more specialized message formats such as an electronic notification of a levy or garnishment of wages by agencies assigned to collect delinquent child support payments.

A voluntary organization, with no legal authority, ANSI is at once a committee-centered business association, a lobbying group, and most of all a forum. Users and vendors work together to resolve the many complex principles and details involved in setting standards. ANSI committees argue, make horse trades, and compromise. Since standards are about details, some standards may require hundreds of pages of specification and several rounds of the propose-publish-vote-approve-implement process. ANSI is a central force in the evolution of standards not only in EDI but in computer programming languages and other areas of information technology. In information technology, however, leading vendors, particularly Microsoft, play a stronger role im-

"The Great Marshmallow Debate flared up on a cold February in Atlanta [at a meeting of an ANSI X12 committee defining Warehouse Information Network Standards]. Marshmallow manufacturers, pitted against retailers . . . turned to the committee to resolve the burning question: Given that the weight of marshmallows changes as they age, should the purchase order note the weight at time of shipment or the weight at time of receipt?" The committee found a compromise—"One more EDI obstacle had been tackled and conquered." (EDI Forum 8, no. 3, 1995)

posing their own preferred standards. For them, cooperation is compromise and at best a reluctant acceptance that the relevant parties can't go it alone. With EDI, cooperation is essential. ANSI has become the main vehicle for this cooperation.

ANSI represents the United States in international standard-setting organizations such as the main one relevant to EDI, called EDIFACT, which is sponsored by the United Nations.

See also **ANSI X12; EDIFACT.**

ANSI   See **American National Standards Institute.**

ANSI X12   The American National Standards Institute (ANSI) X12 Accredited Standards Committee (ASC) is called ANSI X12. The X12 committee is responsible for overseeing a wide range of subcommittees and task groups that develop EDI standards for a growing variety of transactions for business, in general, and for specific business and public sector applications. Think of X12 as the master blueprint by which standards and many other "transaction sets" can be developed systematically and within an overall general framework for the following: purchase orders, mortgage applications, student loan applications, shipment advice, notification of product test results, debit/credit advice, health insurance claims, invoices, and tax remittance.

X12 is by far the most influential and effective force in the development of EDI, to the extent that the term "X12" is virtually synonymous with "EDI." X12 standards cut across industries. Each of its over 200 different types of electronic transaction sets replaces the paper document equivalent. Almost any conceivable business transaction from purchase order to invoice to payment is covered by a standard. Extremely complex exchanges such as the transfer of CAD/CAM designs or student transcripts can be facilitated as well by one of the many standardized X12 document formats.

The ANSI X12 standards began to be used around 1985, when they were evolved to meet the automotive industry's need for

In 1983, when ANSI issued the first X12 EDI standards, there were just 4 transaction sets. By 1986, there were 16. At the end of 1996, there were 273, as much an indication of how influential and respected ANSI X12 has become as of the energy of activity. ANSI has enough clout now to influence the language of major legislation in the healthcare field. For example, the Health Insurance Portability and Accountability Act of 1996 includes requirements for the use of ANSI X12 standards to ensure uniformity of information and transmission of messages. The law, which took effect in January 1997, mandates compliance except in special cases, making X12 a powerful force for coordination of a very fragmented industry with very high administrative costs. Those costs will be cut by compliance with the EDI requirements, simply because EDI slashes the cost of processing interorganizational documents.

highly detailed remittances to accompany orders. X12 represents a merging of a number of similar, industry-specific organizations involved in setting EDI standards, such as VICS (for retailing), WINS (for warehousing), and others. ANSI X12 is primarily a North American standard, used by business and government in the United States and Canada. The international standard is EDIFACT, sponsored by the United Nations. ANSI standards differ from EDIFACT's in the way they are constructed (their syntax) and in the number of documents or messages they cover. However, both use the same data element dictionary (words) and the concept of converting a physical document into a machine-readable electronic file.

To create or contribute to an X12 standard requires an organization to join the ANSI X12 Accredited Standards Committee, participate in one of the many subcommittees, and submit specific changes or additions for review. A typical change can take one to two years to implement and a new transaction can take three to five years. An example of the ANSI process is the ongoing development of a standard to streamline college financial aid. In August 1995, a group representing government agencies, college admissions officers, student organizations, and lending institutions set up Project Easy Access for Students and Institutions (Project EASI) to entirely rethink the national system for delivering student aid. It worked under the aegis of the X12 Education Subcommittee. The aim is to enable students to access information from and apply to multiple colleges without having to provide the same data on many different forms. The new system will include mechanisms for disbursing funds and for repayment of the loans when the student leaves school. The expected savings will be huge. The total sum now spent by the U.S. Department of Education on managing the $35 billion of student loans is $300 million a year. For comparison: The New York Stock Exchange, which manages trillions of dollars of trades, is run on $250 million.

Subcommittee X12A, working in parallel with Project EASI on

student financial aid transaction sets, set up a special task group whose charter was approved in October 1996. Several transaction sets already under development have been transferred to X12A (Education) from X12F (Finance). The leader of the new task group commented that EASI is a project born out of mutual interests among a wide range of communities: "EASI would really change the lives of everybody involved in financial aid. This would cut the cost dramatically from the government's point of view; getting the data from the institutions and the banks and so forth would be much easier [if they could] send and receive [it] electronically. It would be pretty seamless so that things would work much better than they do today from the point of view of the students and it would help parents and students prepare for the costs of their education maybe sooner than they do today" (*EC/EDI Insider*, September 30, 1996). The leader of EASI adds that "It's a massive job, a multi-year effort."

The Project EASI worked full time for 10 weeks to define its goals and vision. It saw X12 as central to the vision. An official from the Department of Education who is on the team comments: "The way the Department does things now is we come up with solutions and we mandate them to our colleges. We say, if you want our money, you'll do it our way: the typical proprietary electronic commerce scenario. . . . [Instead] rather than beating them over the head with it, we take it to X12. Everybody who wants to, everybody's who's concerned enough, has one vote. . . . If you have a standard format, it democratizes the process. We can come up with a standard format and say everybody's got to use it, and maybe everybody would, but X12 democratizes that." The Department of Education is planning to take an active part in X12 TG3 (Task Group 3). Members of the EASI team have taken ANSI's one-day X12 course. A White Paper that is being prepared will lay out the specific transactions, forms, and processes to be included in the new X12 transaction sets. It will serve as the blueprint for the X12 task group's work. The group will then design the standard and formally present it to X12 for review by members. The agreed-on standard will then be sent out for balloting. There are many open information forums along the way, plenty of often intense debate, and reviews with Technical Assessment subcommittees. The many stages toward a final transaction set include several votes: New Project Proposal Approval, Approval to Publish, and Approval for X12 Ballot or Reballot. It's a complex process and, like most committee-dominated operations, X12 suffers from bureaucratic slowness, but it works pretty well. Broad ventures like Project EASI would be very unlikely to accomplish much without it.

In the United States X12 is by far the dominant EDI standard, but internationally EDIFACT is highly influential. EDIFACT is focused on enabling EDI for international trade transactions. It thus includes transaction sets for customs, trade documentation, letters of credit, and the like. Earlier it was thought that the EDIFACT and the ANSI standards would be merged in the late 1990s, but this has not come to pass. One of the reasons is that, given the already substantial investment in ANSI-based EDI systems in North America, the costs for change are not yet seen as justified by any clear business value. Outside North America, the adoption of EDI has been slower but it is not yet clear that EDIFACT will become the standard for electronic international trade. In the meantime X12 and EDIFACT coexist and increasingly cooperate.

See also **EDIFACT; X12 Standards.**

API See **Application Programming Interface.**

Application Interface See **Application Programming Interface.**

Application Programming Interface (API) An application programming interface, or simply "application interface," is the link from an existing software system, such as a firm's accounts payable system, to a system or service that handles the relevant electronic commerce transaction, such as an electronic payment or an EDI message acknowledging receipt of an invoice. This is the single most important and difficult technical and organizational aspect in developing an electronic commerce environment. Even if the base application is a "client" service, such as a system to enter purchase orders or disburse payments, data must flow electronically and directly into or out of the "server" application in order to benefit from the use of electronic commerce. Any rekeying of data at any point risks error and adds more cost (the cost of the rekeying itself and the cost of operating otherwise unnecessary devices such as keyboards and printers, both of which electronic commerce is intended to eliminate). More important, such human intervention entails unnecessary extra administration, steps, and staff that should have been eliminated in the process of streamlining business procedures by means of electronic commerce. An API removes steps and people in the process chain by substituting automatic software links for people and paper links.

Integrating the data from the central transaction management system into the EC service application usually requires a significant effort, particularly if the system is a long-standing one, often referred to as a "legacy" system. Legacy systems often lack adequate documentation, have been updated and "patched" over many years to meet changing business requirements, and have taken on a life of their own, so that the procedures and controls of today are based on the systems and processes of yesterday. An EDI application is both a technical venture requiring an API and a process design innovation requiring careful analysis of the business and organizational logic of those systems and processes. Careful assessment can flush out many operating problems and idiosyncrasies. The firm should take this opportunity to rethink or reengineer the process; often such analysis shows that new data is needed or finds old data to be inconsistent or redundant.

Application of EDI principles can provide far more value than just automating links between software systems. The fundamental

Building a Web site is a fairly simple process, even for a multimedia dazzle display. Linking that Web site to existing transaction systems is not at all simple and involves very different skills. It requires software tools for "interfacing" different systems and technologies. APIs provide the link. When you hear your firm's Webmaster use the acronym API, reach for your budget and add a zero to the estimated cost of development. Perhaps, though, you should also add a few zeroes to the revenue projections. APIs are the base for making the Web a transaction environment rather than an information feed.

tenet of EDI is to standardize the interface between two systems, not the systems themselves. Translation is the operating mechanism for EDI. In other words, your accounts payable system can use whatever terms and procedures you want and my payment system will use whatever terms and procedures I want. However, when you send me an EDI message, you must first translate your terms into the ones we have agreed to adopt for business-to-business communication. Generally, they will be part of the ANSI X12 family of transaction sets. For example, if I'm sending you an invoice, we use X12 810, and if you're informing me of a credit or debit adjustment we use the X12 812 transaction set. In effect, our own accounts payable and payment systems need only know which transaction set the message uses; they can then translate the incoming messages.

Application interfaces are an extension of this approach. Most of the many available commercial EDI translators can be adapted to create suitable file output or receive input from the base application, no matter what the source of the data is. For instance, many convert data created by a specific software data base system into the technical structure required to send it over a network to another system. They provide facilities to check for errors in input data, provide security, and generate reports. Many now include features for linking with the Internet. The technical principle is to keep the interface as "clean" and "transparent" as possible, as shown conceptually in Figure 2.

Both trading partners need to keep the interface between the business process and the EDI application clean and transparent. The conceptual diagram in Figure 2 can be extended to show the process rather than just the software application system, which is a part of it. The process itself should be modified or extended to prevent passing along incorrect, ambiguous, incomplete, or erroneous information into the technical conversion and EDI transaction software that would necessitate intermediaries, duplicate work, or extra administration.

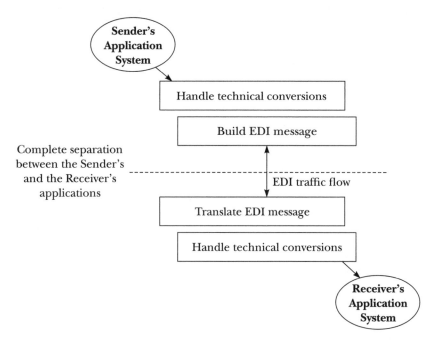

Figure 2

In Figure 3, the sender has applied the principles of the application interface. For the receiver, electronic commerce may be more of a problem than a gain. That situation often occurs when a company adopts EC only because a powerful and important customer demands it. The response is then a halfhearted investment in EC technology rather than a full commitment to EC as a business process. Given that 85 percent of firms report their primary reason for adopting EDI is pressure from a key customer, it is not surprising that few view it as an opportunity to alter business processes fundamentally. As technical necessity, EDI is a cost with at best marginal benefit. As process opportunity, however, it can be a benefit at marginal cost.

It can be hard to separate software from process. The application interface is the boundary between the transaction software and the EDI software/process and must be clearly defined as

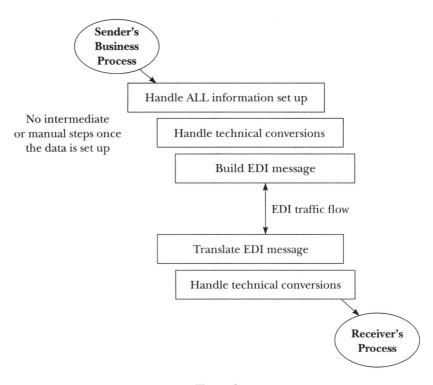

Figure 3

such. The key to an effective electronic commerce implementation is to identify the application interface as the primary point of reference and to build in the controls and management processes that address the business requirements for the service *at the interface.* Whether you are concerned about security or about processing speed, these are the driving factors for the development of an application interface.

What we've discussed here may seem a subtle point, but it's crucial. EDI is both a technology design issue and a process design issue. We've seen many firms blur the two. The application interface is the boundary between transaction management software that usually reflects both old conceptions of processes and the electronic commerce way of doing business.

See also **EDI Translation Software; Value Added Networks.**

ASN See **Advance Shipment Notice.**

ATM See **Automated Teller Machine.**

Auditing Auditing electronic commerce systems is very different from auditing systems built on paper inputs and outputs. Almost all the audit "trail" disappears, as do many control points, the very purpose of EC being to eliminate paper, delays, and administrative levels. When a purchase order is issued electronically, for instance, no printed form arrives on someone's desk and there is no second signature to approve it, no multiple copies to send to Accounting and Sales, and no volumes of files for auditors to peer through.

Electronic commerce thus demands a new philosophy for audit. Auditors are, by habit and perhaps necessity, cautious and tend not to be comfortable with EC as yet, either as technology or as process. One of the authors of this Manager's Guide spent several months working with a leading Big Six accounting firm in 1994 helping a senior partner learn about telecommunications and how electronic commerce transactions may move through a multiplicity of networks. The senior partner was horrified and actually said, "This stuff is out of control. We can't allow this to happen." For him, electronic commerce is a threat. For business, it's a future. His instincts are to impose more controls where he can. For business, the same control can be accomplished by appropriate oversight that doesn't add bureaucracy but makes sure the process is accurate and efficient.

Audit and control go together. The historical approach of auditors to electronic commerce has been to tighten controls at the entry and exit points of transactions. That used to mean where data was keyed into a computer and where it was printed out. Telecommunications changes all this because the transaction begins, is processed, and ends in more and more locations outside the firm's tightly guarded physical premises and computer data center. (On the Internet, who even knows where the customer

Legal skeptics question the reliability of computer records. They say, "Electronic messages and records can be changed. How can we rely on them for legal (or audit) evidence purposes? If there were a disagreement between trading partners A and B, how could we prove who is right? How does an outsider examining electronic records, such as a court, know if they are true?" ("EDI Legal Issues: Important but Not Alarming," EDI Forum, 1995) and company are?) Yet even though EDI, the Internet, and electronic payment systems have been used for many years, the tendency remains to "audit around the computer" at the input–output point, meaning that data contained in transaction logs or storage media is printed and reviewed after the event.

In the world of electronic commerce, transactions move too fast for transaction logs to be much more than historical record-keeping. In general, the creation of a paper replica of an event after the fact has no true value in the control process. For instance, if an error is made in a series of EDI transactions because a supplier's electronic price catalog was not updated or if a hardware device was unable to keep up with the flow of messages and simply missed one, the inputs to and outputs from the computer systems may provide no indication that a problem has occurred. Electronic commerce involves communication across many companies, many networks, and many software and information systems. The audit and control mechanisms need to be built into these, not added on to the first and last components of the message flow. Traditional auditing doesn't fit not-yet-traditional business-to-business electronic commerce.

Auditors are now beginning to place more emphasis on the overall business system and the way it is developed and managed than on printing out vast amounts of transaction data. In the most progressive organizations, the priority for managing purely electronic systems is termed "continuous review" by means of embedded audit modules. Embedded audit modules are software tools used in conjunction with application systems along the process chain. They oversee the process to ensure that all the established audit criteria are met (accuracy, timeliness, authority, recoverability, etc.). This means that audit professionals within the organization must provide advisory inputs to the business and systems development staff so that all parties understand the audit requirements and can manage *processes*—not just input and output steps—consistently and professionally.

Auditors' goals are becoming aligned with the goals of management. Instead of finding fault and focusing on controls, the EC-savvy auditor reviews the application and operation of systems and processes to ensure they meet management's goals for the organization. In most organizations, those goals are growth, profitability, speed, financial stability, and value or equity for the shareholder. To accomplish those goals, management expects all business activities to be done accurately, according to policy and processes established within the parameters of normal or accepted practice, and with an emphasis on speed and responsiveness rather than control. Audit then becomes an integral part of the business process. Much of the recent movement toward international quality standards has been the result of the need for clearly documented—audited—and well-managed processes as a requirement for business survival and success in the future.

EC auditors share these goals, though clearly their view is more specialized. The effective auditor reviews EC activity on the basis of the criteria of accuracy, completeness, security, auditability, timeliness, and recoverability.

- *Accuracy.* What methods and controls are in place to ensure that information is created and maintained in an accurate and controlled state? A business needs to maintain transaction logs and then compare and check them against actual events or conditions. The information chosen for capture along the transaction and message chain should facilitate *management* review of the process.

- *Completeness.* Are all transactions complete and have they been verified? Verifying completeness often requires a response from the message recipient to ensure that an activity has been accomplished. Many telecommunications protocols and EDI standards electronically double-check that messages arrive as sent.

- *Security.* Are the transactions being created and managed by systems or individuals authorized to engage in those transactions? Methods in this area are the use of access controls in active operating systems, segregation of duties between technology developers and operational staff, and the use of dynamic security processes such as message authentication or digital signatures that ensure that the person or device claiming to be the originator of a transaction really *is* and can be legally proven to be so.

- *Auditability.* Is there a verifiable trail and access to key support systems? One of the implications of EC is that it may now be necessary to gain access to systems or records held at either a trading partner's location or by an intermediating organization such as a value added network.

- *Timeliness.* Particularly in financial transactions, has the transaction been completed in a timely manner, with proof of transaction receipt confirmed and corroborated? The electronic equivalent of the teller's stamp is the electronic timestamp from the bank's EDI system, which indicates date and location of receipt of an electronic transaction, thus proving validity. Using a timestamp also prevents late payment penalties.

- *Recoverability.* When electronic systems temporarily "crash," or go "down," what are the procedures to bring them back on-line with sufficient integrity and speed to minimize loss of business? What backup procedures can reasonably be expected? Too often, organizations have a paper-based backup plan; they say, "We'll just do it the old way if something happens." This solution is neither reasonable nor feasible in the world of electronic commerce: paper-based backup systems tend to demand a lot of human input, so if you have to go back to the old ways and there are no humans left in the equation, it will not work. Even if an organization happens to have the staff, they would likely not have the knowledge of the old paper system to substitute for the electronic method.

In many companies, the audit function is reactive rather than anticipatory in its approach to electronic commerce. That has to change.

Authentication Ensuring that a message came from the party who claims to have initiated the message is the process of authentication. In electronic commerce, one of the greatest challenges in processing transactions is to validate that the transacting parties are who they say they are, that they are accepting responsibility for the transaction, and that the transaction has not been altered or changed in any way. Electronic commerce depends on trust. Trust is hard to build when the two parties are computers or anonymous parties unknown to each other. It's even harder to ensure when there's a fraternity, however small, of technology-smart individuals who specialize in "hacking" and "cracking" telecommunications networks and computer systems.

Often the term *encryption* is used for the processes that perform the tasks of verifying the validity and security of a transaction, but the correct tool and term is *authentication*. Cryptography codes a password or message so that it cannot be hijacked on its electronic journey across telecommunications networks and through computer systems; the encoded password or message appears as a random stream of bits. Crypto systems are one of the key tools of security, but they don't ensure authentication.

Consider the case of using your own credit card on the Internet to make a purchase. Lack of security has been the single major inhibitor to the widespread use of the Net for consumer shopping, but now it is virtually certain that the transaction will be encrypted. But will that mean that it really is *you* who is making the purchase? Perhaps your card and password have been stolen. The provider of the Internet service you are using needs to get more information from you, such as the equivalent of your personal signature or a photo ID. In addition, it must be sure that the message came from you and is not the equivalent of a faxed photocopy. Authentication doesn't just apply to people. Any component in an electronic commerce system must be able to conclude that a message came from the party who claims to have originated it, has not been tampered with, and can be accepted. The user must prove his, her, or its identity and the provider must be able to check that proof.

Authentication techniques are added to and use cryptographic techniques to provide this highest level of security. A wide variety of authentication tools exist. The most basic one, routinely employed in electronic commerce, requires the use of a value called a Message Authentication Code (MAC). A MAC is created by encryption but has a different intent and result. The intent of a MAC is to provide an irrefutable "checksum" or value that is calculated by the system at the sender's end of an electronic commerce transaction or message and recalculated at the receiver's end. If the value is the same, the receiver can treat the transaction as valid and correct; it hasn't been tampered with nor has a false one been generated. In some ways, the MAC can be seen as the equivalent of a signature in a transaction.

Figure 4 summarizes the process. The MAC, normally 8 bytes long, but for this example represented by the value "1234," is attached to the message. Change any part of the message, and the receiver will generate a different value and immediately reject it. Keys are like a cipher book; both receiver and sender know that your personal code is, say, the first word in *Moby Dick*—"Call [me Ishmael]"—or the first word in the Bible's Book of Genesis—"In [the beginning]." "Call" indicates that all items in the message shift the alphabet by two positions; "A" becomes "C," "B" becomes "D," and so on. "In" means a shift of eight letters, with "A" becoming "I." The same key is used to code the message at the sender's end and decode it at the receiver's end.

That code could be broken by anyone in a few minutes. The

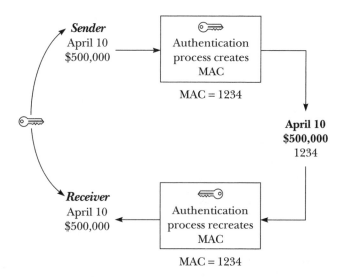

Figure 4

cryptographic tools used for electronic commerce employ won-
derfully exotic procedures that challenge even the most powerful
computers to decipher a message.

A more recent authentication development is digital signatures—encrypted additions to a message which cannot be forged.
They are rather like coded fingerprints. One advantage of digital
signatures is that they cannot be "repudiated," meaning that the
sender cannot disown the message, a key safeguard in electronic
commerce; the digital signature has contractual force. Third-party
authentication is an even newer innovation. Here, the password
that identifies a user of a service is not part of the electronic
commerce transaction but is held on an outside computer—a
"server"—that includes additional information used to verify the
identity of the sender (exactly as credit card firms will ask you for
your mother's maiden name or for the most recent transactions
you have made with the card). The server generates an encrypted
"token" that only the user's system can decode, via special-purpose software. The user is then able to access the desired service
by sending the valid token to it.

All of this is technically and mathematically complex, and there is a whole minilanguage and much more than a minibusiness involved, with terms like Kerberos, Data Encryption Standard (DES), and Pretty Good Privacy (PGP), which are publicly available software tools, as well as SHEN, a system that allows multiple levels of authentication security, from weak to strong, or from private to top secret. Obviously, no business manager can be expected to or needs to be conversant with all this, but authentication is so fundamental to the reliability, security, and public acceptability of electronic commerce that all managers involved in an activity that is part of electronic commerce or that depends on electronic commerce must be sure that it's addressed in their firm's business and technical planning.

See also **Public Key Encryption; Security.**

Automated Clearing Houses (ACH) Automated clearing houses are the main system for handling bank payments in the United States. There are around thirty regional ACH, owned by associations of banks, and a growing number of private ACH, owned by large banks or groups of banks. Ninety percent of U.S. banks are members of an ACH. Institutions that accept deposits, such as credit unions and savings and loan associations, may also be members. The National Automated Clearing House Association (NACHA) sets overall policies, and the Federal Reserve operates but does not own most of the regional ACH.

ACH were originally set up to handle huge numbers of government payments; the first ones processed Social Security payments in California starting in 1972. As electronic business has grown, the proportion of government versus corporate transactions has shifted, with government transactions now representing under half the total and corporate payments growing at over 30 percent a year, twice that of government transfers. The main use of ACH has been for regularly scheduled processing of large volumes of payments that go from the company to payee accounts

General Motors uses the banking system's automated clearing houses to pay its vendors and to receive payments from dealers for vehicles. In 1993, it made 700,000 ACH credit payments amounting to $38 billion and received 600,000 debit payments from dealers, for $12 billion. The payments average $54,000 and $20,000 respectively, making the ACH

in many banks; payroll is one such. Some government agencies pay vendors via the ACH Vendor Express service.

ACH transactions provide a range of processing options and message types. Payers can specify next-day or two-day settlement. The computer file sent to the bank will indicate the type of processing required for each transaction or each group of transactions. Among the common message formats are the following:

- *Prearranged Payments and Deposits (PPD)*. Direct deposit of payroll, monthly government transfers, and others
- *Cash Concentration and Disbursement (CCD)*. Instructions as to where incoming cash is to be transferred
- *Corporate Trade Payments (CTP)*. Payment plus limited remittance information
- *Corporate Trade Exchange (CTX)*. The only ACH format that combines a payment and full remittance advice

Every developed country has its ACH system; without clearing houses, it would be difficult to be a player in international trade or to develop an efficient commercial banking system. In most countries, the ACH is run under the supervision of the country's central banking agency and provides both transaction processing for the commercial banks and settlement reporting to the central bank for risk management. ACH associations in the United States develop the rules and framework for transaction exchange, end-of-day cut-offs, and other administrative management activities.

The use of EFT and ACHs worldwide is growing at a significant rate and, since 1989, has eclipsed the growth of paper in the 11 largest payment systems in the world. The main limitations of most systems reflect their origins as just check-clearing factories: lack of space on the messages to add information about the transaction needed for management, communication, and control. In addition, in the United States the Federal Reserve has a strong vested interest in preserving the paper-dominated ACH system. It has invested huge sums in image-processing systems—

processing fees of $0.05 to $1.20 highly cost effective—lower than the price of a postage stamp in most instances. According to a Federal Reserve Study, the administrative cost of an ACH transaction is roughly one-third that for issuing a check.

ones that read paper documents—and large buildings for doing so. ACH are really semielectronic commerce; they are for handling checks. Much of electronic commerce is about *replacing* checks.

Automated Teller Machine (ATM) An ATM is a 24-hour, stand-alone minibank located outside branch bank offices or in public places like shopping malls. Through ATMs, clients can make deposits to their accounts, withdrawals, account inquiries, and transfers. Typically, the ATM network comprises two spheres: a proprietary sphere, in which the bank manages the transactions of its clients, and the public or shared domain, in which a client of one financial institution can use another's ATMs. The shared networks are regulated by national standards (the ANSI X9 series). ATM networks in North America make extensive use of cryptography.

The ATM was one of the harbingers of personal electronic commerce because it created the market for plastic cards and on-line, real-time banking service systems. Although at first it may have appeared as simply a convenience, the ATM created a new environment:

- Clients came to expect financial services to be available 24 hours a day, 7 days a week.

- Access was at the client's discretion, not limited to the bank branch's open hours; clients became accustomed to "instant access."

- On-line customer files and electronic databases on customer activity and entitlements became the foundation for access to home banking services and related electronic services.

- Most important, ATMs made computers routine for people who had never used them and were often afraid of them. Now, very few people have any fear of electronic transaction systems if the systems are secure and easy to use.

Without the ATM, true electronic commerce would have taken much longer to evolve. The ATM profoundly changed the basics of banking over a short time, roughly 15 years. It thus provides some pointers for the likely future of electronic commerce. The first lesson is that electronic commerce will take off fastest when it offers something that directly affects simple, everyday transactions. There is nothing glamorous or innovative about ATMs by now, and none of the efforts to offer glamorous and innovative new services over them have as yet succeeded. A second lesson is that electronic commerce will inevitably generate unanticipated side effects that will be very different for different communities and even different nationalities. For example, ATMs have greatly added to the circulation of cash in the United States, where 130,000 ATMs handle 100 million transactions a month. By contrast, in China, where bank accounts are limited to organizations not individuals, the credit card has become the main vehicle of electronic commerce; this is Visa's second largest market. In Germany, most ATMs dish out a fixed amount of 400 Deutsche marks, because Germans will not tolerate waiting in line long. In Brussels, a journalist reports opening a bank account. Having asked for a two-year supply of checks, he received a checkbook containing just 40—the bank added a note that it had sent this amount to make sure he had extras!

One of the most interesting aspects of ATMs is that even after over 20 years of use, there's been very little extension of them. Home banking, widely touted in the 1980s, was a solution looking for a problem. It is only in the past few years that Intuit's Quicken system has begun to build a market that banks spent many millions on but failed to build. Intuit is a *software* company, not a bank. For all the talk about the Internet becoming a $150 billion mass market, in 1997 there are very few examples of large-scale use of electronic commerce by consumers. There are plenty of examples, though, of widespread adoption of simple tools for use in everyday life: fax machines, 1-800 telephone numbers, catalog ordering—and ATMs. Much of electronic commerce isn't yet simple to use and doesn't add much to everyday life; phones, credit cards, and faxes beat PCs and the Internet for most people and will for many years.

A final lesson from the evolution of ATMs is how easy it is for experts in an industry to underestimate the market for a new technology. Here are just a few examples:

- The founder and chairman of IBM, then the leader in tabulating machines, once stated that he saw the world market for computers being at most three systems.

- Xerox turned down the chance to manufacture machines for reading the now ubiquitous numbers on checks because there was no need whatever for banks to sort checks automatically; it was essential, Xerox believed, for humans to process checks in order to verify the signature (most banks now do this only for large payments).

- The chairman of Digital Equipment Corporation, a force in the computer industry second only to IBM at the time, stated in public that there was no reason or wish for people to have computers in their homes.

- Executives at Bank of America expressed their worry that the introduction of ATMs would bankrupt Citibank and damage the banking industry.

It's very hard to make predictions about the consumer side of electronic commerce. Hence we suggest that managers follow what we call the Braudel rule. Braudel was the French historian who advocated a shift of focus in history from events to *la longue durée,* the long-term rhythms of social and economic change. He stated that these rhythms are driven by changes in the limits of the possible in the structures of everyday life. Each of those words is key: *change* the *limits* of the *possible* in the *structures* of *everyday life.* ATMs did indeed, in the long term, do just that. The Internet, in the long term, looks like it is doing so. Home banking didn't do this in the 1980s, despite many expensive efforts. Nor did airline reservations via PCs or smart cards, nor have digital cash or smart wallets. Rapid technology innovation doesn't mean rapid social innovation. Even ATMs took a decade to make an impact.

Automotive Industry Action Group (AIAG) Founded in 1982, the Automotive Industry Action Group established a standard method for electronic data interchange throughout the U.S. automotive industry, eliminating the multiplicity of systems created when each major manufacturer and supplier developed its own message formats and software. AIAG's executive director captures the Group's purpose succinctly: "In today's industry, communication and interaction throughout the supply chain is critical. More than 60 percent of the cost of a new vehicle comes from the supply chain. . . . and the way to minimize that cost while protecting profits is to work together as an industry on pre-competitive issues, eliminating waste and streamlining processes. . . . and that is why AIAG was created" (*EDI Insider*, November 10, 1996).

AIAG was one of the very first associations to assemble all major players in an industry's business-to-business commerce to address their shared data needs and requirements and plan how to combine their differing systems. That cooperative approach is becoming the norm as companies realize they can't go it alone but need to adopt the philosophy of Walter Wriston, the legendary chairman of Citibank, who more than anyone moved banking into the electronic era. Wriston's adage: Cooperate in the morning so you can compete in the afternoon.

AIAG membership includes not only automobile manufacturers but also suppliers, transportation companies, petrochemical companies, banks, and many other organizations that support the industry's operations. Over 1,200 companies pay dues to AIAG, which is a nonprofit trade association whose main activities are (1) to identify, prioritize, and address existing and emerging

The Automotive Industry Action Group shows the degree to which cost savings can be huge when an entire industry works together. Conservative estimates are that streamlining customer–supplier electronic links has saved well over a billion dollars a year. ec.com Magazine *cites the following as typical benefits for firms cooperating in the AIAG Manufacturing Assembly Pilot initiative launched in 1994: material release processing, from 1 month to 11 days; inventory turns, up by 17–24 percent; and transaction error rates down by 75 percent.*

common issues and apply technology to increase the efficiency of the industry; and (2) to promote a sense of urgency in adopting EDI-based business processes. The group meets regularly to discuss issues and update its Implementation Guide, which provides practical advice on implementing ANSI X12 EDI standards (the main generic EDI standards) and other relevant documentation. The group also establishes and validates the industry's positions on new and emerging EDI standards. It works with relevant non-automotive ANSI X12 committees that may be developing new transaction sets for, say, insurance or warehousing applications. AIAG is thus at once a clearing house for information and advice, a coordinator for industry action, and a communication link to other industries.

One lesson the automotive industry's experience provides for all businesses is that the industry, not the individual company, is the main lever for progress in electronic commerce. The AIAG is effective because its members view it as a force for making decisions and setting directions, not just as a committee. The impetus for cooperation and real action was the crisis of the 1970s and 1980s when the U.S. car industry lost market position to Japanese competitors. The American firms had to entirely rethink the basics of their business: quality, cost, design, time to market, employee relationships, training, and the supply chain. To regain their position vis-à-vis foreign competition, they had to act as an industry, not just individual firms.

Once the new business structure and methods were thought out, individual companies could take advantage of the opportunity to transform their own supply chains. Chrysler illustrates the role of electronic commerce in this process. *Business Week* (November 25, 1996) describes the automaker as "Detroit's profitability champion" which has "rewritten the book on supplier relations." Chrysler's development of what the *Harvard Business Review* calls a "U.S. *keiretsu*" took around seven years—*keiretsu* being the Japanese term for the typical Japanese business structure of a holding company and its operating units, which is built around a set of close relationships with suppliers and subsidiaries. The first step did not involve basic changes in relationships, but Chrysler both encouraged more open communication and provided suppliers with more information. This became the base for bringing suppliers into Chrysler's own initiatives in product development and process improvement. Chrysler stopped pitting suppliers against each other, a reversal of the previous, adversarial tradition, in which the power players, the big automakers, pushed suppliers every year to beat each others' prices and terms. Chrysler developed a formal system for planning and measuring joint cost improvement programs, called SCORE. In SCORE's first two years, fiscal 1990 and 1991, the firm recorded 875 ideas generated by suppliers, which resulted in savings of $171 million. By the end of 1995, the total was 5,300 ideas, worth $1.7 billion a year.

Between 1989 and 1996, Chrysler cut its supplier base from 2,500 to 1,140. This simplification of the supply chain contributed to the firm's success in slashing time to develop a new vehicle from 234 weeks to 160 and development costs by 20 to 40 percent. Profit per car increased from $250 to $2,110! The goal has been to add value in design without adding costs. Success is indicated by Chrysler's 1996 engineering costs of 2.7 percent of revenues as compared with over 5 percent for Ford and General Motors. It was the AIAG standards that provided the industrywide foundation on which Chrysler could build its combination of business strategy, supplier relationship strategy, and company-specific information systems.

Other industries have organizations comparable to AIAG. Much of the development of EDI has been driven by voluntary committees within industry associations. One of the most effective of these efforts has been the Petroleum Industry Data Exchange group (PIDX), whose chairman summarized the key issues for the future as follows (*ec.com* Magazine, November/December 1996), highlighting pitfalls as well as needs:

- After defining standards, help members address the practical issues of implementing them. "Standards enable implementation, [but] they are not implementation." That's a point often ignored by users and suppliers. Once a standard has been precisely defined, approved, and published, it has to be embodied in software, hardware, and telecommunications systems. Often, this leads to "minor" differences in interpretation, programming, and so on. The typical standard-setting organization lacks the ability, interest, resources, or reason to play an active role in implementation. The PIDX experience suggests that such groups should play an active role.

- Drop the hype. Get beyond promising benefits to identifying measurable results.

- Encourage frequent and meaningful *business-level* interaction. One of the problems "technical people" involved in EDI often emphasize is the need to get the message to top management so it can affect the core of the business as well as relationships with the firm's trading partners. The very success and cohesion of industry standard-setting groups can too easily lead to insularity. For example, only a tiny fraction of business managers have even heard of ANSI X12 (see Glossary entry), even though its activities are opening up new opportunities for them and changing processes and relationships dramatically.

- Move to managed expectations. Never mind the "Vision of the Future," and promises that the Internet will take over the world.

Don't even try to hype electronic commerce; just look at the proven benefits, provide plenty of examples, and build the business case on the expectation of 20 percent improvements in operational measures of business performance. We recommend to all firms that they draw on any strong industry association in their strategies for electronic commerce and make sure that they are well represented in the association. Cooperate in the morning to compete in the afternoon.

Bar Coding   A bar code is a graphic representation of numbers or a code that can be read by an automated scanner device, usually using a laser that illuminates the code. Its simplest feature is a product number that can be scanned at the checkout counter of a supermarket or in a warehouse. The more far-reaching aspect of bar coding is that the coded information moves with the goods. More and more information can be added if it can be compressed into a small enough space for a scanning device to pick it up. Newer versions of the bar codes you see on soup cans or pharmaceutical products, for instance, store information about the origin of a production batch plus its composition and quality control data—basically anything and everything the manufacturers and vendors want to track.

The most prevalent method of representation of bar code information is governed by Universal Product Code (UPC), a bar code managed by the Uniform Code Council (UCC), which represents hundreds of companies, mostly in manufacturing industries. The UCC assigns the first six digits in the code to the manufacturer, and then the manufacturer assigns the next five, covering such values as size, color, and lengths (all of which are governed by the UPC standard for terminology and metrics). The twelfth and final character is a check digit calculated from the other digits; if one of them is altered or misread, the recalculation won't produce the original check digit, thus alerting the system to the error. The bar code or UPC, now very familiar to consumers, looks like a striped box and can be found on virtually any consumer product.

Bar codes have become an integral element of electronic data interchange for matching actual physical goods received with the sender's information about goods shipped. The logic of bar coding is that information about goods travels with the goods,

Bar codes can be placed on just about anything. One of the most unusual examples is the tagging of honeybees for scientists to track their movements, sexual behavior, and entry and exit to hives. The codes are positioned between the bees' shoulder blades, so that the bees can't rub them off.

A typical department store will maintain in its computer files data on around 2 million unique items—called Stock Keeping Units (SKUs), each with its own Universal Product Code (UPC). Ten shirt styles, 10 colors, 10 collar sizes, 10 sleeve lengths, and 2 collar styles adds up to 20,000 SKU's—all for one set of display shelves. Without bar codes, inventory management would be a muddle.

Most UPC bar codes contain 12 digits. The first indicates how the item is priced—by the unit (0, 6, 7), by the pound (2), or with a coupon (5). The next 5 digits identify the manufacturer (it costs $300 to $10,000 to obtain a number from the Uniform Code Council in Ohio). The next 5 digits are the product number, which the manufacturer assigns. The final digit is a "check" digit that is calculated from the other 11 and used to detect scanner errors; the scanner repeats the calculation and if any digit has been misread it will generate a different result for the check digit.

whereas EDI messages travel without the goods. Putting the two together means that if, for instance, a supplier has sent the wrong parts, the EDI information flags the problem. By using bar codes, a significant increase can also be made in controlling the accuracy and speed of data entry at the physical product level. Bar coding is the basis for automating many functions in the movement of goods, including ordering, shipping, receiving, and inventory management, as well as at the consumer level by gathering data at point of sale (the cash register).

The recent introduction of two-dimensional (2-D) bar coding has significant implications for the future of data management at the physical product level. Developed by Symbol Technologies, the 2-D bar code can store over 1,000 characters of data in the same physical space as a standard bar code and thus can be used to represent much more information about a product. Applications of 2-D bar coding will be useful in the healthcare industry, where certain scientific data about batches of medicine or drugs is critical, and also in the metals industry, where detailed metallurgical data about production techniques is needed.

Bar coding is often used at two levels in the supply chain's logistical process: the item level and the carton level. Item-level bar coding is for recording data at point of sale, accurately capturing sales data on consumer purchases. Carton-level bar coding, also referred to as "shipping container marking," is used so that the receiver does not have to open boxes to confirm the goods contained within. Checking carton bar codes, known as blind receiving, relies on an excellent supplier–buyer relationship and good security measures at the receiving area more than on the application of technology alone. As in all successful electronic commerce applications, it is critical that a mutually beneficial and Win/Win attitude is in place to ensure the processes work.

See also **Advance Shipment Notice.**

Blind Signature   A recently developed means of ensuring privacy in electronic commerce transaction is the blind signature, which is the equivalent of a pseudonym. The bank that processes a payment or purchase over the Internet does not get the real name of the person; instead the bank receives a coded, disguised identifier. The software used to generate and decode the blind signature guarantees its validity. This ID system works something like a Swiss bank account; the bank doesn't know who exactly you are and requires only enough identification to permit you to make transactions. It does not release information about your account to anyone. In effect, you are an anonymous customer.

Blind signatures are a clever mathematical trick that accomplishes the electronic equivalent of the Swiss bank privacy. Whereas credit card transactions, for instance, identify the user of the card, transactions with blind signatures are like cash; when you use a $10 bill, it is anonymous. Given the widespread public concern about how often what should be private transactions end up in a data base that is sold to many parties and used for telemarketing and mass mailings, advocates of blind signatures believe that privacy has to become a priority in electronic commerce.

DigiCash, Inc., one of the major innovators in what is termed electronic cash—the substitution of computer bits for paper and coin—uses blind signatures.

See also **DigiCash; Digital Signature.**

CA See **Certification Authority.**

Cash Cash is a medium of exchange that is a token—something accepted as having a specific value in commerce dealings. Historically, the token has been a seashell, bean, coin, paper note, or some other unit of exchange in various societies. Cash is something that anyone will accept as "money." In the United States, a dollar bill is cash, but you're very unlikely to be able to get a shopkeeper to accept a dollar's worth of Swedish krone when you try to pay for a soda. You may also have trouble offering a thousand dollar bill and asking for change.

There are 300 billion cash purchases made each year in the United States. $1.8 trillion is spent in transactions under $10.

"It really is not electronic cash unless your privacy is protected. That's the idea of cash. You don't have to reveal your identity to pay. Cash is the most popular payment system on the planet. It's something even kids know how to use. Its particular structure may have had one technological origin, but it's now established as a fundamental payment system and certainly the most prevalent one. If you want to create an electronic thing that will replace cash, at least in cyberspace, then it should have all the features that cash has. It can have more features, but it can't have fewer." [Dr. David Chaum, founder of DigiCash, Inc., quoted in Seth Godin, Presenting Digital Cash *(Indianapolis: Sams Net Publishing, 1995), 226.]*

Electronic commerce utilizes credit cards and electronic fund transfers as its currencies of trade. The costs of handling these forms of payment prevent their being practical for very small transactions, such as buying a 25 cent electronic newspaper. Many observers believe that Internet commerce will not become popular until the costs of electronic transactions permit such payments. The race is on to create digital money—electronic cash. Some of the proposals suggest a mechanism like buying a prepaid phone card—you obtain the electronic cash from an on-line "bank" and store it on your computer to use for Internet purchases. Other proposals aim at resolving one of the major problems for Internet commerce: how to enable providers of information, software, and publications to recover their costs by charging very small amounts, as little as a hundredth of a cent.

The immediate future of innovation in electronic commerce is more about cash and security than anything else. For business-to-business commerce, most of the needed mechanisms are in place: EDI and EDI standards, payment systems, protection of information and company networks, and procedures for establishing contracts and liabilities. Already well established are value added networks that offer electronic commerce services efficiently for small and large companies. Firms are rapidly learning how to use the Internet and to adapt its technology to create their own intranets. Businesses have used electronic forms of currency for decades for funds transfers, automated clearing houses, netting, and the like. They routinely do billions of dollars of transactions in the form of electronic bits that never turn into bank notes.

For business-to-consumer electronic commerce, progress in many areas has been just as rapid, inhibited only by consumers' perceptions of security. But, until there is a form of digital currency as readily acceptable and liquid as cash, the variety of transactions that can be conveniently and cheaply handled over the

Internet and on-line information services like America Online will be limited. There will be a mass market but not a massive market.

See also **Consumer EDI; CyberCash; DigiCash; Mondex.**

Cash Concentration   The process of transferring funds from many bank accounts into a single account is known as cash concentration. The goal is to provide a single point of management, for funding disbursements, optimizing short-term loans and investments, and making sure that the local operations do not, for instance, have surplus funds while other local accounts are overdrawn.

The tools of electronic commerce are useful for this purpose. Electronic cash management systems provide the software both for accessing timely information from the user companies' bank accounts, including balances and receipts, and for transferring funds. Electronic payment systems move funds as required, through the domestic and international banking systems. Risk management software analyzes the company's exposure to volatility in foreign exchange rates. The term *lockbox* is applied to the electronic equivalent of a physical lockbox into which funds flow securely and with appropriate audit and management controls.

In itself, cash concentration is part of efficient cash management. Its broader impacts are on business logistics, where it aids in managing the flows of the firm's money inventory in the same way as managing physical flows of inventories. Thus cash concentration is an important tool in the new style of business, which focuses on processes and how to streamline them.

See also **Cash Management.**

Cash concentration is a warehouse for money, analogous to a retailer's management of the distribution flows of goods. Historically, "logistics" meant the flow of physical goods. Now, it means the management of processes that move information, money, and goods along the supply chain. The companies that have most successfully moved to just-in-time inventory and production and Quick Response and point-of-sale in selling naturally move on to apply the same principles of logistical management to their cash.

Cash Concentration and Disbursement (CCD)   One of the transaction services the U.S. Automated Clearing House offers to corporations for electronic funds transfers (EFT) is cash concentration and disbursement. The service creates electronic deposi-

As of 1995, only 750 of the 11,000 U.S. banks could accept and transmit electronic data interchange messages. Part of the problem is that the main electronic banking services, such as FedWire and automated clearing houses, were designed as direct substitutes for paper checks and the banks' own systems are check-clearing factories. These cannot handle the content and distribution of information inherent in EDI messages and related processes.

tory transfer checks, which are a means for companies to sweep all the money from their accounts at various banks and place the funds in one single account at their main cash management financial institution. The CCD format, and its sibling, the CCD+, can convey a limited amount of data about the payment (about 80 characters). The U.S. Treasury uses the CCD+ format extensively, as do large corporate payers, because its simplicity, flexibility, and ease enables it to reach almost every financial institution and account in the United States. This is not true of some of the other, more complex, transactions.

CCD resulted from the need for an electronic payment transaction that would deliver some data along with the value. Since they are simpler and more easily defined transactions, the CCD and the CCD+ are now the predominant transactions for financial EDI in the United States. Any organization involved in providing services or products to the U.S. government must be able to receive one of these transactions.

Cash Management Cash management is the management of the firm's cash inventory by techniques akin to management of physical inventories—tracking its flows, forecasting cash needs and foreign exchange needs, and managing short-term investments in order both to minimize finance costs and maximize the return available from putting the money to work.

In the late 1970s, the emergence of electronic cash management services enabled corporations to manage their financial positions electronically. Before that time, corporate treasurers gave instructions to banks and in many instances relied on banks to keep them informed of funds flows, payments, and balances. Many banks developed mainframe computer systems and offered their larger corporate clients electronic access via special-purpose computer terminals. These systems provided the facility to handle balance and transaction reporting, money transfers, and reconciliation as well as investment management and collections. As an extension to this service, many banks offered electronic lockboxes and management of accounts payable as well. These were proprietary, bank-specific systems. In the mid-1980s, the treasurer of Exxon complained that his department had 17 different terminals—one for Chase's cash management, one for Citibank's, one for Britain's Midland Bank, and so on.

Proprietary hardware is a thing of the past. Since the 1980s, banks have changed their centralized systems to PC-based applications and numerous third parties have developed software to amalgamate and integrate information from many different banks and financial institutions. Very sophisticated tools are now available to forecast cash flows and exposure to risk and to provide easy and accurate views of the funds flows within and between companies. Some of the more powerful tools are *treasury management workstations*; their name reflects the role of the corporate treasurer's office in coordinating a firm's cash inventories and funds flows.

Payment cycle changes can have serious impact on a firm's bottom line. For example, at an annual interest rate of 10 percent, a three-day reduction of the payment cycle time on a single payment of $1 million translates into $822 savings to the receiving firm. The same reduction in processing, say, $100 million in customer payments of monthly credit card bills amounts to savings of close to $1 million a year. This economic opportunity largely explains the growing use of more time-efficient manual collection methods, such as bank lockbox services and check pick-up/courier systems.

The gains are not just the direct interest savings. As the predictability of payments increases, an organization—as either payer or receiver—can manage its cash flows more effectively. For example, the corporate payer may be in a position to negotiate more favorable product terms or credit terms with its supplier by making a firm commitment to pay "on time"—promptly, by a contractually agreed date. This form of leverage has begun to emerge because many accounts-payable systems need to be restructured to provide flexibility and programmability for applying

Banking has been losing customers to firms from outside its previously well-bounded industry for decades now. Electronic commerce will surely accelerate that process, simply because fewer and fewer transactions legally require the banking system, except as a payments processing vehicle. Customers look for convenience and service that can more easily be provided by auto makers (General Motors and Ford together account for 60% of all consumer loans in the U.S.), retailers (credit cards), mutual fund companies (Fidelity, among many others, offers full-service banking with no bank branches), and even corporate customers (British Petroleum set up its own financial institution that offers many wholesale banking services without having to buy deposits).

the best terms for each particular supplier situation. Many of the more recent developments in financial EDI add information to payments and collections that enable better planning, mutually beneficial relationships between customer and supplier, and reliability and efficiency along the entire supply chain. They provide for more effective risk management. Among these developments are evaluated receipts settlements, payment on production, and cash concentration.

Money is inventory. From the perspective of cash management, reducing variability of payments means that a firm needs a lower cash buffer or threshold cash inventory. Companies do not need to keep a safety reserve just in case a funds transfer doesn't arrive, for instance. This cuts the need for financing costs or the risk of a check clearing faster than its anticipated term. Cash forecasting tools are reasonably reliable and have been improved over recent years. Nonetheless, there are still occasional "surprises" that can negate any value created by float.

Float is the time gap between the date a firm issues a check as payment and the date the funds are actually debited to the payer's bank account. Many of us rely on it at the end of the month in sending off a mortgage payment, for instance, on the 30th, when the pay check that will cover it won't be deposited until the 2nd. Companies use the float, too. Historically, firms have produced checks on or before the actual due date, but the conscientious payer usually put the check payment in the mail a day or two prior to actual value date, in order to avoid late payment penalties and ensure that checks are in line with the firm's policy for disbursing accounts payable (A/P). Typically, once an invoice has been received, approved, and keyed into the buyer's A/P system, it is held in the system until it comes due for payment according to the firm's due date algorithm. Due date algorithms typically include two basic parameters: a baseline payment date and payment time lag.

In paper-based business systems, payment due dates are often computed either from the invoice date or from the invoice receipt date. Most originators base their due date calculations on the invoice date, while the invoice receipt date is used by the smaller proportion of payers. This can lead to some significant delays to the supplier getting paid.

In many real-world cases it can take up to seven days before the invoice is mailed, after goods have been delivered and the necessary paperwork gets back to the billing office. Consider that in many firms invoicing is not done on a daily basis, which creates additional delay. Adding postal delays once the invoice has been created leads to potential time lags of up to 10 days or more between the delivery of goods and the customer's receipt of the invoice.

Some suppliers create the invoice at the same time as the bill of lading so that the invoice accompanies the customer's actual receipt of goods. The majority of invoicing applications, however, issue the invoice after goods have been shipped and, often, after they have been received. The resulting time lags between the date goods are received and the date goods are billed increase uncertainty about cash flow and can lead to errors. To use electronic commerce to optimize the supply chain and integrate logistics, which is the imperative of modern manufacturing, retailing, and distribution, requires coordinating *all* the elements of a transaction and information about it. Cash management then becomes more than just an aspect of the central corporate treasury function. It becomes an integral element of business logistics.

Applying the tools of electronic cash management has become mandatory in order for corporations to manage their money effectively and be successful. It allows firms to manage cash as inventory and apply other proven tools—total quality management, just-in-time inventory, and process reengineering. Although originally the cost of technology, expertise, and banking relationships necessary for electronic cash management largely limited its use to large organizations, now with the PC, accessible software, and the Internet, even the smallest firm can exploit cash management and financial electronic data interchange. It's an opportunity not to be missed. The Internet provides the telecommunications reach the small firm could not hitherto afford, and the personal computer provides the access and processing capabilities. All that is needed to seize the opportunity is the firm's commitment to make cash management a business priority.

See also **Automated Clearing Houses; Evaluated Receipt Settlement; Financial EDI.**

CCD   See **Cash Concentration and Disbursement.**

Certification Authority (CA)   In proposed applications of public key based cryptographic security now undergoing pilot studies, an unbiased third party, termed the *certification authority*, intermediates the exchange of "keys"—coded data—between two entities. A *key* is the secure code used to encrypt and decrypt data to protect it from prying eyes. Cryptography is the method of applying complex mathematical procedures in order to turn, say, the number "$1,000,000" or the statement or command "Buy 20,000 shares of IBM" into a stream of bits that can't be interpreted, altered, or misused. The resulting encrypted message then looks like a random jumble of electronic garbage.

The CA is a trusted entity who determines the identity of a party, say a potential trading partner, seeking access to electronic information, and confirms that identity to others. In other words, a CA is an organization that verifies and certifies that you, or your organization, exist and are who you say you are. The CA can then provide a "certificate" for this verification—in the form of an electronic key or value—which you can present electronically to the CA for verification and confirmation at any time by a trading partner. This method makes conduct of electronic commerce anonymously, or without a prior relationship, practical. It's analogous to being able to have your credit card accepted and payment authorized in thousands of stores and restaurants around the world. The merchant doesn't know who you are but can verify your identity and the validity of your use of the card. Certification authorities provide the equivalent guarantee. By the same token, there is a need for a standardized and recognized methodology and "directory" for CAs; this has not yet come to pass—there is not yet the CA equivalent of a MasterCard.

Organizations perceived as candidates for this essential role in extending electronic commerce to the widest market are the U.S. Postal Service or other quasigovernmental organizations that can be seen as unbiased, comfortable, and legitimate in the role. As well, a number of trade or industry associations are also considering serving as CA on behalf of their constituents or members. As the application of public key-based cryptography grows, it is likely that there will emerge a specialty field for providing such a service for a fee. This is still an unresolved aspect of the concept of public key cryptography and will likely result in the emergence of a number of competing schemes and CAs.

See also **Public Key Cryptography.**

Checks   Checks remain the cornerstone of today's commerce systems, with complex payment mechanisms in place for banks to process the huge volumes of paper they comprise. By the very fact that checks are paper, they represent a main target of opportunity for electronic commerce in general and electronic data interchange in particular. Every paper check replaced by an electronic transaction provides tangible benefits in terms of cost, speed, avoidance of errors, and administration. The cost of an electronic funds transfer is typically one-tenth the cost of a paper check. The infrastructures needed to process the more than 300 checks issued annually per U.S. household are immense and constitute much of banks' investment in real estate, staff, and information technology. The Federal Reserve Bank charters close to 50 airplanes every day of the year to fly bundles of checks that banks have sorted and tabulated to a central location where they are retabulated. Checks take days to clear, are very vulnerable to errors and fraud, and require complex equipment to handle what looks like a very simple task.

In 1993, 96% of all noncash transactions in the United States were made by check. Consumers issued 55% of these, businesses 40%, and the government 5%. Electronic processing accounted for only 0.2% of the total noncash transactions. However, it amounted to almost 90% of the total value.

The days of checks are numbered. Every innovation in payments and most innovations in business-to-business commerce displace checks. The mainstream of developments for business-to-consumer commerce via the Internet is obviously to use electronic service instead of paper. Among the proposed electronic alternatives to checks are credit cards, digital cash, smart wallets, and electronic data interchange. The main obstacles are (1) tradition and habit, and (2) the heavy investment in the check-processing, accounting, and clearing systems that are now the base for commerce.

In 1992, over 80 percent of consumer bills were paid by credit transfer, where one check for the total of a set of household bills is written and the public "giro" banking system disburses the funds to the various accounts. In countries like Sweden and Germany, the figure varies between 50 and 80 percent. In the United States, it is under 2 percent.

Tradition and habit can be thought of by believers in the Something of the Future as "resistance to change," or inertia, or some other undesirable response. In fact, very often the tools we use today are good enough and the cost of adapting to new ones is expensive—even if the new ones work as promised—and the likely payoff from the change is not worth the effort. That's certainly the case with checks. Anyone with a credit card and checkbook can wander through their everyday life quite comfortably. Why switch? To date, there's little incentive to change.

For this reason, there are many ongoing efforts that aim at evolution from paper to electronic checks, rather than substitution. Quicken and Microsoft Money, for instance, offer users of their financial software for the home and the small business the option to write electronic checks and send them by electronic mail (e-mail) to banks that process them exactly as if they were paper checks. NetCheque and CheckFree offer electronic checks that are rather like a cashier's check; they are endorsed as valid by the service provider, which also adds security features. Several electronic payment services provide the float, the feature that many customers see as an advantage of traditional checks. Customers rely on float—the time gap between the date they mail a check and the date it is debited to their account. A customer's bank account is usually debited two to five days after the person mails the check, allowing the person use of the money until then or, more often, ensuring that the check is honored even though it was mailed before the person deposited the monthly pay check or other funds to cover it.

It will probably be another 10 years before there is a widespread replacement of checks in everyday life. The pace of change will vary widely across the world, too. In Japan, checks are rare, with the average family writing four or less a *year.* In much of Europe, too, cash dominates; credit cards are still uncommon in Germany and the Netherlands. In Sweden, sending checks abroad requires approval from tax authorities and such checks may be made out only to companies, not individuals.

In terms of infrastructures, the existing check payment and processing systems are well established, widespread, reliable, and highly efficient. The banking system, automated clearing houses, and the like constitute a giant check factory. It will take plenty of time for anything to supersede them.

CHIPS   See Clearing House Interbank Payments System.

Clearing House Interbank Payments System (CHIPS)

CHIPS is one of a number of bank-to-bank exchange systems that have evolved in the United States over the past several decades. As in other countries, this relatively specialized component of the nation's payments systems was built to track and manage transactions that have special attributes or concerns, such as the need to convey a large amount or to be able to deliver the transaction faster than normal bank clearing channels can accommodate.

Operated by the New York Clearing House Association, which also operates private automated clearing houses (ACH), CHIPS is used primarily to manage the settlement risk between banks while handling large dollar payments among a relatively small number of banks (around 150). Processing a CHIPS payment entails comparing the transaction against a threshold or limit that has been established between the two banks involved in the transfer. The level of this threshold may affect the actual conveyance

Around a trillion dollars a day passes through the CHIPS system in settlement of electronic foreign exchange transactions—in other words, a trillion dollars of FX deals generates a trillion dollars of bank payments. At least one side of these payments— payer or payee—is almost sure to be in dollars, the international unit of currency.

Most CHIPS transactions relate to foreign exchange trade settlements (65 percent) or government bond and interest rate derivatives (20 percent). That means that only about 15 percent of the 200,000 daily transactions amounting to $1.3 trillion have anything to do with payments for "real" goods and services.

or release of funds. For example, two large and well-funded banks would likely set a higher limit between themselves than a large bank would with a smaller, or less well-funded, bank. If the transaction exceeds the prescribed limit, the receiving bank will hold the funds until settlement from the other bank has occurred through the Federal Reserve Bank or until some other risk reduction takes place. The float, or delay in funds reaching the recipient's account, would therefore affect funds available to the ultimate recipient. If an organization is concerned about timely delivery of funds, it can choose the more expensive, but higher-performance FedWire system to convey its payment instruction.

All CHIPS transactions relate to domestic U.S. payments; however, a large proportion of them are settlements for international transactions between correspondent banks and their respective U.S.-based relationships. Unlike the FedWire system, CHIPS transactions are accumulated throughout the day and settled at the end of the day, similar to ACH transactions. In the FedWire system, the sending bank must fund the transaction with the Federal Reserve prior to its release to the recipient bank.

CHIPS resolves an issue that electronic complements or replacements must address: risk management. A party involved in a CHIPS transaction can be sure that if it is accepted, the funds will flow and the payment be honored. With every single innovation in electronic payments, that guarantee must be assured to all parties in a transaction. In many instances, software companies like Microsoft, startup firms such as CyberCash, and small banks like Mark Twain are among the pacesetters in the use of the technology for payments, replacement of checks, and creation of electronic currencies. They will need acceptance, commitment, and in many cases investment in their firms from the power players in today's financial markets.

Clipper Chip The Clipper Chip is a computer chip that encrypts—that is, codes—messages so they cannot be read by unauthorized parties. It was developed as part of a U.S. government project that was and remains highly controversial and that has significant implications for electronic commerce. Cryptographic techniques make it virtually impossible and perhaps even literally impossible for anyone to work out the "keys" that are used to code and decode the data. These keys are massive numbers used in arcane calculations that even the largest computer could not replicate by systematically trying out all possibilities.

The Clipper Chip is one product of the government's 30-year-long struggle with the problem of how to balance the conflicting concerns of, on the one hand, companies and individuals who wish to preserve the privacy of their electronic communications and, on the other, police and intelligence agencies who fear that criminals and terrorist groups will be able to operate with complete security, safe from all surveillance. Wiretaps, for instance, would be useless if a chip encrypted everything that was being spoken over it and only the receiving party could decrypt it. Such a use of encryption is technically fully feasible today. If Mafia don John Gotti had had a computer science adviser, he could have negated all the many hours of wiretapped conversations that put him in jail.

Accordingly, the government proposed in 1993 that the Clipper Chip would be required for all encryption, in personal computers, bank payments systems, hardware devices, and the like. The communications would still be encrypted with a secure key, but a copy of the key would be kept by an authorized third party—an "escrow agency." The agency would make the key available to law enforcement authorities if and only if the courts issued a warrant for them to hand over the key.

The government's proposal unleashed a flood of protest in the computer science community. Some of the objections concerned the intrusion on the right to privacy, some concerned fears that the (unpublished and secret) mathematical procedures proposed for encrypting data were potentially not secure, and some objections were raised on the economic grounds that by restricting the development, use, and export of "strong" encrypted

Powerful arguments exist for freedom from government interference in and intrusion on electronic communications, as well as for controlled government rights to prevent secrecy that damages national security or facilitates crime. There are equally powerful arguments against, and few arguments for, the government's imposing the use of the Clipper Chip in every piece of hardware sold in the U.S., imposing Skipjack, its own mathematical encryption "algorithm," and making its Capstone project literally that—the capstone for security in electronic commerce. The government has gotten bad press but the issues are very complex and consequential: freedom versus protection, individual versus national rights, and information use versus control of information misuse.

chips, the government would be hampering U.S. business and handing over the market to Japanese competitors.

In 1996, the Clinton administration relaxed the restrictions on the use and export of cryptographic chips and software. It now looks like the original proposal for the Clipper Chip is dormant if not dead. However, the issue it reflects won't go away: privacy versus national security.

See also **Data Encryption Standard; Public Key Cryptography.**

CommerceNet   Launched in Silicon Valley in April 1994, CommerceNet is a not-for-profit market and business development organization. Its stated mission is "to accelerate the growth of Internet Commerce, and create business opportunities for our members." Membership includes 200 leading banks, electronics firms, telecommunications companies, providers of on-line services, Internet Service Providers (ISPs), software and services companies, as well as major end-users.

In November, 1996, CommerceNet and the Electronic Frontier Foundation (EFF) joined together to form ETrust, which aims at establishing consumer confidence and trust in electronic transactions. It will certify companies that meet specific security requirements; they will be allowed to post the ETrust logo—"trustmark"—on their Internet Web sites. Today, distrust is high among consumers— distrust that their privacy will be respected and protected and that the Net is secure. The Executive Director of the EFF claims that when

CommerceNet creates value by bringing together vendors and end-users who possess key pieces of the Internet Commerce puzzle, thus helping them to seize important market opportunities jointly. The series of services—vision, technology, project management, public relations, and legal/policy advocacy—CommerceNet delivers in partnership with its members creates business opportunities for them. Because of its membership, CommerceNet is expected to be a major player in the evolution of the Internet to a highly profitable electronic mall of the future.

Evidence of its likely impacts is shown by the announcement in October 1996, that the World Wide Web Consortium (W3C) and CommerceNet had finalized the specifications for the Joint Electronic Payments Initiative (JEPI). W3C is an association of leading Internet scientists whose mission is to help evolve, through influence and expertise rather than formal authority, the next generation of Internet technology and standards. JEPI is a universal payments platform that will allow merchants and consumers to carry out transactions over the Internet using many different forms of payment. W3C and CommerceNet spearheaded the effort to agree on a specification for JEPI that is being implemented by such providers of hardware, software, telecommunications, and electronic commerce services as IBM, Microsoft, British Telecommunications, and CyberCash. The principle behind JEPI is that the relevant Internet component systems—those of the merchant, the bank, and the customer—negotiate what types of payment are acceptable, including credit cards, bank account debits, or the more exotic forms of digital "cash" being piloted across the world, and handle the technical issues of communication of information and payments among the parties.

JEPI is a significant move forward in the progress of the Internet as the base for consumer rather than corporate electronic commerce. The prestige of CommerceNet's membership makes it a strong force. Whether that force will result in implementation is hard to predict. The field of electronic commerce is moving so rapidly that changes in the technology itself and the wishes of individual players in the marketplace to establish their own products as the standard often get in the way of cooperation. Microsoft, for instance, is both participating as a CommerceNet member and at the same time pushing several of its own schemes for merchant and consumer purchasing and payments via the Internet.

See also **Digital Cash.**

you ask a roomful of people if they immediately leave a Web site that asks them to register their names, half the room will say yes, and those who do register input bogus data. (Gary H. Anthes, "In Web E-Trust," Computerworld, *18 November 1996)*

Consumer EDI   Consumer EDI denotes the extension of electronic data interchange in business for the purpose of reducing the costs of processing the routine paper documents a firm sends to its customers, most obviously monthly bills. Many utilities and insurance companies now send invoices via EDI to their large commercial customers. Now that more and more households have PCs and are linked to the Internet, the infrastructure is in place for those businesses to begin adding consumers to their electronic commerce bases.

The key word here is "begin." In early 1996, an ANSI X12

In 1995, American Express launched and soon abandoned a payment plan for consumers to write "One Check" to cover all their utility bills. Four years of market research concluded that 10 percent of U.S. households would adopt the service. It was a dud. Utilities pulled out on the grounds that they would lose the opportunity to include ads and promotions with the bill. The system had taken far longer than expected to get started because it involved close to 100 electricity and gas companies, each with its own billing statement format. As often happens in the application of information technology, a good idea failed because there was no compelling benefit—the current systems worked well enough—to offset tradition and habit.

working committee published guidelines for consumer billing via EDI. It has developed three X12 transaction sets: one for invoicing, one for payment, and one for requesting bill-paying services from a "Consumer Service Provider" (CSP). The committee envisions the CSP as the intermediary between company and consumer. They would provide a single point of communication for consumers. Your phone bill, insurance renewal invoice, and credit card statement would be sent to your CSP, which is most likely to be your bank. The CSP would forward each bill to you via the Internet or an on-line service provider like CompuServe. You would review the electronic bills and then authorize a direct debit from your bank account.

The new transaction sets will be tested by just a handful of companies. Companies have been cautious about trying out an innovation for which no evidence exists that consumers are interested. Unless most consumer billing were to be transacted in this electronic way, there would be little value to the consumer. If just your phone bill and payment, say, are handled electronically but not your credit card, insurance, electricity, bank, and other monthly statements, why bother? If they were all handled through a CSP, though, both you and the billing party would each save the cost of a stamp, and payment would be made immediately and reliably. For companies that send out large volumes of small bills, the savings should be substantial. That is because one of the problems of processing payments by check is that every envelope and its contents has to be treated as a special case; people forget to put their account number on the check, forget to enclose the original bill, leave out data and so on.

One of the first implementers of consumer EDI is CheckFree, which began to roll out an Internet bill delivery service in late 1996. It began with just seven billers, for whom it handles a range of technical functions, including setting up data bases and inserting promotional material in the electronic bills that customers see on their PC screens. Queried about problems of security on the Internet, which have greatly inhibited its widespread use, a

CheckFree executive replied, "Yes, there are security concerns, but what security do you have today? You get your bill in the mail and how many stories are there about people rifling through envelopes?" (*EC/EDI Insider,* September 16, 1996).

CheckFree is cautiously phasing in its system and reckons it will need several years, plenty of marketing, and education of both companies and consumers for consumer EDI to take off. It clearly *will* take off at some point. For anyone who checks his or her electronic mail daily and links to the Internet even once a week, consumer EDI is just another type of message. For the millions of people using such software packages as Quicken for managing their finances, it's more convenient than messing around with bills, checks, envelopes, and stamps scattered on the desk on which your PC sits.

The Internet will be integral to the success, or lack of it, of consumer EDI, because of costs. There are many EDI systems provided via value added networks (VANs) or via bank clearing house networks, but the cost per transaction is 5 to 30 cents. Via the Internet, the incremental cost is basically zero, though the setup costs may be high. The new ANSI X12F WG4 committee's guidelines provide the standardized base for consumer billing. The Internet provides the established infrastructure and the PC the access point.

Continuous Replenishment (CR) The dynamic, constant matching of the flow of materials and parts to their usage in manufacturing production or to sales in retail stores is called continuous replenishment (CR). As part of just-in-time (JIT) inventory management, which has become the foundation of modern manufacturing, continuous replenishment is the physical logistics of JIT. CR defines and refines the parameters for the cycle time, the relationship between how long a product remains "on the shelf" and the time it takes for it to be replaced. Often, one of the most challenging aspects of implementing JIT is not in whether or not a supplier can deliver the goods in a timely and speedy manner,

In April 1997, American International Group, a large, profitable, and innovative insurer, began offering liability coverage to U.S.-based Web sites—up to $250,000 against liability suits from credit card holders whose card numbers are stolen and up to $1 million against personal injury suits for unauthorized use of private information. AIG also offers coverage for damage caused by hackers to Web sites, as well as for business interruption costs. (Information Week, *28 April 1997, 67)*

Benchmarking Consultants estimates that there is well over $700 billion in goods in the retailing supply pipeline. Experience in supply chain management suggests that this can be halved, resulting in huge savings in the cost of working capital.

Wal-Mart and Warner-Lambert, for instance, cut the forecast to production to delivery cycle time from 12 to 6 weeks, using an emerging extension of Quick Response technology called Collaborative Forecasting and Replenishment (CFAR). In essence, CFAR focuses on using shared information for early forecasting, whereas QR focuses on EDI for ordering and delivery.

but whether the goods, once delivered to the buyer, quickly find their way to the actual use point.

In manufacturing, this means delivering the part or item as close as possible to the production line where that item will be used. In many cases, the plant requires physical modification to accommodate this approach. Ford Motor Company has dozens of delivery points along the production line for automobiles, so that preassembled components such as engines or dashboards can be delivered directly to their installation point, in some cases less than 50 feet from the loading dock. In retail apparel, continuous replenishment means the efficient and accurate use of bar coding—in some cases packing the boxes in the same sequence as they will be placed on shelves during restocking—with the point-of-sale register accurately recording changes in inventory up to the minute.

Continuous replenishment is a key impetus motivating the application of electronic commerce. Only with the speed and accuracy of electronic messaging can suppliers be expected to deliver replacements for goods consumed only a few days, or sometimes hours, before. Furthermore, CR depends on direct interchange of purchase information from the point of sale, directly from the electronic cash register, through EDI links from the inventory management system of the retailer to the order entry system of the vendor.

Contracts Every aspect of business involves implicit or explicit contracts, ranging from the implicit one involved when you go into a supermarket and buy a pound of butter to the much lengthier and more formal process of completing all the forms for settlement in closing on the purchase of a house. In the supermarket, you know that you must pay for the butter and that the shop must charge you the displayed price. With the house purchase, the contract includes disclaimers about liability, terms and conditions for your mortgage, and legal clauses that cover issues of discrimination, truth in lending, and the like.

Electronic commerce involves explicit and implicit contracts. In many instances, though, many uncertainties remain about the extent to which existing contract law applies. U.S. law distinguishes three modes of communication that establish a contract:

- *Instantaneous.* If the parties meet face to face or negotiate over the phone, an offer or acceptance is regarded as made when it is spoken and thus legally "operable."

- *Delayed* (U.S. Postal Service). The offer/acceptance is made when the mail is dispatched or physically deposited in a mailbox.

- *Delayed* (non-U.S. Postal Service). In this case, which is increasingly the base for electronic business, offers and acceptances are deemed as having been communicated and hence being operable when the message is *received,* not sent. This applies to faxes, electronic mail, and couriers.

It is unclear where liability applies in such instances as an EDI network failing to transmit or receive a document. There has not yet been a precedent-setting court case. The divergence between the date of effectiveness or legitimacy of the contract delivered by the U.S. Postal Service and that of the contract delivered by some non-U.S. Postal Service carrier is a major issue for the future of EDI. Is the contract determined by when I send it to you or when you get it?

Electronic contracts are surrounded by uncertainties, especially concerning legal liability in payments and credit card transactions, as well as jurisdiction. For example, where does state tax law apply with Internet commerce, given that the buyer and seller may be in different states or countries and the computer that links them may be in yet another state or country? For business-to-business electronic commerce, the solution is to require a formal document, generally termed a trading partner agreement, that lays out mutual expectations and mechanisms for handling problems and errors, and that is designed as a statement about how

U.S. trademarks can be violated in cyberspace even if the site is not in the U.S. One Italian publisher found himself at odds with the U.S. courts when he published a Web site that offered a quick peek at its "male sophisticate" magazine, Playman. *Because Playboy Enterprises had only registered the Playboy trademark in the U.S., no conflict existed in Italy, where the server and the publisher were located. He was ordered by the court to restrict U.S. Internet access to his site. Trademark holders in the U.S. were elated by this judgement, until it was expanded to other jurisdictions. "This nationalistic concept of Internet resources is a double-edged sword: a Tokyo court could just as easily justify that a U.S. trademark holder's Web*

site violates some Japanese trademark. How can a Web site realistically and pragmatically screen all foreign access?" Any unauthorized use of a Japanese trademark generated from a software program and visible on a computer screen is considered a violation by Japanese courts. It remains unclear whether Japan will extend domestic trademark rights to foreign sites.
(Computing Japan, *March 1997, 26)*

the partners will work together, rather than as a "legal contract." All the experience accumulated by companies over the past 20 years in applying EDI to the basics of their trading partner relationships shows that trust and joint discussion of processes is more important than the technical issues that get the priority and all the attention and resources.

Discussions are frequent in the press and in business about our society moving to an information economy. In many ways, the issue is how to move toward a trusting economy; it is trust that makes electronic commerce work, with shared information the foundation for trust in a contractual relationship. The consistent pattern of customer–supplier relationships in EDI is that customers implementing electronic commerce first narrow down their list of suppliers, dropping those who are not equipped for EDI. As the remaining trading partners extend EDI across the supply chain and use it to transform their business processes, they add forms of transaction that go well beyond the traditional control- and contract-dominated ways of doing business. Customers pay for goods on receipt without invoices (using evaluated receipt settlement), they allow vendors to decide what goods to deliver and when (vendor-managed inventory), and they give vendors access to what used to be tightly guarded in-house data about sales and trends. They add information for mutual coordination, such as advance shipment notices, corporate trade exchange data, and disbursement services. Focus on process replaces focus on the transaction. The parties work interactively together; reducing the number of parties is part of increasing the quality of interaction.

See also **Trading Partner Agreement.**

Selling personal information is a $3B-a-year business—with at least 10,000 lists for sale that contain very private information about people.

Cookies   Cookies are entries in a computer file on your hard disk that list the address of a World Wide Web site plus some data. You or other users of the computer did not put them there and probably don't even know about them. It is the originator or operator of the Web site that creates the cookie in visitors' computers when computer users "visit" the Web site. If you have filled out a form on the Web, as many service and information providers request you to do, the site can track the other pages you have visited, match your cookie to your exact name and address, and sell the information to advertisers and others.

This really is an invasion of privacy and may violate laws that require informed consent. People who are informed about it can take simple action. Browsers like Netscape Navigator and Microsoft Explorer include a feature that informs you when a Web site wants to leave a cookie on your system. CommerceNet, the not-for-profit group set up to build consumer trust in the security, privacy, and safety of the Internet, and the Electronic Frontier Foundation, an advocacy group for the protection of both privacy rights and freedom of expression on the Internet, have established an organization called eTrust, for rating the privacy of Web sites. The organization issues an eTrust logo the Web site can display that shows its rating: holders of rating 1 pledge not to collect any data on their users; holders of rating 2 collect data only for use by the owner of the Web site; and holders of rating 3 disclose the terms under which they provide data to outside parties.

It is obviously the responsibility of businesses to obey the spirit and letter of privacy regulations. They should certainly both ensure that their own accesses to the Web are suitably private and encourage the eTrust initiative, including setting clear policies for their own Internet and intranet sites.

"Many people surf the Web under the illusion that their actions are private and anonymous. Unfortunately, it isn't so. Every time you visit a site, you leave a calling card that reveals where you're coming from, what kind of computer you have, and other details. Most sites keep track of all your visits. In many cases, this logging may constitute an invasion of your privacy." (PC World, *February 1997, 227)*

Corporate Trade Exchange (CTX)   The Corporate Trade Exchange message format is one of the options provided for electronically sending payments and accompanying information through the U.S. banking Automated Clearing House (ACH) system. CTX has been around since 1987 and is seen as superior to the more established Corporate Trade Payments (CTP) format for the transportation of remittance detail. A number of attributes make this so. Although the CTX is an ACH format, in essence it is an electronic envelope around an ANSI X12 820 transaction—a standardized message containing payment and remittance data. This means that it has much greater data-carrying capability than any of the other ACH formats. As well, because it envelopes an 820 message, corporations can feel a greater level of comfort in using a "nonproprietary" format (that is, a format not limited to specific networks and to banking, but widely implemented across electronic commerce service providers and users), for which they can choose a much wider variety of software and banking providers.

Overall, CTX has seen increasing use, at the expense of the CTP. There is still the problem of acceptance and capability within the banking community; less than 10 percent of the banks in the United States are capable of receiving the CTX and processing the remittance data properly to the end receiver.

See also **Corporate Trade Payments.**

Corporate Trade Payments (CTP)   The CTP is an electronic payment message format used by the U.S. Automated Clearing House (ACH) electronic banking system, which handles many large companies' routine payments. It evolved to meet the needs for corporate users of the ACH to include information with their payment messages for purposes of coordination with the recipients as part of their wider electronic commerce activities or for their own management purposes. CTP payment messages can contain a substantially larger amount of data than the alternative ACH CCD+ format—as many as 4,990 addenda records. Each addenda record typically refers to an order and invoice.

Since its introduction in 1983, CTP has attracted only limited use by the corporate market although it has found favor with a number of special-interest groups. A few key factors have limited its use:

- Few banks in the National Automated Clearing House Association (NACHA) have implemented it, and transaction volumes have continued to be low, with only the largest and most advanced companies needing it.

- The format is limited to a fixed-length data field and therefore is viewed as inefficient from a telecommunications perspective. Instead of sending just the data included in the message, each transmission also includes any empty space in the data fields.

- There are concerns that it does not offer the appropriate levels of security and encryption that are desired by the corporate market.

The banks' reluctance to adopt CTP, despite their need for it, indicates the shift from electronic payments to electronic money management and integrated logistics. This reluctance also indicates the shift of ownership of electronic money management from banks, the effective owners and drivers of the payment system, to the banks' customers—business companies—the drivers of today's electronic commerce. Banks have billions of dollars and decades of experience and tradition invested in the existing payment systems. Consequently they have tried to stick with these, reacting to demands for change rather than taking the lead. Retailers and manufacturers have used current technologies to improve their business processes, and as a result are way ahead of their banks in their thinking about the logistics of banking-related processes. Nonetheless, given the sheer volumes and values of transactions that banks have to process, and given that their proven infrastructures will remain the foundation of commerce, if the system works well, why change it? The answer to this question for a business pushing the frontiers of electronic commerce is that the traditional payment system may work well for banks, but it's slow, expensive, and built around paper and doesn't work well enough for business.

See also **Automated Clearing Houses; Cash Concentration and Disbursement; Corporate Trade Exchange.**

Costs of EDI Electronic data interchange (EDI) has three obvious areas of cost and one of hidden cost. The obvious costs are for the physical and organizational implementation and include software, hardware, training, and support. The hidden cost is the cost of reviewing and (re)designing the business process itself.

Obviously, a key issue in electronic commerce is the relative cost of processing the transaction versus its value. For credit cards, the cost is around 2%, a significant percentage of which goes towards covering the cost of fraud. Banks typically add a charge of 2% to their own cost of funds, paying depositors X% and charging X+2% for loans, though, of course, the figures vary according to customer, product, and risk. Telephone companies have the highest transaction cost differential. About 30% of the cost of a phone call is for accounting and billing. The average price of a call is 30 cents, so roughly 10 cents is for processing.

- *Software.* A translator and application interface system which can derive the data from the source system (such as purchasing or accounts payable) or deliver to the receiving system (order entry or accounts receivable) and convert it from proprietary complex data formats to standardized EDI message format. Typical costs for EDI translation software range from $300 to $3,000 on a PC, to $5,000–$10,000 on a midrange computer, to well over $40,000 for a mainframe computer. This does not include the costs necessary to map, test, and integrate the product into a specific application.

- *Hardware.* The appropriate hardware for the application is whatever platform and technology makes sense for the volumes of data to be handled and the systems architecture already in place. Whatever makes sense does not necessarily support the use of mainframe technology for relatively low EDI volumes, but it may be practical to prepare to upgrade from a PC-based solution if volume increases. Adding EDI will not raise costs significantly if the base applications are already automated.

- *Training and education.* Most companies need to place a great deal of emphasis and commitment on preparing employees for the switch to EDI, far more than most companies plan for. Without proper training and education of staff, EDI too often becomes an organizational disruption, and makes people feel uncertain and incompetent. Staff need to gain new skills in understanding the methodology of EDI and see evidence of its benefits for themselves and customers, not just be shown how to use the software tools effectively.

The largest hidden cost is the need to review the business process itself. The most effective applications of EDI occur in the areas most affected by business process change. These include efficient consumer response (ECR) in the retailing and food and grocery industries, vendor-managed inventory (VMI), advance shipment notice (ASN), and lean production. None of these processes can be implemented without using the tools of EDI. The costs of designing or redesigning them should be recognized as the real costs of EDI, but this is also where the real benefits can be obtained. When managers think of the costs of EDI as being those of software, hardware, and training alone, they tend to automate the status quo—to simply create a parallel system that replicates the paper process and in some cases increases overall operating costs. The lack of focus on process and people is the main reason for disappointments and lack of benefit from EDI investments. That's really common sense, but in every area of information technology, managers tend to focus on the technical work and overlook "soft" issues or put them on the back burner. A rule of thumb is that education for the business process and training in the use of the technology itself should be budgeted together as 20 percent of the total project cost. You can never start education too early or make it too pervasive.

Apple Computer's summary of the lessons it learned in implementing EDI point to the hidden costs over and above the technology itself. Apple's transaction cost has decreased from $1.07 per purchase order to about 27 cents through EDI, so that the investment provided substantial returns. But it took time and resources. Here are suggestions a manager provided from Apple's experience [*EDI Forum* 8, no. 3 (1995)]:

- Make sure EDI is driven by business, not technology.
- Accomplish goals quickly by keeping the scope of your pilot narrow.
- Test your relationship with trading partners prior to implementation.

- Choose partners with long-term commitment to EDI. To ensure that your partners' commitment matches your reality, meet regularly with them in person.
- Continually educate your customers and stakeholders.
- Define with your partner assumptions and agreements regarding standards, technical issues, business issues, and objectives.
- Require participation from your stakeholders at an early stage in the EDI implementation process, especially for legal and Information Systems and Technology (IS&T) departments.
- Do not underestimate the amount of "tweaking" that will be required for the software.
- Be aware of the many requirements necessary to fully integrate the application to the host central system.
- Understand that EDI is more than a piece of translation software.
- Encompass technical and business issues when developing and obtaining a consensus on a corporate EDI strategy.

Some of these suggestions may seem like common sense, but again and again and throughout the forty-year history of information technology in organizations, the same patterns appear: the costs and time of the organizational work are underestimated, the costs of installing, integrating, and supporting the software are greater than assumed, education has to be pervasive and sustained, and communication isn't automatic.

CR See **Continuous Replenishment.**

Credit Cards Credit cards are the main vehicle for purchases when the buyer and seller do not have an established relationship, as well as for non–face-to-face transactions such as ordering goods by phone, and for nearly all noncash transactions away from home. Besides convenience in paying for hotels, restaurants, shopping, and foreign travel, they offer you the ability to buy on impulse or make purchases for which you don't have the funds in your checking account. Credit cards are a form of currency. They offer merchants more of a guarantee than do checks. The card issuer underwrites the risk. If the merchant accepts a dud check, it is the merchant who gets burnt. But if the merchant accepts a credit card purchase, and has gotten authorization from the card issuer, any loss is the issuer's problem. Credit cards are, for consumers, an almost ideal currency: money literally in hand and even in advance (many people in the United States carry credit card balances that are around half their annual salaries), and a means of routinely roaming across the international landscape without carrying francs, marks, pounds, or pesos. "Charge it" is the "Open Sesame" of our age.

All these features make credit cards a key element of what is practical for electronic commerce if and only if their users feel safe in giving their card numbers over a network, most obviously the Internet. Merchants want consumers to charge their purchases and orders electronically; they want secure transactions from anywhere across the world, and fast and flexible payment mechanisms. The key word once again is "secure." Until consumers feel safe entering their credit card numbers on the Internet, there will be no mass market for electronic commerce.

As a result of this concern, 1996 saw large-scale and massive investments by companies and industries in making the Net more secure and in trying to persuade consumers that it really is secure. Security depends on cryptography, a set of mathematical techniques for coding information so that it cannot be tampered with, corrupted, or copied. There are many tools for encryption. Each varies in exactly how safe the coded message is from hackers with plenty of computing power at their fingertips and in

"There is still not a single recorded case of a [credit] card number being stolen during a transaction on the Internet." (The Economist, 27 July 1996)

"As for me, I don't feel ready to trust my Visa number to the cyberspace datastream, even with promises of security. That's a curious conclusion, considering that I hardly ever worry that giving my credit card number to a restaurant waiter or telephone sales agent will result in financial disorder. But it's how I—and I suspect loads of other Internet shoppers —feel. Maybe next year I'll be willing to cast caution to the wind. Meanwhile, my check is in the mail." (Washington Post, 15 December 1995)

For most of this decade, credit cards have been a money machine for leading providers. Now they are becoming a risk machine. Each of the more than 1 million personal bankruptcies per year in the United States almost invariably involves credit card debt write-offs. Bad debts grew by almost 80 percent between 1995 and 1997 and credit card debt has doubled since 1995. That will increase rapidly if the more optimistic predictions of on-line consumer electronic commerce turn out to be on target. Credit card risk added to Internet uncertainty amounts to a very unstable future.

the cost of computer hardware and software needed for processing the message. The most widely used techniques here are SET, which has the endorsement of Microsoft; SSL, Netscape's choice; DES, the oldest and most proven encryption method; and RSA, the most complex and exotic. In addition to cryptography, there are a growing number of services which act as guarantors for a transaction, authenticating the sender's identity and adding a "digital signature" that is the equivalent of a real signature but, unlike physical signatures, unforgeable.

The Internet is now very secure for credit card use, far more so than the everyday use of the physical plastic card, which is handed over without thought to waiters and store clerks, and far safer than giving out the credit card number over the phone, or authorizing "signature on file." There's a big difference, though, between the Internet being secure and people feeling safe in using it. Over time, as more and more transactions are handled on the Net, the same people who daily read their card numbers over the phone in making purchases via 1-800 lines will routinely enter their credit card numbers via the PC keyboard. Providing the service uses one of the many available encryption techniques, consumers should feel safe even now using credit cards for electronic purchases. It's the responsibility of service providers and sellers to make it clear on their Web page that the buyer is protected. The rule is simple and obligatory: never offer or accept a transaction over an on-line service that is not encrypted.

The Credit Card Research Group, London, provides the estimates of credit card usage in North America and Europe as of the end of 1996 listed in Table 1. The variations between countries are striking. Britain, for instance, has five times as many cards per person than France and Germany. The United States and Canada are way ahead of the rest of the world in credit card use (in addition to the 365 million Visa and Mastercard accounts, there are another 75 million other credit cards in use), but the average annual charges per card are much lower than elsewhere, $1,471 per account holder versus $6,198 in France. The differ-

Table 1   Total Visa and MasterCard use

	Number of cards (millions)	Total charges (billion $)	Cards per person	Annual charge per card ($)
United States	365	537	1.4	1,471
Britain	30	72	0.5	2,424
Canada	29	51	1.0	1,755
Germany	9	25	0.1	2,707
Italy	6	9	0.09	1,695
France	4	24	0.07	6,198

ence reflects the huge number of cards issued in the United States but also shows how little market penetration there is elsewhere.

The differences in the table also, though, relate to major cultural differences in the use of cash and checks as well as credit cards, different banking systems, and different consumer preferences. Electronic commerce developments for consumers, particularly on the Internet, are largely built on the U.S. model, with a reliance on secure transmission of credit card information as the basic payment mechanism and widespread ownership of personal computers. Those assumptions don't hold for most of the world, including Japan. Even in Japan's businesses, there are just 10 PCs per hundred workers compared to 42 in the United States.

Credit cards are now so widely used that it's easy to overlook the scale of the business they represent. Visa, for instance, handles 10 billion transactions annually, amounting to $750 billion of purchases. The card is accepted by 12 million merchants in over 200 countries. Visa's networks add up to 9 million miles of fiber optics cable and many thousands of computer data centers. The average total cost per transaction is less than 1 cent. That includes the cost of currency conversion and settlement of payment between financial institutions. Visa handles around 400 times more electronic transactions than the Federal Reserve banking system.

Visa is less than 30 years old. Its average growth rate has been 20% a year. That has been the typical *sustained* rate of increase of the major innovations in telecommunications and computers and thus is likely to be the rate of sustained growth for major developments in electronic commerce. Just as Visa had growth rates of as much as 50% for periods of several years, electronic commerce will see some rapid bursts. But wild-eyed predictions of Internet electronic commerce growing from millions to billions of dollars in the next decade need to be cautiously compared with history. At the same time, the impacts of a compounded 20% a year growth in an economy where 3% growth is positive and 8% an economic "miracle" point to the massive opportunity of successful electronic commerce innovations, including EDI, which is moving rapidly along the 20% curve and the many others that are at the base of the curve.

Here are the 5-, 10-, and 15-year results of a $10 million business growing by 20% a year: Year 5: $24 million, Year 10: $61 million and Year 15: $154 million. For comparison, here are the 10-year figures for other rates of growth: 5%: $16 million, 10%: $25 million, 30%: $137 million, 40%: $289 million, 50%: $576 million.

CTP See **Corporate Trade Payments.**

CTX See **Corporate Trade Exchange.**

Currency Server A currency server is a computer that in effect issues money on-line and in real time—that is, immediately. It's a hardware bank. Instead of your going to your bank to get a cashier's check or draw out cash, your message authorizing a purchase is sent to the server, where you have previously set up an account. The funds in the account will have previously been transferred from your bank account or paid in by credit card. The server will pay out your transaction request through another electronic mail message that the seller receives and can redeem through its bank; it will add the equivalent of a bank note's serial number, uniquely identifying the payment. It will add security features. As with the use of bank notes and unlike the use of checks and credit cards, these electronic tokens maintain anonymity and privacy; the merchant has no idea of who made the payment.

See also **Blind Signature; Digital Cash; Public Key Cryptography.**

CyberCash   CyberCash, a company founded in August 1994, is focused on providing secure financial transactions services over the Internet, including credit card transactions, electronic checks, and microtransactions. (Purchases costing just a few cents or even a fraction of a cent, buying a snippet of information on-line, for instance, are microtransactions.) The CyberCash approach has two key elements: encryption for security and the "CyberCash wallet."

The security of CyberCash transactions is assured by application of a 1,024-bit RSA encryption algorithm. Consumers, merchants, banks, and any other appropriate party who wishes a part in the transaction must adopt this unbreakable code. (At least it is unbreakable within the perceived capabilities of computers today and for many years to come.) RSA, which is an acronym composed of the first initials of the three people who invented it, is a set of mathematical procedures which both encodes a message so it can't be tampered with or decoded by trial and error and makes it simple for authorized users to decode it. The size of the algorithm means that the number used to generate the code is larger than the physical number of atoms in our universe, meaning that a computer would have to explore more combinations of numbers to break the code than computation power could work out in the history of humankind.

The CyberCash "wallet" can be thought of as a portable, cryptographically secured, electronic device containing a consumer's credit card data. In use on the Internet, the CyberCash system

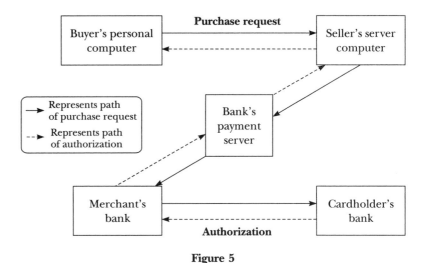

Figure 5
Source: CyberCash Inc., 1996

uses the RSA-based security process to place a digital signature—
the equivalent of a set of fingerprints—on a credit card transaction, ensuring that the party using the card is valid and has the
authority to use that card.

Now in the pilot stage CyberCash consumer transactions
would proceed as shown in Figure 5.

In this illustration the consumer has been viewing information about goods from the merchant's on-line service and "clicks"
on the screen to make the decision to purchase. The CyberCash
wallet window opens on the PC display. The sequence shown in
the diagram has six steps:

1. The customer has shopped the merchant's site and
   decided what it is that he or she wishes to purchase,
   where it is to be shipped, and so forth. The merchant
   server returns a summary of the item, price,
   transaction ID, and so forth to the consumer.

2. The customer then clicks on the "Pay" Button, which
   launches the CyberCash, Checkfree, or Compuserve
   Wallet software processing. The customer chooses a

credit card from his or her "wallet" with which to pay and clicks "OK" to forward the order and encrypted payment information to the merchant.

3. The merchant receives the packet, strips off the order information, and forwards to the CyberCash server the encrypted payment information that is digitally signed with its own private key, an electronic code key. The merchant cannot see the consumer's credit card information. The transaction is private.

4. The CyberCash server receives the packet, takes the transaction behind its "firewall"—the hardware/software system that screens incoming messages and protects against intruders—and thus pulls it off the Internet into its own secure processing environment, "unwraps" (that is, decodes) the data within a hardware-based crypto box (the same ones the banks use to handle PINs as they are shipped from ATM network to ATM network), reformats the transaction, and forwards it to the merchant's bank over special "dedicated" telecommunications lines.

5. The merchant's bank then forwards the authorization request to the issuing bank via the credit card association's telecommunications facilities, such as Visa, or directly to the nonbank card issuer, such as American Express or Discover. The approval or denial code then is sent back to CyberCash.

6. CyberCash then returns the approval or denial code to the merchant, who then passes it on to the consumer. From step 1 to step 6 takes approximately 15 to 20 seconds. All encryption is at the message level and is therefore independent of the Internet software browser technology used; it makes no difference if the customer got onto the World Wide Web through Netscape Navigator, America Online, or Microsoft

Internet Explorer. CyberCash manages the processing within its own boundaries.

CyberCash is designed to combine ease of access, simplicity of use, speed of service, and absolute security. It employs the strongest tools of cryptography and processes the key elements of transactions offline, meaning that the many hackers roaming the Web can't sabotage it to show off their technical expertise, make some political or social statement, or commit fraud. CyberCash may or may not become a market standard, but its basic strategy seems to be a blueprint for secure electronic commerce on the Internet.

See also **Digital Cash; Mondex.**

Data Element   A data element in an EDI transaction is the same as a word in a sentence. Even the simplest data elements may have numerous interpretations, just as even the simplest words do in human speech ("set," for example, has over 30 distinct meanings in the English language). In the application of EDI, ambiguity is thus a substantial potential problem. In order to reduce the risk of misunderstanding or confusion, a dictionary for virtually all the data elements has to be created, to define each element's specific meaning and application clearly. For instance, since the element CA could mean Carton or Case, a data element dictionary would specifically define its meaning as, say, Case, to prevent misinterpretation. A common data element dictionary is shared by the two main EDI standards, EDIFACT and ANSI. However, their segments and transaction sets/messages are constructed differently, so that while their messages can be interchanged, software is needed to convert their data elements from one standard's electronic dictionary to the other.

Obviously, defining data elements precisely and comprehensively, without ambiguity, requires both close cooperation between trading partners, usually a group from within an industry, and a formal process for resolving disagreements and concerns. The

ANSI X12 committee has become the main forum for this purpose in the United States. Parties interested in a new EDI application can apply to form a working group, and then use the ANSI procedures to define, publish, and vote on standards following the well-proven X12 basic EDI model. The process can be slow because it must be so precise. The end product dictionary of data elements becomes the working document for implementing the EDI application.

See also **ANSI X12; Transaction Set.**

Data Encryption Standard (DES) DES is part of the mathematics of security. Data encryption converts numbers and text such as your name, account number, purchase amount, and accompanying message into a stream of apparently meaningless digital bits. The purpose of cryptography is to find techniques that quickly and reliably code the data so that it cannot be decoded by some saboteur or thief. DES is the grandparent of the growing progeny of tools that aim at making the communication of information across networks totally secure. The challenge cryptographers face is that some very powerful computer could crack the code by brute force and trial and error; given that today's supercomputer is tomorrow's desktop, the mathematical procedures—"algorithms"—must become more and more complex to keep the good guys ahead of potential or real bad guys. DES is safe enough to be in widespread use, though it could be broken by someone throwing enough computing power at it.

The DES algorithm has been invisibly securing electronic transactions for decades—and few people knew it was happening. Virtually every ATM in North America, and most around the world, use the DES algorithm to protect the Personal Identification Number or PIN that is the electronic signature for consumer transactions. Use of the DES algorithm has also found its way into commercial applications, such as EDI, where there is a need for securing the electronic payment transaction through cryptographic means.

"Depending on whom you ask, the widely used Data Encryption Standard (DES) is either dangerously outdated or good for another decade" (Gary H. Anthes, "Push Is on for Safer Standard," Computerworld, *25 November 1996). Given the widespread use of DES in bank ATMs, point-of-sale and funds transfer systems, it's rather important which opinion turns out to be correct. There is no known case of anyone breaking the DES coding procedures, but experts believe that "brute force" use of computer power could successfully attack the systems that use*

shorter "keys," the large numbers that are the result of very complex mathematical calculations. The basic idea underlying DES and other more secure encryption techniques is that the large numbers and calculations prevent any intruder being able to work out how to replicate them. The issue is how large the numbers have to be (key length) and how complex the calculations. Banks are reluctant to spend a lot of money on giving up DES, which has worked well for close to 20 years. The argument of many computer scientists is that they may well have to.

Adopted by ANSI in 1981, the U.S. National Bureau of Standards authorized the use of the DES algorithm for use by a variety of groups. It was developed jointly by IBM and the U.S. Department of Defense in the 1970s for use in both military and commercial applications, and has found its way into many everyday electronic devices and applications. The algorithm itself must be combined with two other elements in order to be effective: the message data itself, and a set of electronic keys. Think of the key as equivalent to the following instruction to a nineteenth-century spy who didn't have access to computers and needed a simple way of coding messages: "105, 3, 6." The spy and his or her contacts knew that this referred to a book, say, *The Works of William Shakespeare*, published by Scruton Press in 1876. Go to page 105, line 3, letter 6. That's an "M," the 13th letter of the alphabet, which means the alphabet should be shifted 13 places, with A becoming M, B becoming N, and so on. Obviously, such a simple code—called a Caesar code since it was used by Julius Caesar in his private writings—would be absurdly easy to crack. Modern cryptography relies on massively complex ways of generating massively big key numbers. DES is in the midrange of massiveness.

DES is known as a symmetrical or private-key cryptographic scheme because both sides or partners in a transaction must use the same electronic key values as well as the DES algorithm in order to encrypt and decrypt messages. (In the simple example above, both spy and contact use the same 105, 3, 6 key.) This is in contrast with a public, or asymmetrical, key process that allows each party to use a different key but requires the use of a third party, key certification authority, or agent who looks after the keys.

Figure 6 summarizes the basics of DES encryption. *Encryption* is the technique used to ensure that data privacy is maintained. Data is translated into the standard format and passed through the data encryption standard algorithm, or set of mathematical procedures, in this case involving the use of prime numbers larger than anything you ever came across in high school math. There are additional values added to the result of the algorithm called

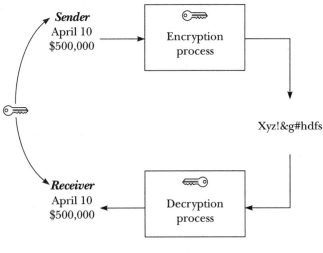

Banks are reluctant to spend a lot of money on giving up DES, which has worked well for close to 20 years. Many computer scientists feel that they may well have to.

Figure 6

keys which, calculated against the data itself, create the process by which the data is scrambled.

Figure 7 summarizes the basics of authentication in exactly the same technical manner as encryption, where the *authentica-*

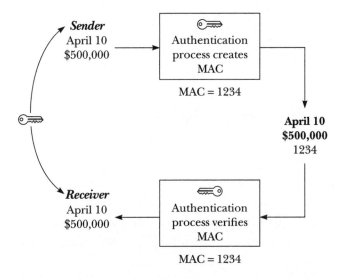

Figure 7

tion process is used to create a value or checksum for the data. It resides in the main part of the data and, because it is calculated using the DES algorithm and the private keys, can only be determined and checked by the sender and receiver who set the keys in the first place. It is called a Message Authentication Code (MAC).

Data Mapping Data mapping is a process of converting data from one format to another. In EDI, it is the process whereby one company's proprietary system is converted into some standardized format, usually an ANSI X12 or EDIFACT transaction set so that it can be read by another company's computer. For example, a previously printed purchase order generated by the firm's transaction systems is realigned into a specific EDI order defined by the ANSI X12 standard as shown in Figure 8.

As you can see, the same information is contained in the "standard" format on the right as is on the physical document on the left. The data has been reorganized, based on the rules of the X12 standards and coded so that a computer can read the data, locate the essential pieces of information, and act on the instructions.

Accomplishing this takes several steps:

1. First, someone must map the data requirements and current available data to the business process and precisely document the connections. Next, the analyst must compare the output and input variables in place with the data requirements necessary for the EDI business transaction.

2. "Mapping" software is then used to identify firm-specific data by location in the structure of the computer file that generates it. The standardized EDI file that passes it on to the relevant trading partner is constructed or deconstructed accordingly.

3. Finally, a comprehensive test is carried out in which

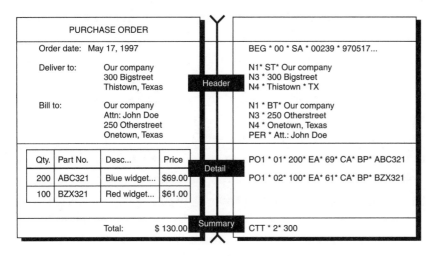

Figure 8

a variety of transactions and situations (such as an incomplete order) are tested and confirmed to the actual expected output.

This process is one that developers of information systems are used to. It's complex, must be rigorous and well-documented, and almost invariably takes more time than anticipated. Even with well-established processes and proven software tools, there's no "plug-in and go" system for EDI. Business-to-business electronic relationships mean process-to-process communication. Data mapping is the basic requirement and skill for achieving this translation.

Data Mining   The analysis of massive aggregations of computer data while looking for nuggets of gold—patterns, anomalies, exceptions, and trends that can be used to target customers, identify market niches, and detect new opportunities—is called "data mining." It's a new term for a not-so-new market research practice—companies have been analyzing customer data for this purpose since the 1980s. What's really new is the combination of masses of data automatically generated as a by-product of elec-

Companies have massive stores of data—sales figures, customer records, inventory figures, orders, credit card payments, and the like. These may contain nuggets of gold that give them insights into customer needs, behavior, and preferences. Metaphorical miners sift the data without any preconceived ideas of what they are looking for. They are prospectors. Once in a while they will find pay dirt. An often-quoted example is the retailer whose miners found that there was a strong correlation between sales of disposable diapers and six-packs of beer when the two goods were placed close to each other in the store. Their interpretation was that daddy was sent out to buy diapers in the evening and naturally picked up some beer. The obvious action agenda then was to put the beer in reach of the diapers.

tronic commerce operations and massive low-cost computer power to process it.

By definition, electronic commerce transactions *automatically* generate large amounts of data. In a sense, data comes for free in that no extra effort is needed to create and store it; it's already there as a result of various transactions. An example is a credit card transaction over the Internet. Think of all the information that one purchase generates as a computer record that can be stored and analyzed: time of day, merchant, origination point, type of purchase, number of items bought, and so on. With EDI and store point of sale, the data may be even more detailed: the shelf the goods are stored on, the color of the buttons on the shirt, and so on. This collection of detailed data on consumer preference is a potential gold mine. Of course, panning through mud and stones to find flakes of gold takes time and money.

Until a few years ago, data mining cost too much time and too much money to be practical. Only supercomputers had the speed to plow through the volumes of data, much of which might contain little of interest or value, or to apply mathematical formulae and statistical techniques. In the late 1980s, a few computer hardware and software vendors began to exploit low-cost microprocessor technology to soup up commercial computers by linking together computer processors so that they would work in parallel. Think of the difference between you working to locate every name in the Manhattan phone book that begins with "Joan" versus having 300 people each checking an allocated smaller number of pages. In late 1996, Intel demonstrated a parallel processing system built out of its main commercial product for personal computers that broke the barrier of 1 trillion computer instructions per second. In the 1970s, the most powerful machines operated in millions of instructions a second.

As data mining becomes routine, electronic commerce is evolving into a "data warehouse." The information technology trade is using the term "data warehouse" to describe the aggregation of multiple data bases as an enterprise resource that can be accessed by more and more people for more and more purposes. Examples are the routine use of credit card data to analyze purchase patterns in order to offer targeted marketing, the sifting of point-of-sale data in stores, and the bringing together of information on airline and hotel reservations and car rentals to build profiles of travelers.

Data mining requires data, obviously. This makes just about any computer-gathered information on consumers valuable to companies. In the same way that when you subscribe to a magazine you can be pretty certain your name and address will be sold to a marketer of goods advertised in that magazine, you can expect in the future that any transaction you carry out on the Internet where you fill out a form and give your real name will generate an entry in a data base. That data base will be sold to someone. Increasingly, Web sites automatically download a "cookie" to your computer's hard disk drive that identifies it; when you next log onto the site, the cookie provides information about your being a repeat visitor. If you've filled out a form that gives information about you, the cookie can be cross-referenced to you.

Cookies are mostly harmless, but few users of the Internet have ever heard of them and even fewer have consented to cookies being placed on their personal computers. Is this a violation of the rules of informed consent that are a requirement in everyday commerce? Do you yourself particularly care about what data about you is being mined by retailers, manufacturers, credit card firms, phone companies, and others?

See also **Cookies; Data Warehousing.**

Data Warehousing   Data warehousing is a fairly new term in the information technology field that refers to the assembly of large volumes of data that may be spread across many software data bases and that constitute a business information inventory that can be retrieved, searched, analyzed, and reported.

The goal of data warehousing is information on demand.

The logic of data warehousing is to make available information accessible. Any large organization generates masses of data and then wastes it. The data is put away in "jailhouses" rather than warehouses; its use is impractical except for in simple queries and fixed reports. Data warehousing frees data by providing tools that make it easy to ask free-form questions, search for patterns and trends, help decision makers visualize information, and bring together data from many sources. It makes data a capital resource that can be reused again and again; the data is already paid for. Currently, most databases are an expense, not a capital asset.

Business cycles move at faster and faster speeds—just-in-time manufacturing, Quick Response retailing, and on-line service. The computer-based information systems that support these operations were not designed for time-based competition and management. Most of the time, particularly with financial systems, there is a tendency to run the system on a "batch" basis, producing all of the output for a forthcoming period at once. For example, it is quite common for an accounts payable system to produce all of the checks for the next week, postdated to their respective value dates. With the usual delays in mail and in-house processing, this is usually not a problem. In fact, the convenience of producing a series of checks prior to their actual value date gave rise to the practice of "holding back the check" in the proverbial drawer, for the purpose of providing an incentive to the vendor or recipient to act in a certain way.

In electronic commerce, there is no electronic drawer per se. In fact, delaying payments can cause significant problems with the trading relationship. Many terms and conditions in an electronic relationship are so tightly wound to a time schedule that a delayed payment can cause significant loss of discounts, and in some cases, can incur severe financial penalties. At the same time, releasing payments earlier than they are due can cause loss of financial float to the paying organization, also undesirable. To address this problem, many banks and some value-added networks provide a data warehousing service whereby they hold the transactions until they reach their valid processing date—and then release them on the correct date into the payment system. Most such data warehousing systems can store data for up to 30 calendar days without difficulty.

Electronic commerce is about relationships. Transactions such as EDI messages, purchases, and payments are its core but so, too, is the provision of information. The information most obviously needed here is about products and services, with electronic catalogs and Web pages the main resource. Increasingly, though, companies are using data generated as part of electronic commerce and by their other computer-based transactions to facilitate the relationship. The basic concept of a data warehouse is that all information should be viewed as an inventory, to be combined, analyzed, and reported in many ways, for many purposes, often in unanticipated situations.

An example is GlaxoWellcome's GWis system. GlaxoWellcome is the largest international pharmaceutical firm in the world. In the summer of 1996, when the company announced that a combination of two of its drugs had been proven to be effective in treating AIDS, physicians immediately started writing prescriptions en masse. GlaxoWellcome feared it could not keep up with demand. However, GWis enabled the firm to rapidly track the sources of demand and their sizes and use the reports to reallocate production and distribution. Wholesalers around the world never ran out of supplies.

Debit Cards   A debit card looks like a credit card but acts like an ATM card that is also a check. The payment you make with it is immediately debited to your bank account, as with an ATM cash withdrawal. Debit cards are well suited to small, routine purchases, such as buying gas and groceries. They have been around for over a decade but a variety of issues has slowed their growth: security, merchant acceptance, and consumer dislike of loss of float.

Their use is now growing rapidly. In greater Washington, D.C., the number of merchants accepting debit cards grew 80 percent in 1996, to over 16,000. Almost 25 percent of U.S. households now use a debit card at least once a month. In 1991, the figure was under 10 percent.

Table 2 shows the breakdown of U.S. debit card use as of late 1996. The cost per debit card transaction is typically 25 cents. Some banks charge a monthly fee of $1 to $2.

One-fifth of the world's 8.5 million pay phones in 160 countries now accept prepayment cards.

Processing a check costs banks five times more than making an on-line debit transaction. "From the bank's standpoint, we would love to put a debit card in everybody's hand." (An executive in NationsBank, which has over a million Visa check card holders)

Table 2 U.S. debit card use

	Percentage of cardholders using debit cards for transactions	Average transaction ($)
Supermarkets	67	63
Gas stations	39	19
Department stores	27	42
Convenience stores	9	15

Source: *Card Monthly* 2 (February 1997) 17.

One estimate is that documents generate 20 to 45 percent of an organization's labor costs, which amounts to as much as 15 percent of revenues. The average business document is copied 19 times. (Computer Dealer News, *4 October 1993)*

Around $250 billion or 5 percent of total U.S. gross domestic product is spent on processing commercial paper documents. Many of these documents are eliminated by electronic commerce, through EDI and electronic payments in particular. The main blockage is the legal

Dematerialization Dematerialization is a legal and regulatory term that originated in the securities industry. It means that there is no requirement that when a stock is sold, the share certificate must be physically transferred to the buyer's broker—in other words, the certificate is dematerialized. This is a specialized financial services issue, but one with substantial general industry-independent and long-term implications. Electronic commerce is part of the battle against paper and all the administration and bureaucracy that goes with it. The cost of handling not just stock certificates, but invoices, insurance policies, ownership documents, application forms, and the like is immense.

In planning an electronic commerce strategy, a document is often the driver for designing or redesigning a business process, from the birth of a piece of paper—a purchase order, mortgage application, health insurance claim form, or request for information—through its cloning as multiple copies wend their way through many departments to its final death and burial in a filing cabinet. The combination of technology and process innovation is the base for the electronic commerce approach which eliminates steps—if it can eliminate the physical paper.

Much of the paper in everyday transactions is not legally required and can be removed with the agreement of the parties involved. For instance, many of us routinely use our credit cards over the phone or have an ongoing relationship with a travel agent which adds "credit card signature on file" to the payment receipt. When automotive firms like General Motors and Ford decided to eliminate the need for suppliers to send any invoice, paper or electronic, but to pay them on the basis of the bar coded information on the goods as they are delivered, all they needed was an agreement between the trading partners. In financial services, matters can be more complicated and firms need to take into account the legal issues of paper. The more that transaction documents can be dematerialized, the more the business process they address can be made faster, more convenient, cheaper, and more reliable.

Many of the systems and telecommunications networks needed for dematerialization in electronic commerce are already in place. They include banking's automated clearing houses and international funds transfer systems such as CHIPS and SWIFT, value-added networks for EDI, and the ubiquitous Internet. Others, though, both need to be developed and pose large problems of design and implementation. Businesses engaged in international trade want to eliminate paper certificates and trade documents, which add administration costs, delays, errors, and fraud, and move toward an electronic share settlement system, where instead of a certificate changing hands, the relevant data base records are updated. In the United States, stock certificates have been "immobilized" or placed in a central depository but not yet dematerialized.

The complexity of the systems needed to dematerialize an entire stock market is immense in terms of technical design, operations, as well as process change. The failure rate has been high. In the United Kingdom, whose stock exchange handles greater volume than the rest of Europe combined, a massive investment in the Taurus system for paperless trading had to be abandoned in 1994, with a write-off amounting to hundreds of millions of dollars. The Crest share settlement system ran into major problems in late 1996, and did not meet its target date for "going live" in April 1997. Smaller firms have had particular

requirement for some physical piece of paper. One Norwegian bank cut the costs of its securities administration function by 30 percent when regulators permitted the elimination of physical stock certificates in favor of electronic records of ownership.

In some ways, the substantial benefits of EDI reflect the dreadful waste and administrative complexity paper-based systems create and maintain. The U.S. Department of Defense identified $1.2 billion in likely savings over 10 years just from automating its 16 most-used forms. When Texas Instruments can lower its average cost to process a purchase order from $49 to $4.70, the question has to be, how on earth did a form grow to cost almost $50 in one of the world's best users of telecommunications over the past 30 years?

The answer has to be paper power. Electronic commerce is not just about war on paper but it's a high-payoff first step. It's not the elimination of the paper that matters as much as the rethinking and streamlining of the processes that electronic commerce enables.

trouble trying to use readymade, off-the-shelf software packages to connect to Crest. The heavy transaction load demands of the complex system have led to very slow processing for the very small volumes of settlements currently being handled by it.

Electronic commerce systems fall into two very different categories: systems that are basically message-handling services and those that provide transaction processing. Message handling systems include the bulk of EDI applications, fund transfers, and related electronic payment systems. In these the overhead costs for software are small and the functions the system performs are stable and the processing demands simple. The opposite is true for systems mainly devoted to processing transactions, such as those for mutual funds management, ATM networks, credit card authorization, global custody, securities trading, and share settlement. The estimated developmental cost for the proposed CEDEL system for clearing international securities trades in real time is $100 million. Wherever an electronic commerce application mostly involves the movement of messages with little processing, the technical risks are predictable and limited. Wherever it requires fast on-line processing following complicated procedures and rules, there is a big risk.

DES See **Data Encryption Standard.**

DigiCash DigiCash is one of the companies aiming to establish itself as a leader in providing electronic money for use in transactions on the Internet. DigiCash's Ecash provides users with electronic currency that they can use anonymously, as with paper currency but unlike credit cards. Most other proposed Internet payment innovations add security and processing features to credit cards, so that they can be used for transactions on the Net.

Ecash is like a stored-value card, such as a prepaid phone card that contains $10 of credit coded into a magnetic strip. As the phone card is used for calls, the balance encoded on the strip is updated. The Ecash value is stored on the hard drive of your personal computer. Extra value is downloaded by your bank at your request; you pay for this through a traditional vehicle, such as a credit card. You can then use the funds to buy goods and services from merchants who engage in electronic commerce. The Ecash software transfers money from the buyer's to the seller's Ecash account. A distinctive feature of Ecash is the way it ensures privacy. The bank that provides the service moves money from your real account to the Ecash Mint, where it is now available to you as digital currency. It moves electronic coins from the Ecash Mint—the equivalent of withdrawing money from an ATM. The coin is tagged with a unique identification code and tucked into electronic envelopes that encrypt the information. The merchant can cash in the coins but cannot recognize from which person they come.

Mark Twain Bank, a small bank operating in Illinois, Missouri, and Kansas, was the first to implement Ecash, in October 1995. Essentially, it is the U.S. clearinghouse for Ecash. It is unusual in standard banking in that it offers consumers accounts in 25 currencies. For Mark Twain, Ecash is just one more of those. The bank had signed up 10 merchants prior to launching Ecash. By late 1996, the number had grown to 200, with 1,000 customers. The most difficult issue for Mark Twain was pricing—"the cause of much angst," according to bank officials. Fees for consumers include a setup cost of $10 to $100 plus a monthly charge of $2 to $5. The main fees are for transactions, with consumers paying 2–5 percent and merchants 2–4 percent. There are four packages for merchants and four for consumers to choose from.

DigiCash's technology is based on patented methods in public key cryptography developed by the company's founder and chairman, Dr. David Chaum. Founded in 1990, DigiCash has pioneered development of electronic payment mechanisms for open, closed, and network systems that provide security and privacy.

DigiCash's first product was a road toll system developed for the Dutch government. It is now being tested in Japan and marketed in other countries. DigiCash has developed a number of other technologies. Other leading organizations that DigiCash has worked with in technology development include Visa International, IBM, and Siemens, as well as various European telecommunications service providers.

See also **Digital Cash; Mondex.**

The lifetime of a U.S. bank note is now 22 months, down from 60 months 10 years ago. There are 450 to 600 coins in circulation per person.

The 1996 estimated consumer sales over the Internet of $500 million were roughly equal to the money spent on computer magazines lauding the wonders of Internet electronic commerce. The Economist *(10 May 1997) described the software problems, complexity of interfaces, and limited range of goods as making "even the corner store look like a miracle of*

Digital Cash   Digital cash refers to a "token based" currency that translates into equivalent real currency units that are backed by a bank. This payment system usually involves a trusted authority that allows users to conduct and pay for transactions with digital cash after a predetermined relationship has been established. The main purpose of this payment form is to enable commercial transactions over the Internet for amounts too small to justify the cost of credit card payment processing, and, more generally, to create the electronic equivalent of cash: convenient, private, widely accepted, and legal currency.

There are many candidate approaches to digital cash and many companies pushing hard to establish their products and services as the leaders when electronic consumer commerce becomes popular. They include:

- *First Virtual Holdings.* Customers sign up for the service by providing credit card information, which First Virtual stores offline, so that it cannot be tapped into over the Internet. Customers receive an ID number to use for transactions over the Net. The merchant does not know who the purchaser is. Transactions are handled by a private telecommunications network, which updates the credit card account information. They are confirmed by the system sending an electronic mail one second or so after the purchase is made; the buyer must reply to it before it is consummated. The merchant pays 29 cents per transaction plus 2 percent of the price of the goods sold. Since there is no transfer of funds over the Net, this is a simple and safe system, built on well-established infrastructures and processes. First Virtual had signed up close to 150,000 customers and 2,000 merchants by late 1996.

- *CyberCash*. Customers set up bank accounts with funds specifically for spending on the Net. When purchases are made, money is directly transferred from the buyer's to the seller's CyberCash account. Both parties pay a fee of 30 cents per transaction.

- *DigiCash*. Customers purchase digital cash, which has been likened to "the serial number on a dollar bill that has shed its paper body and entered the ether" (*Wired*, August 1996), via their credit cards or bank accounts. The serial numbers are maintained by the merchant and bank. The merchant has no idea whatever of who the buyer is. The transaction cost is targeted to be one-tenth of a cent. Credit cards provide convenience but not privacy. Anonymity and privacy mean cash. DigiCash represents the most radical approach to combining privacy, convenience, low cost per transaction, and security over the Net.

- *Mondex*. One of the most ambitious schemes and the most international, Mondex aims at establishing its "smart purse" or "electronic wallet" as the base for a new worldwide electronic currency. The purse will be preloaded with digital cash that may be used in many ways, including offline—not on a telecommunications network. Users will be able to transfer funds from one wallet to another, rather like, but obviously far more securely than, transferring a file from one PC to another. Funds stored on a PC may be used over the Internet or such services as America Online.

organization and choice. . . . For most consumers today's Internet, far from being a perfect market, is the high street from hell." But the magazine is very bullish on the long-term opportunity and quotes the chairman of Intel: "What's my ROI on e-commerce? Are you crazy? This is Columbus in the New World. What was his ROI?" Neither he nor The Economist *mention that Columbus did not in fact make much money for himself, that the colonists he left in the New World revolted because they found little of the promised gold, that the governor sent Columbus back to Spain in chains, and that on his fourth and final voyage he had to abandon his rotting ships and was marooned in Jamaica for a year.*

Congressman Wright Patman, Chairman of the House Banking Committee in the 1960s and 1970s, liked to define legal tender in the following way: if you take it out of your pocket and offer it in payment to someone and that person refuses to accept it, you can put the money back in your pocket and declare that you have paid your bill and the courts will agree that you have done so. It will take a lot of legislation and customer confidence before digital cash meets that criterion.

- *Millicent.* A system is being developed to handle very small purchases at very low cost. Today, the cost of processing, say, a one-cent fee for downloading a short piece of information from the Net is many times more than the fee. Web advocates anticipate that the ability to handle microcents or even nanocents—billionths of a cent—will be key in the longer term if it is to become a major base for electronic commerce. *Wired* comments that "Would-be barons of digital microeconomics say there is a potential annual market of several hundred billion dollars" (August 1996). But that market will never develop if transactions cost several hundreds of billions of dollars to process. *Wired* adds "the only thing missing is the technology to really make it fly." Millicent involves "scrip," fake money, like two-for-one coupons, food stamps, or gift certificates. Merchants create their own scrips that they sell to small brokers, who will be well established and well trusted banks. Buyers buy currency from these brokers who have the scale of operations to spread their own costs over a wide customer base. Anyone could tap into the requests for and transfer of the scrip, but it is so small in value that the cost will be more than it's worth. The targeted transactions are as low as a cent, and the fee one-tenth of a cent.

Digital Signature An unforgeable signature is needed for the electronic document to guarantee that a specific person agreed to the sending of the document, in effect signing it. There are three requirements for a digital signature: (1) it must be reliable and safe—that is, it cannot be forged, (2) it must be verifiable—it can be directly attributed to the person, and (3) it offers "nonrepudiation," which means that the signer cannot disown it later and claim that he or she did not in fact sign the document in this way.

As so often is the case in the rapidly emerging field of electronic payments and contracts, where the need for security is vital and the technology is moving fast, there are several competing designs for electronic signatures, each of which exploits a different technique. The Internal Revenue Service has been the main proponent of Digital Signature Standard (DSS) as the base for electronic commerce in government. The IRS's own expensive, belated, and largely ineffectual efforts to modernize the paper-based tax system obviously will require electronic signatures for electronic filing of taxes to become routine.

Supporters claim that DSS has an advantage over the main alternative, RSA (named for its three inventors, Rivest, Shamir, and Adelman), from the user's perspective: DSS signatures can be generated quickly, though verifying them is slow. For RSA, a public-key cryptography system, the advantage claimed is the reverse. RSA has been in use for close to 20 years now, which means that it has withstood repeated and skilled attempts to break the secret mathematical algorithm used to generate the signature. DSS is relatively new, and part of the reason that it generates signatures faster than RSA is that it uses a less complex calculation. That, in the view of the proponents of RSA, makes it more vulnerable to efforts to crack it.

The computer industry has largely adopted RSA, so that any switch to DSS would be complex and costly. Clearly the government, and more particularly the IRS, is in the driver's seat in determining the direction and speed of digital signatures, but it may be trying to overtake a race car. RSA looks like the winner here.

Digital signatures require a management infrastructure. A small industry is emerging here, with the expectation of a vast industry growing as the Internet becomes the base for electronic commerce. Verisign, a California firm started in mid-1995, quickly built a business that sells two types of digital signature—the electronic equivalent of your physical signature backed up by a driver's license or some other evidence of who you are. Its site certificates identify a company as being a legitimate firm that is

Digital signatures are not a matter of imitating handwriting. Forging a signature that will pass casual inspection is not especially difficult. Making an electronic equivalent forgery-proof involves esoteric mathematics and very fast computer chips for encoding and decoding. The math is a little beyond high school calculus. It's based on the axiom that $x^{(p-1)(q-1)} = 1 \ (mod \ pq)$, where x is not divisible by p or q. That's the simple part of the algorithm. Mod(pq) is, in the terms of the crypto trade, "quite large"—at least 150 digits.

A digital signature electronically "seals" a message so that it cannot be changed or forged and uniquely identifies its originator.

safe to do business with. Personal certificates identify you as the person you say you are and not a hacker who has carried out the electronic equivalent of stealing your credit card or ATM card. These signatures authenticate the person, but do not handle the transfer of money, only make it safer for the parties that process the financial transaction to do so. Verisign entered a joint venture with Visa in July 1996, to expand on its existing base of 10,000 site certificates and 100,000 personal certificates.

The debate about electronic signatures and electronic commerce security in general tends to be rather purist. Experts are concerned that crypto schemes may not be perfect and that, with massive enough computer power, even the best systems can be compromised. Business managers need to heed the concerns. Security demands digital signatures, for legal reasons, for reliability in business relationships, and for the elimination of controls, administration, and delays associated with paper-based commerce. The issue is what is secure *enough*? An RSA-based digital signature is far safer than most paper signatures and, so far at least, there has been no large-scale electronic break-in of established EC networks that use it.

Disbursement Services   Disbursement services are part of the streamlining of payments made practical by electronic networks. One of the impacts of electronic commerce has been the search by banks to find new or additional services they can provide to the market. One of the more obvious ways is for them to assume the operational and technical support for managing the accounts-payable (AP) systems of their clients, as an outsourced services provider. Over the past several decades, financial institutions have become consequential players in the human resources and payroll services business, and many banks see the offering of AP as a natural extension of their product line.

This does not mean that they simply produce and mail checks on behalf of their customers. Rather, they provide a variety of processes and outputs designed to lower costs and increase efficiency. Obviously, if a bank is to offer these services, it must achieve a profitability and economy of scale to do so: the business rests on volumes and operational efficiency. Typically, a bank provides a series of payment disbursement options, ranging from a simple EFT (electronic funds transfer) to an EDI payment or even a check, depending on the recipients' requirements. As banks continue their search for value added services, to add value and to increase transaction flows through their systems, the disbursement service will be a critical element.

The logic of disbursement is one of management rather than transaction processing. The person who sits in front of the computer screen is *managing* disbursements, drawing on a wide variety of options. The bank's key is to increase those management options; that's a major product base for electronic commerce in banking. It's also a major option for telecommunications and other companies aiming to displace banks; they want the volumes of messages as part of their own large-scale operational advantage.

Disintermediation   One of the terms that became part of common usage in the 1980s as a direct result of the electronic commerce phenomenon is disintermediation. This is the concept of an organization being displaced, or outright replaced, in a chain of activities by a third party not traditionally associated with the business that the organization is in. It's a major consequence of electronic commerce's making communication direct between trading partners instead of via brokers, wholesalers, and other intermediaries.

For example, there has been significant concern in the banking industry that third-party processors will take away a lot of the bank's traditional processing business and, as a result, client loyalty. This view is substantiated by the fact that already a significant amount of the check processing and credit card business has been outsourced to third parties such as Deluxe Data and National Data Corp. Furthermore, the two largest credit card issuers are now a telephone company (AT&T) and a retailer (Sears Discover

When you buy a sweater at a high fashion boutique for $100, about 80 percent is absorbed by the distribution channel, leaving a mere $15 for the manufacturer. The interactive medium diminishes the need for intermediaries, resulting in great potential savings for both the consumer and the manufacturer. (Martin, Chuck, The Digital Estate: Strategies for Competing, Surviving, and Thriving in an Internetworked World, *New York: McGraw Hill, 1997.)*

Card). Neither of these organizations were seen as serious threats in 1980.

Disintermediation is also a real concern in other industries. Travel agents, for instance, could easily by displaced by direct customer access through the Internet to airlines, hotels, and resorts reservation systems. Access to these facilities can be accommodated through the use of a WWW page and some effort by the respective airlines and hotels. Savings of the commissions usually payable to travel agents would more than offset the development costs for such a facility and would allow a more direct relationship with the buyer of the flight or room.

The concept of disintermediation is simple: a complacent existing intermediary or even industry is displaced by a non-traditional competitor using electronic commerce as the leverage point. In 1997, for example, there was growing evidence that the almost century-old car dealership structure will be more and more disintermediated by the car buyers' use of the Internet to locate the best deals and get highly detailed information about cars, prices, and inventories. So far, the travel agency system has held up as the central intermediary between airlines and passengers. The industry well understands the threat of disintermediation and has for almost two decades been very much on guard against intrusions on its traditional territory; whenever airlines like American tried to introduce self-ticketing machines in the 1980s, travel agent associations opposed them and informally many agents made it clear they would stop booking flights on American where they could.

Note that there is a major difference in customers' use of the car dealer and the travel agent. The travel agent provides a valuable information service and skills in working through the complexities of airline options and deals. So, even though anyone with a personal computer and access to the Internet can make his or her own reservations, most travelers prefer to have an agent do it instead. In buying a car, however, most people prefer to seek out their own information and can go to any depth or breadth of search very easily. They zero in on a model and options and search electronically or by phone for the availability and best price. The car dealer adds little if any value to the search beyond handing over the keys for the necessary test drive.

A number of defensive strategies are emerging in the businesses most vulnerable to such disintermediation. Banks offer electronic commerce services, such as on-line processing of loans, but still have a personal touch in their branches and over the phone; they aim to add value by becoming financial advisers. The key solution to any threat of disintermediation is the creation of value added and innovative new services within the affected industry or group. As disintermediation increases, firms also have little choice but to become part of the new infrastructures that contribute to the disintermediation; car dealers have to join the electronic wheeling and dealing on the Internet. Even the banks, who are convinced that the Internet will take away their business, are moving onto the Net.

Businesses thus are searching for ways to add value to services in order to prevent disintermediation. Sometimes, the value comes from information, sometimes from convenience, sometimes from new products and services, and sometimes from the nature of the personal contact and relationship. In a way, electronic commerce is forcing companies to reassert electronically the personal touch, the very thing many people feared would get lost in on-line commerce and culture. Electronic commerce is fundamentally about information, convenience, new products and services, and new forms of relationship. It's both the generator of and the answer to disintermediation.

Many elements of electronic commerce will directly contribute to disintermediation. Others, though, will create new forms of intermediation. Nets Inc., founded in 1990, brings buyers and sellers together in an interactive environment on the Internet. It offers 25 on-line services, provides electronic business centers for over 4,000 companies with information on 250,000 suppliers, and has grown at a rate of 200 percent a year from its inception. The

In March 1997, Charles Schwab and Co., the world's leading securities discount broker, announced that it now had 700,000 active on-line accounts totalling $50 billion in customer assets. The main attraction is price— $29.95 a trade plus 3 cents a share. On-line services offer a cheaper version of existing discount brokerage and appeal to the same community of knowledgeable customers who want to manage their own portfolios and be able to make trades when and where they wish. It is unclear as yet how many new customers the Internet-based services will attract, and how many existing telephone customers will switch to the new medium.

annual buying power of its members is close to $200 billion. Just shifting 1 percent of this into its network amounts to $2 billion. Nets Inc. makes a lot of money just charging annual fees of a few hundred dollars. That said, Nets went bankrupt in mid-1997; its growth was too costly to sustain.

One of the most attractive features of information as a product is that the only inventory is disk space and thus the incremental margins can be very high—if, and only if, you have information that people want and are willing to pay for.

Double Spending   Double spending is a recent and as yet specialized term that refers to the problems of updating computer records on-line in order to reflect a transaction that reduces a balance in a financial account. It's the electronic equivalent of bouncing a check. For instance, proposed forms of digital cash that substitute some form of electronic token for physical money may require the issuer's data base, usually a bank account, to be updated as its user makes a purchase over the Internet. It's possible in some situations that the holder of the digital cash could simultaneously make purchases from, say, Germany, Greece, Hong Kong, and the United States. Even a minute's delay in updating the account that shows the available value of the token is too long and too late to stop the double spending.

For systems of the future that are expected to process millions of Internet purchases and payments per day, often for small amounts, it will also be too expensive to match information across multiple countries and financial institutions. In addition, banks would have to spend large sums to upgrade their software systems to add new checks, controls, and audit logs. Preventing double spending really means adding on-line, real-time information management to transaction systems. That's expensive.

Ecash   See **Electronic Cash.**

ECR   See **Efficient Consumer Response.**

EDGAR   See **Electronic Data Gathering, Analysis, Retrieval.**

EDI   See **Electronic Data Interchange.**

EDIBANX   EDIBANX is a 1994 proposal by a consortium of banks to provide the variety of and level of information detail in electronic commerce messages and transactions that businesses need for using EDI and FEDI for the integration of their logistical processes. EDIBANX should mark the move to the next generation of electronic commerce services, one where those services become more and more integrated, too.

Even though financial EDI and EDI payments have been operating in the United States longer than anywhere else, there has still been slow growth and uptake in the application of these technologies. One of the concerns that often has been expressed about the limited usage is the inability of the vast majority of the over 10,000 banks in the United States to *receive* EDI payment transactions. Generally, there has been no problem in moving the value from originator to receiver. As the remittance detail becomes increasingly important to the successful completion of the business transaction, the frustration of not having "qualified receivers" is of greater importance than ever before.

This frustration, and the need to develop a complete, end-to-end capability, led to the creation of the EDI Bank Alliance Network Exchange (EDIBANX) initiative, which acts as a payment network within a payment network. The mission statement for this group is: "to become the dominant electronic commerce service provider to link U.S.-based corporations with their trading partners." This is an especially interesting statement because it doesn't specifically limit the organization to financial applications of EDI, although that is EDIBANX's first objective.

Most of the EDI payments processed through the U.S. Automated Clearing House System are done so without any specific management requirements beyond those established at the "lowest common denominator" level, meaning the bank with the least technical capability forces all the others to accommodate it; if that bank can't handle a given message format, the customer can't use it even though all the other banks involved in the payments offer it. It is quite common for remittance detail sent as an addenda record attached to a payment to fail to reach the receiving organization at all; it gets dropped along the processing chain. With business demand for an effective financial EDI solution growing, more and more financial institutions with a significant investment in the EDI and electronic services business realized they needed to develop a more effective and far-reaching solution for corporations requiring financial EDI and information-based financial exchange.

That's why in 1994, a group of the most active and prominent banks in the business of cash management and payments processing in the United States joined together under the EDIBANX arrangement. These 14 member banks are the largest transaction handlers in the U.S. payment systems; together they process more than 60 percent of the corporate lockbox transactions and over 50 percent of controlled disbursements.

All the EDIBANX transactions retain an ANSI X12 EDI message format, but corporations or their banks must enclose these "native" X12 transactions in an ACH format "envelope" such as a CCD or a CTX before sending them through the ACH system. The primary purpose of this envelope is to place the financial and bank routing and transit data in prominence so that they flow through the ACH payment system as a financial transaction (with the "addenda" record). This is part of the problem in the system of the ACH—some receiver banks just don't think addenda is a critical deliverable, especially if there is any difficulty in getting a client to pay for the service.

The payment transportation structure that the group uses relies on the application of the ANSI X12 standard 820, Payment with Remittance Detail, and the 835 Health Care payment as the key transactions sets. Each transaction receives a series of acknowledgment transactions based on the ANSI 996, 997, 824, and 831.

One of the design features of the EDIBANX initiative is the creation of a Trading Partner Directory, essentially a list of declared EDI-capable corporations, which can help companies starting or expanding their EDI programs to identify and qualify trading partners capable of sending and receiving transactions electronically. Locating electronic trading partners has proven to be both expensive and time-consuming for many organizations; it is the intent of the initiative to resolve that problem. This list is available to subscribers on diskette, paper, or over the Internet.

Key to the success of the EDIBANX initiative is the ability to deliver transactions in an effective manner to the diverse types of receiver organizations who subscribe to the service. For example, an EDI-capable customer might transmit its payable or billing file to a member bank. The bank would query the authorized payment or billing stream and identify EDI-capable receivers from the EDIBANX data base. For those trading partners listed as being capable of receiving EDI transactions, the bank would distribute the payments or billing documents through the EDIBANX network. The receiving financial institution would report the activity to the corporation using existing reporting links such as direct transmission, balance reporting, fax, e-mail, or paper advice. If there is a trading partner who is not included in the EDIBANX directory, the bank would create paper documentation and distribute it via the post or courier.

By offering a collective, integrated service capability, the EDIBANX members remove much of the difficulty that corporations have had in rolling out their EDI programs. They often have initial success as the more aggressive trading partners all work together to implement a process for their own strategic needs. But after that level, the next layer of reluctant participants begins to cost more than expected and bogs down the process. The EDIBANX solution is one more partnership to motivate the recalcitrant supplier.

One of the long-term goals of the EDIBANX members is to offer true value added services, which step beyond the traditional boundaries of banking by acting as a true value added bank (VAB). For example, in collections, it is possible for a member bank not only to receive payment and detail but also to reconcile the client's accounts receivable. The bank would download and update the client's receivables file for more effective management of cash and credit. The bank can even take over more of the management of the billing cycle, issuing and tracking invoices on behalf of its client. This would lead to a full outsource service for management of accounts receivable. If done effectively and at reasonable economies of scale, this results in savings for the client corporation and efficiencies in the overall collections process, as well as—of course—profit for the VAB.

The converse of receivables management is outsourced payables management. Banks can also play a more obvious role as companies streamline their payables operations. During the past years, many companies have outsourced check printing to their banks. In the future, banks also may handle the routine processes involved with payment authorizations. This would require the establishment of a procedure for referral for certain "unusual value or payee" payments, but these generally could be managed either by the bank receiving and adjudicating an invoice or paying a regular amount for utilities and periodic services.

One of the mission statements of the EDIBANX group is to "expand the scope of transaction types processed to include those transactions that are beyond the scope of financial EDI." This goal has yet to be interpreted in specific terms but clearly suggests that the conveyance and management of trade documents, invoices, advance shipment notices, and more are likely to be included. This indicates the true breadth of this initiative and is an example of what financial institutions worldwide may have to develop to remain competitive in their own marketplace.

It will take time for EDIBANX to move from proposal to full-scale implementation and rollout. The implementation is fully practical and breaks no new ground technologically. The proposed applications have already been proven in other contexts and the needed standards and message formats are fully defined and in use. It's important in ensuring that the banking industry will move from piecemeal to coherent electronic commerce.

EDIFACT   The EDIFACT EDI standard is seen by most experts on electronic commerce as the emerging global standard that will form the basis for a common language for electronic commerce between the great trading blocs of North America, Europe, and Asia/Pacific. It is still less used in North America than in Europe, mainly because of the large investment already made in the more mature ANSI standard. Technically, both EDIFACT and ANSI standards carry similar data elements, which means they can be interfaced. Structurally, however, both in the way the data elements are organized and the way they are applied, they differ significantly and it has often been difficult to convert messages from one to the other.

It was between 1980 and 1985 that the ANSI X12 EDI standard was developed by U.S. businesses for their immediate domestic business needs, while the European and U.N. standards were developed primarily by government and trade associations. A few industry-oriented EDI standards were developed, such as TRADACOM, designed for retailers by the European Article Numbering Association (ANA) in the United Kingdom and the Netherlands, and the ODETTE standard, developed by the European auto industry. These had no future. ANSI and EDIFACT took over from them.

EDIFACT, the product of the United Nations, is somewhat bureaucratic and labored in its standard-setting deliberations, perhaps because of its international nature. Many parties must be involved, from many countries with many regulatory differences. In any case, it generates a lot of alphabet soup acronyms. In the mid to late 1970s, an ad hoc group of countries under the banner of the United Nations ECE Working Party 4 (UN WP4) for the

Facilitation of International Trade Procedures, formed two committees to define the information required for the interchange of business documents electronically. In March 1987, drafts of the international EDI syntax, called Universal Standard Message (UNSM), for the International Invoice, were submitted to UN WP4. The EDIFACT syntax was approved, and the final draft was submitted in September 1987. After being approved first with "Draft for Trial Use" status, the Invoice UNSM received the final status of "Registered Message" in September 1988. In September 1987, the EDIFACT Syntax was submitted to the International Standards Organization ISO TC154, where it was unanimously approved as an ISO Standard (DIN 9735).

The U.S. ISO Technical Advisory Group (TAG) to TC154 met prior to this ISO meeting under the direction of ANSI. The TAG voted to approve EDIFACT but with the stipulation that specific X12 comments and modifications be addressed before final ISO approval. These comments were admitted and added to the approved syntax document.

Since that time much effort has been spent on both sides of the Atlantic developing complementary messages and providing guidelines for message design as well as standards maintenance. Today, ANSI, EDIFACT, and ISO work cooperatively, thus avoiding surprises and conflicts.

Some of the more commonly used EDIFACT transactions are:

- CREADV (*Cre*dit *Advi*ce)
- CREEXT (*Ext*ended *Cre*dit *Advi*ce)
- CUSDEC (*Cus*toms *De*claration)
- DEBADV (*Deb*it *Adv*ice)
- DELJIT (*Deli*very *Ju*st *in* *T*ime)
- ORDERS (Purchase *Orders*)
- INVOIC (*Invoi*ce)
- PAYORD (*Pa*yment *Ord*er)
- REMADV (*Rem*ittance *Advi*ce)

EDI Gateways Gateway is the term used in the telecommunications field for a hardware/software combination that manages the information and application link between networks and services. There are many devices that handle the physical links—bridges and routers being the main ones—but they cannot manage the many translations and reformatting required in linking applications between dissimilar systems. Gateways do this, operating as interpreters, traffic coordinators, and record keepers. They are complex and expensive but essential for business-to-business electronic commerce. Some of the functions of an EDI gateway are as follows:

- Translates messages from one software application so that the receiving software can accept them; in most instances, this means translating them into one of the main EDI standard transaction sets, such as ANSI X12 or EDIFACT.
- Manages the queuing and transmission of the messages over the relevant networks, rather like an air traffic controller.
- Checks for errors before transmitting the message.
- Captures information needed for call logging, auditing, billing, and security.

Generally, the provider of the EDI service, such as a value added network, will provide and manage the gateway. The gateway determines the range of applications that can make use of the network.

EDI Hubs Hubs are computer complexes accessed over a telecommunications network, that provide a processing center for electronic commerce transactions. The term is commonly applied to the buyer side of a trading partner relationship in electronic commerce. The customer sends a message from the hub, for instance, to place a purchase order. Historically, such hubs have been large, generally multinational companies, which can com-

"One of the biggest values from an administrative perspective is that the Internet provides a common carrier . . . the cost of adding new partners is

almost zero. We [can] support a higher level of functionality while spending a lot less. . . . No one can do business on a competitive schedule without [Internet] access; it just takes too much time to deal with communication any other way. If other companies say they want to exchange data on tapes, we are more and more likely to say no and look for someone already on the Internet." (Mark Silbernagle, Mgr. for Corporate IS, in Mary J. Cronin, Doing More Business on the Internet, *New York: Van Nostrand Reinhold, 1995, 170)*

mand their suppliers, referred to as spokes, to do their electronic bidding. Companies like General Motors, Sears, and the U.S. Department of Defense are examples of powerful hub players.

There has, however, been a significant change in the definition of the term over the past five years. As defined by The EDI Group, Ltd., of Oak Park, Illinois, a leading research firm in the area of EDI and electronic commerce, a hub is now defined as any group of organizations that has 100 trading partners connected electronically to it, no matter if they are buying or selling goods. This change in definition reflects a significant power shift from the traditional, nonelectronic, buyer/seller relationship to an electronic relationship governed by the importance of controlling the information channel and the access to goods that results. The hub is the control and coordination vehicle in the management of the electronic commerce relationships.

Spokes in this context might be the buyers rather than sellers in a trading relationship of the future, simply because without electronic connection to their suppliers, they cannot operate effectively. Certainly, this is beginning to be the case with small, independent retail food stores who cannot command any advantage from their suppliers on their own. At the same time, retail buying groups who use electronic inventory and ordering procedures can command significant discounts by exerting their joint buying power—not just in the volume they purchase, but by consolidating and electronically linking their orders into one smooth flow of information. Ultimately, the term "hub" in electronic commerce will mean the organization that controls the development and information flows in the trading relationship.

EDI Translation Software   Translation software examines a sender's message and reformats it so that it can be processed by the software systems of the receiver, a trading partner. EDI is accomplished through the use of a common, standardized, format. This almost always requires translating the outputs from the sender's computer system into the format used by the receiving trading partner. For example, a firm's purchasing system will produce printed order forms that display its name and address in, say, the right-hand top corner, the item number on line 12 and the quantity on line 13. The supplier's form for processing the order may have the item as line 4 and the quantity on line 6. The terms they use to refer to the same item of data may differ slightly—"Salesperson" vs. "Sales rep" vs. "Staff ID. Number," for instance.

Regardless of the format of the output, it has to be converted to the formats that allow the recipient's system to interpret its contents accurately and completely. This is done through translation software, which is commercially available for nearly any computer system of any size. The cost can range from a few hundred dollars for a simple PC version to tens of thousands of dollars for a mainframe computer version. The function, though, is the same and relatively straightforward in all cases—to convert data from the structure that exists within your system to a common, recognized, standard form of data. From this standard structure, a receiver of the data can pass the information through its translator and then read and convert it into its own system, without having to modify its own software application.

The use of a translator also allows organizations to make changes to their own systems without affecting any of their trading partners. This is possible because the changes are made between the base application and the translator within the company while the translator remains unaffected.

A commercial translator should be able to:

- Process transactions in all relevant standards, most obviously the ANSI X12 transaction sets that are the core of EDI.

- Manage the transfer of computer files (electronic catalogs, price lists, etc.).

- Provide user-defined input screens (for a PC, for example) for entering data and filling out forms.

- Automatically forward messages to and from a mailbox, with automatic trading partner setups.
- Convert incoming and outgoing documents to the relevant format.
- Print out all transactions.
- Provide automatic acknowledgments of receipt of messages.
- Provide audit trails.

Efficient Consumer Response (ECR)   Efficient consumer response, or ECR, is the name applied to a process of electronic order and inventory management in the retail food industry. It is an application of just-in-time (JIT) principles. JIT focuses on manufacturers' inventory management and the matching of materials and parts to production. In the food industry, ECR has adapted the same basic concept to the specific needs and product-handling requirements of food stores and their suppliers. One of the key differences between inventory in the retail food industry and inventory in other industries is, of course, the highly perishable nature of many of the goods in the supply chain. Milk, eggs, bread, and lettuce are not able to be "warehoused" for any significant period of time, nor are the cows and chickens able to be turned off and on at will.

The food industry has managed a JIT environment for virtually all of its existence without calling it such. (Indeed, the Toyota executive who coined the term "just-in-time" and first applied it as the base for the car company's "lean" production, launching the Japanese car industry's 20-year global dominance, first thought up the idea when visiting a U.S. supermarket. He observed how the shelves were continuously replenished as goods were bought, neither running out of stock nor piling them up and thus avoiding waste of expensive space.) The key element of ECR is that it creates a formal methodology for inventory management, ordering, and replenishment that can be implemented in a computerized system.

Prior to ECR, issues such as shrinkage (missing products from the shipment), special offers, tax adjustments, and other variances wreaked havoc on the efforts to automate the interchange between the buyer and seller's computers. A seemingly simple matter of calculating tax or terms would create major problems for the software programming effort. In the case of tax, if a certain tax is charged to a buyer who is exempt, recalculating to remove the tax from the amount due proved very difficult because deducting a percentage from a bill would end up leaving a small variance. This variance would cause the seller's computer to reject the payment—even for one cent—unless the software designers reprogrammed the program to have sophisticated parameters.

ECR involves both complex software development and complex process analysis and transformation. It is obviously as much the future of food retailing as JIT was the future of car manufacturing. It will take as much effort, time, and management commitment as JIT did.

EFT See **Electronic Funds Transfer.**

EFTPOS See **Electronic Funds Transfer; Point of Sale.**

Electronic Cash Electronic cash is based on the increasingly used cryptographic systems for "digital signatures." Cryptography codes and decodes information via complex mathematical procedures. One such system involves a pair of numeric "keys" that work like the halves of a code book: messages are encoded with one key and decoded with the other key. One key is made public, while the other is kept private. By supplying all users with its public key, a bank can allow them to decode any message encoded with its private key. If decoding by a user yields a meaningful message, the user can be sure that only the bank could have encoded

Electronic transactions in core business operations generally reduce the number of suppliers a firm chooses to work with. That has been the case with electronic data interchange, where companies build tight

relationships with a select group of suppliers. It has been the same with cash management. In the 1980s, the number of banks with whom a Fortune 500 firm maintained primary relationships dropped from 13 to 10. (Thomas D. Steiner and Diogo B. Teixeira, Technology in Banking, Illinois: Dow-Jones Irwin, *1990, 158)*

"Money may no longer be controlled exclusively by central authorities—like the U.S. Treasury—that are tied to individual political systems. In its place will be digital currency "minted" by companies responsible for keeping it secure and valuable." ("Electric Money," Byte Magazine, *June 1996)*

it. These digital signatures are far more resistant to forgery than handwritten ones.

Electronic cash schemes are oriented to the use of tokens of value—a fancy name for a short data item that resembles a traveler's check in being widely acceptable as a valid form of payment. A token is a representation of value that is exchanged between parties, all of whom subscribe to the same scheme. All accept that the token is a real substitute for cash value and not like play money in the game of Monopoly. Electronic cash is no different than physical cash in that the token of value must be agreeable to the receiver before it is truly usable. For example, to offer to pay for a good or service with a U.S. dollar or British pound sterling is, in most countries, an agreeable alternative to domestic cash. To attempt to pay with a Russian ruble would likely not be met with success (during the collapse of the Russian economy in the early 1990s, even Moscow taxi drivers refused rubles and insisted on packs of cigarettes as a much more valid currency). Both dollars and rubles are valid and legal forms of tender, but the ruble is not seen as desirable currency. The same situation is true for electronic cash—if the provider and supporters of the token are not trusted or seen as relevant, then the acceptability of electronic cash will not be broad. The issue is what type of token and what provider/guarantor of its value will meet these requirements?

On a more technical level, in the basic electronic cash systems that have been proposed, software at the user end would generate a random number, which would serve as the token or "note." His or her system would then "blind" the note, using a random factor, so that it could not be read, and would transmit it to a bank. In exchange for money debited from the user's account or otherwise supplied, the bank would use its private key to digitally sign the blinded note, in effect making it like a cashier's check guaranteed by a bank officer's signature, and would digitally transmit the result back to the user. The user's system would unblind the note, which would now constitute its payment. After checking that the note's digital signature is authentic, the payee would electronically send the note on to the bank, which in turn would check the signature and credit the payee accordingly.

See also **Digital Cash; Digital Signature.**

Electronic Catalogs   Electronic Catalogs are, as the term implies, data files that contain product and pricing information (and, in many instances, inventory data). They have emerged as a major application of electronic commerce, especially as accessibility improves by way of the Internet and value added networks. The pharmaceutical industry for example is replacing its drug catalogs printed on paper with electronic catalogs, which not only cut down on the cost of production and updating, but also provide a much easier and more effective method for ordering and shipping. Electronic catalogs can be kept updated by the hour, which explains why Netscape's World Wide Web gets 15 million "hits" a day; software and telecommunications developers need today's product information. They can't get it by mail.

For corporate purchasing departments, on-line catalogs greatly widen the range of potential suppliers and products they can choose from. Just how big that wider range can be is indicated by a Dallas consultant's review of information about electrical transformer equipment. The local telephone Yellow Pages listed 11 suppliers. The AT&T National 800 Directory Shopper's Guide had none. Internet search engines turned up between 13 (Yahoo) and 23,975 (Altavista). While the Altavista list obviously included much irrelevant information (there's a line of toys called "Transformers" that shows up in the search, for instance), the consultant took just seven minutes to narrow down the huge list to product specification sheets showing size and voltages and to print out a list of information on six different transformers that met his requirements.

Surveys and press articles strongly suggest that the heaviest users of the Internet in business are people who need a constant flow of information about products: engineers, software and

One of the longest-established and most successful electronic catalog services is Computer-U-Card, which has revenues of close to $1 billion. It does not sell products directly but offers its 30 million subscribers unlimited access to a data base of information on 250,000 thousand items, including automobiles and appliances, for purposes of comparison shopping. Computer-U-Card forwards subscriber orders to the manufacturer. The CEO commented (Fortune, 18 April 1994) that "This is virtual-reality inventory. We stock nothing, but we sell everything."

hardware specialists, and corporate purchasing groups. The World Wide Web sites of such companies as Hewlett-Packard, Netscape, and Sun Microsystems are accessed millions of times a day. The combination of up-to-the-minute information on products and prices is the draw here.

The importance of electronic catalogs as the data resource needed to ensure accurate processing of EDI transactions is also growing. With such applications as vendor-managed inventory, continuous replenishment, and evaluated receipts settlement, EDI systems handle purchase orders and deliveries of goods automatically, with no human intervention. The EDI system generates invoices, for instance, based on the information in the electronic catalog. If that information is not kept fully updated, the catalog may list an incorrect price.

Electronic catalogs differ from electronic commerce messages in size and complexity of structure. Catalogs often have very large data files, whereas an EC message is both shorter and simpler in structure. A manufacturer of electronic components or a supermarket wholesaler will have thousands of products in its catalog. Whereas the formats for EDI messages are increasingly standardized, file formats are determined by the software that generates them and their structures often make it impossible for other software systems to read them without converting them. That conversion can be extremely complex; it isn't just a matter of converting the data but of translating all the extra information that goes with it: indexes, data base management aids, cross-reference links, and the like. Keeping the catalog updated means transferring it on a timely basis.

The cost of electronic catalogs obviously depends on their size, complexity, and use of such multimedia as video clips and high-quality photographs. A growing number of companies offer Internet "hosting" for merchants, providing both a World Wide Web site and all the software needed to give them an electronic presence on the Internet. An example is Best Internet's Best/iCat

Electronic Commerce Suite, which costs $400 to $1,000 a month, with a setup fee of $500.

An example of the impact electronic catalogs can have is shown in the experience of AMP, the largest manufacturer of electronic and electrical interconnection devices in the world, with 40,000 employees and sales of over $5 billion a year. AMP won an award from CommerceNet for its implementation of an electronic catalog, which now contains information on 65,000 items. The immediate savings in reducing the number of copies of the 400 paper catalogs that must be printed have been substantial. AMP spends close to $10 million on publishing them. The electronic catalog was put up on the World Wide Web in January 1996. By year's end, there were 55,000 registered users in 100 countries, including 1,200 AMP employees. Around 200 new users sign up daily. AMP summarized what it has learned from the development and implementation of the catalog:

- User acceptance is very positive; the catalog fills a real need. There's no selling required to get them to make regular use of it.

- It's essential to phase the implementation via a pilot and not try to do everything in one Great Leap Forward.

- The priority for users is a fast and accurate search capability that displays the products that meet the specified user criteria—they need efficient search, not just "browsing" or Internet "surfing."

- There are wide variations in the capabilities of the software that handles the search and in the data base management tools. Choosing and implementing these requires careful evaluation and planning.

- Users place a high value on pictures, even though these take longer—often much longer—to download than text. Visualization is essential.

- Experienced users are hungry for product information and repeatedly request additions.

- Strong project management is vital. The bulk of the effort goes into planning and phasing of the data base implementation. The data has to be well organized and structured. A paper catalog can be fairly free-form and grouped by broad categories. The data base of an electronic catalog has to be as tightly and comprehensively structured as a data base for customer information or sales information.

AMP reports numerous benefits gained: the electronic catalogs get information about new products out immediately; firms that put their catalogs on-line can track trends in customer interest, as well as identify repeat customers and the information they want; putting its catalog on-line also makes it easier for the firm's own employees to learn and keep up to date about its many and fast-changing products; and users can download and print data and pictures themselves instead of waiting for AMP to mail the information.

Electronic Checks   As the name indicates, electronic checks are versions of the standard paper check sent electronically. The person or organization that wishes to use this convenient mode of payment must register with a third-party service that verifies that the payment is valid and authorized. The third party functions like a travel agent who has a customer's credit card number and signature on file so the customer can book tickets with the agency by phone.

In the processing cycle for electronic checks, the buyer sends the check to the payee by electronic mail or EDI, which (rather than who, since typically this is a piece of software) forwards it to the third party's on-line computer system, called a server, which contains the information needed to authorize the payment. The server sends the check for deposit to the seller's bank, which handles it as a normal check. The information will be encrypted and an electronic equivalent of the payer's physical signature added to the message.

Electronic checks may well turn out to be more widely adopted than more innovative forms of electronic payment, just as the fax machine is far more widely used than electronic mail. Like the fax, electronic checking has the advantage of familiarity, convenience, and ease of use. There are several other advantages:

- Electronic checks are well-suited to the existing banking systems.
- Consumers still can depend on the float, since their accounts are not immediately debited and there is still a delay before each check clears.
- Financial risk is assumed by the third party, via its server.
- Security is achieved via simple and well-established encryption tools.

Quicken, by far the most widely used financial software system for personal computers, employs electronic checks. It links to a number of banks that combine the third-party and traditional banking role.

See also **Cash; Checks.**

Electronic Commerce Standard-Setting One of the most important, and often the lengthiest and most tedious activity related to EDI and electronic commerce, is the development and distribution of standards. Standards are agreed upon, published, precise, and openly available agreements on the formats of messages and procedures for sending and receiving them. They are the key to electronic commerce.

There are several layers involved in the standard-setting process:

1. A group of firms that shares communications and transactions realizes that all parties need to operate

Since the technology of the Internet and the wider electronic commerce base changes so quickly and so constantly, it can be very hard indeed to reach cooperative agreements. Such agreements need a neutral venue, such as ANSI, the main coordinator of EDI standards-setting in the United States, and industry groups like the influential and successful Automotive Industry Action Group (AIAG) and the World Wide Web Consortium (W3C). That said, the leaders still look for a proprietary edge. Microsoft's offer is always (paraphrased), 'Since we are the inevitable winner, sign up with us or lose.' IBM succeeded with this strategy for almost forty years.

within a consistent framework for communication and transactions. The group needs to agree that their competition as individual firms should not be based on infrastructure, but in the quality and differentiation they can bring to their customers in using that infrastructure. For example, hundreds of years ago, different railways used to operate on different-gauge rails. Sometimes there would have to be a change of cars from one county to the next. This might mean transferring the cargo from one car to another, or in some cases, changing the actual axles and wheels of the cars so that they could continue on the new rails. In any event, what was seen by some in the railway business as competitive differentiation was simply an inefficiency that was passed on to the consumer.

2. After identifying common industry needs and opportunities for mutual benefit from cooperation, firms in the group often form an industry-specific standards body to provide the tools for the rest. This happened in the grocery, warehousing, transportation, and other industries. These proprietary, vertical, industry standards were of limited value because as soon as the groups that developed them began to deal with other industries they were unable to communicate. This leads to the need for cross-industry standards.

3. Cross-industry, or generic, standards are ones such as ANSI or EDIFACT. While each of these covers the needs of virtually all possible users, even these standards are seen as somewhat regional since ANSI is the standard in North America while EDIFACT is used in Europe. The key issue is that a cross-industry purchase order standard has the flexibility and detail to allow a manufacturer, a transportation company, and a

supplier all to use the same electronic document structure effectively. The ultimate goal is to provide a lower overall infrastructure cost for all parties in the transaction flow.

ANSI and EDIFACT are examples of standards developed through collaboration, consensus, and negotiation. Other standards emerge from the market's adoption of a power player's "proprietary" system or product. For decades, IBM set the de facto standards for computing, and phone company monopolies across the world imposed their own standards because customers had no other choices. The owner of a de facto standard has immense power in the market. As electronic commerce both grows rapidly and promises potential aggregate revenues in the range of billions of dollars and even hundreds of billions of dollars annually, companies like Microsoft, IBM, Netscape, AT&T, and many others recognize that, first, they cannot succeed if their proprietary standards are not widely used, and, second, that they must convince other vendors, service providers, and software developers to adopt *their* standards. That makes the standard-setting process intensely political, often adversarial, and highly self-serving.

The progress of electronic commerce is and will always be dominated by standard-setting. For instance, the many companies competing to establish secure transactions over the Internet fully recognize that any product that is not adopted as a standard by merchants, on-line information services, PC software and hardware providers, and Internet users can gain at most a niche position. Naturally, they will tout their own as the best option and the inevitable standard. Naturally, they will seek deals with firms that already own a large customer base or dominate the tools customers use. When a Microsoft or Netscape adopts their offering, they are on the way to making it a standard.

The list of major standards that are the base of today's electronic commerce, and those under development that will be part of the platform for tomorrow's, would fill an entire book. The ones that will have the most impact on business planning are the ANSI X12 family of standards and industry-specific standards. For the typical business manager, it's useful to have a sense of the standard-setting process, of ANSI X12 and of the basics of EDI. It's also useful to maintain a cautious view of proposed initiatives and innovations in standards, especially in such areas as consumers' electronic commerce on the Internet. Standards take years in most instances to define and implement and for every proposed five standards, maybe one will emerge as a building block of everyday electronic commerce. If the proposal is for an X12 standard, then the odds are much better—close in fact to one for one.

Electronic Commerce Tax Law Existing tax laws do not easily accommodate the special feature of electronic commerce—buyers and sellers may be widely separated in geographic distance. An EC transaction may link a buyer in one tax jurisdiction to a seller in another, with the transaction and information handled on a computer "server" somewhere else—buyer, seller, and computer server being anywhere in the world. When you buy a VCR in Virginia, you pay Virginia sales tax and the Virginia merchant pays state and Federal taxes. Who pays what when you order the VCR over the Internet from a Virginia retailer, using your PC, which connects to the retailer's computer server, which is located in Atlanta? What about downloading a piece of software over the Net?

There are two often conflicting issues that national and state or regional governments wrestle with in evolving new forms of taxation needed to address EC—a market where goods may be ordered from Texas, reside in Italy, be processed over a web site in Canada, and be paid for through digital cash on the buyer's hard disk. (1) What jurisdiction should apply—is the item

In November 1996 the U.S. Treasury Department issued the first report on the government's intended tax policy for the Internet. The policy is: where possible, apply existing tax rules to Internet transactions, protect companies from being taxed in two jurisdictions for the same transaction, and resist new tariffs on downloaded goods and services, most obviously software and information. The deputy secretary of the Treasury stated: "This is a case where tax policy is trying to support the development of a technology, not impede it."

A key issue that remains to be resolved is whether taxes will be imposed depending on the residency of the buyer or the seller. The stakes are large. Most sellers are companies in the United States; the U.S. government wants to tax them. Many foreign countries want to levy their own taxes, which means focusing on the buyer. Other countries also show strong indications of wanting to discourage low-cost U.S. companies from undercutting their often protected domestic high-technology firms—a personal computer priced at the competitive U.S. levels being a bargain almost everywhere in the world. The European Community wants to place a value added tax in the buyer's country of residence.

A fundamental question underlies these tax questions: Where exactly is the Internet located and when is it in a given state or nation? Italy and Belgium see it very much as a highway and intend to tax every digital bit that travels across their borders. U.S. states are considering any Internet server—computer—physically within their borders as constituting a tax location.

Record-keeping and documentation are concerns for tax agencies. A spokesman for the IRS summarizes the Service's general position on these issues (*EDI Forum*, 1995):

> We need to educate our folks that an electronic record can be relied upon to the same extent as any paper document the taxpayer might pull out of the stack. . . . First of all, EDI is an outstanding technology, and we at the IRS don't want to be a barrier to taxpayer use of EDI. We want to empower taxpayers to use EDI, to make good business decisions as to its use, and at the same time to have comfort that they would be meeting our requirements. . . . Yet the truth is that public networks are not secure; information carried over them cannot be confidential and integrity is not guaranteed. . . . I'd make sure the audit control department works with MIS to ensure that proper controls are in place as the EDI system is being installed. EDI's elimination of order processing steps, for example, automatically changes internal auditing procedures.

taxable at the location of the buyer, the seller, or the distributor? (2) Should the focus in taxation be to grab the money and risk encouraging the seller to find a way to bypass the system, or encourage electronic commerce growth in a state's own area of jurisdiction? It's too early to predict the outcome, but the emerging pattern in the United States is to support EC growth and avoid tax systems that constrain it. In Europe, the bureaucratic ethos is looking to regulate EC and ensure that no more advantage is afforded to buyers using the Internet than to those using physical—and easily monitored—channels.

Note the IRS's view of the security (or insecurity) of government networks.

Electronic Commerce Transaction Costs A key issue in electronic commerce is the relative cost of processing the transaction versus its value. For credit cards, the cost is around 2 percent, a significant portion of which goes toward covering the cost of fraud. Banks typically add a charge of 2 percent to their own cost of funds, paying depositors x percent and charging $(x + 2)$ percent for loans, though, of course, the figures vary according to customer, product, and risk.

Telephone companies have the highest transaction cost differential. About 30 percent of the cost of a phone call is for accounting and billing. The average price of a call is 30 cents, so that 10 cents is for processing.

It is difficult to estimate the cost of Internet transactions. Transfer of messages via Internet is free, but when hardware, software, security, and data base management are added in, costs can soar. Value added EDI networks generally price transactions on a combination of setup fees, a monthly service fee, and message fees. The cost of a message may be fixed or priced by the byte, with surcharges for priority delivery and time of day. Long distance carriers seem to offer as many prices and packages as there are customers.

Wall Street brokerage firms, lawyers, and investors previously paid $250 million a year to obtain information filed with the SEC by public companies. They can now access it electronically. "Easy Internet access to EDGAR

Electronic Data Gathering, Analysis, Retrieval (EDGAR) A database that is intended to automate the filing of over 12 million pages of the financial information by public companies that is required by law is EDGAR. The reports are the annual 10K, quarterly 10G, shareholder proxies, and many other forms. They are filed by 15,000 public companies for the dual purpose of preventing investor fraud and ensuring that investors, regulators, and others have accurate information on the companies.

The U.S. Securities and Exchange Commission (SEC) set up the project to reduce the paperwork for companies providing the required information and for parties using it. It cost over $100 million to implement, double the budget allocated. Before EDGAR, it took up to six weeks for the SEC to enter documents into their archive and a week for inquiries to be processed. Now, the information can be obtained over the Internet, and when the system becomes fully operational (only around 5,000 out of 15,000 companies are in the data base as of early 1997), information will be accessible within 24 hours of the SEC receiving it. Getting the paper documents costs about $50, using the many SEC data vendors who specialize in this service. The Internet access is free.

has fundamentally changed a business that was closed, costly, and profitable to an open, inexpensive and competitive market."
(*T. Kalakota and A. Whinston,* Frontiers of Electronic Commerce, *570)*

Electronic Data Interchange (EDI) Electronic data interchange is the intercompany, computer-to-computer transmission of business information in a standard format. For EDI purists, "computer-to-computer" means direct transmission from the originating application program to the receiving, or processing, application program, and an EDI transmission consists only of business data, not any accompanying verbiage or free-form messages. Purists might also contend that a standard format is one that is approved by a national or international standards organization, as opposed to formats developed by industry groups or companies.

One of the key factors in achieving success in the use of EDI is recognizing that EDI improves business efficiency, not just technical efficiency. The use of EDI, and all forms of electronic commerce, is based on the clear and established intent to accomplish a *business* objective such as reducing inventory, lowering personnel costs, speeding up access to information, or reducing errors. EDI is a tool, facilitated through technology. In fact, the components of EDI technology are becoming readily available commodities, thanks to the need for them in the business process.

There are four elements in any EDI system:

- *Electronic store and retrieve facilities.* An electronic mailbox receives and holds messages sent by all parties to its

"Contrary to popular assumptions, the majority of EDI applications will be built out of competitive necessity, providing little if any competitive advantage for most users. These systems will become a cost of doing business. To be sure, many firms enjoy competitive advantage from EDI, however short-lived. But only a rare few maintain this advantage, and when they do, it is not from the technology but by instilling a mindset that focuses on customer value and then supports

a process that continually innovates and adds features valuable to the customer." ("The Realities of Electronic Data Interchange: How Much Competitive Advantage," Benjamin De Long and Scott Morton, EDI Forum 8, No. 3, 1995)

owner. The messages remain in the mailbox until they are picked up by the owner.

- *Communications.* A network both transmits and receives the message, provides security and control information, and handles its efficient routing.

- *Translation software.* This converts a firm's purchase order, for example, into a structured, formatted message that its supplier's order processing software can interpret automatically via its own input formats.

- *Application programming interface software.* This links the firm's transaction processing software to the EDI translation software.

As the focus in EDI has shifted from technological aspects to business functions it supports, enables, or adds value to, the need has increased to understand the impacts on the organization and the procedural changes it will have to make. Many value added networks, along with a growing number of consulting firms, are providing reviews of changing business processes and management-oriented education in the area of EDI and electronic commerce.

See also **Application Programming Interface; EDI Translation Software.**

Electronic Data Interchange Association   The Electronic Data Interchange Association is the longest-established cooperative industry group in EDI and the pioneer of most EDI innovations in the 1970s and 1980s.

Electronic Funds Transfer (EFT)   Electronic funds transfer refers to the movement of funds electronically through banking payment systems. The term covers both the payment of funds or the collection of money. Where information and funds move together, the transfer is more generally referred to as financial EDI (FEDI). A common application of EFT is direct payroll deposit. Many companies pay their employees through an EFT payroll credit, primarily because the costs for issuing an EFT are substantially less than the cost of issuing a check, with a greater level of control and security. As well, for the purpose of collecting recurring payments for loans or for insurance premiums, many organizations offer automated electronic collection options, which result in lower cost for the handling and management of the collections process.

Typically, the direct costs for an EFT are about one-third the cost of a paper check, and the indirect costs for managing, storing, and retrieving the physical check can be much higher. The intrinsic value in electronic payments, and EFT in particular, is the greater control and security that now is part of most EFT systems. Ironically, since the introduction of high-resolution color scanners and printing, it is easier than ever before to produce forged or fraudulent paper checks. And with the ever declining cost of these technologies, even the smallest criminal operation can get into the act. With the current state of electronic payment systems and cryptographic techniques, it is virtually impossible to create a fraudulent payment in an EFT system.

Since 1989, EFT and electronic payments such as ATM and debit cards have exceeded the total volume of paper-based payments in North America. There is a similar trend internationally, where most Western European countries are experiencing a comparable trend.

See also **Financial EDI; Automated Clearing Houses.**

Electronic Mail Electronic mail is basically the simple transfer of messages in text form. Many options are emerging that attach files and include such nontext information as graphics files and voice annotations. At the core of electronic mail is the concept of *store and forward*. A message is sent over a telecommunications network which interprets the recipient's electronic address—on the Internet, it will be something like "PGWK@aol.com"—and routes it to the equivalent of a post office box, not unsurprisingly termed a mailbox, where it is stored. When the addressee logs onto the system, he or she will be informed that there is a message, which the network then forwards.

Electronic mail took several decades to move beyond being a tool many academics and scientists relied on and some companies encouraged for internal communication. Obstacles to its growth included the complexity of many e-mail systems; incompatibility between them, which was like having to use five different phones, none of which could receive calls from the other types; the public's initial fear of computers and the consequent paucity of correspondents equipped for electronic communication.

All these problems have disappeared. Electronic mail is now the simplest, most popular, and most widespread use of the Internet and on-line services. For an employee not to use a large firm's e-mail system is to choose to be locked out of many informal and formal communication networks. It is increasingly rare to get handed a business card that doesn't list both a fax number and an electronic mail address besides the phone number. The fax number is a reminder of the limitations of e-mail. Electronic mail predates the arrival of low-cost fax machines, but fax transmission became enormously popular because fax machines are so easy to use. E-mail began to catch up only when it too became simple, though even now the effort needed to fax a document is still far less than the effort to log onto a PC and then the network, create a message, and send it. The massive advantage of e-mail, though, is its ability to store the message until it is picked up by the recipient. And whereas e-mail goes to a person, the fax message goes to a machine. If the recipient is not present at the fax machine's location, he or she does not get the message or must rely on others to deliver it. An electronic mail message gets delivered to you whether you're in Italy or India. That is, it gets delivered to you wherever you can log onto the relevant network, which increasingly means the Internet. Nonetheless, given all the differences across the world in phone systems, access to the Internet, wire connections and technical requirements for connecting a personal computer to a telecommunications network, the fax machine is still easier to use and more likely to get your message through.

The growth in electronic mail volumes has been around 20 percent a year in the 1990s, roughly the same as the increase in electronic commerce in general. Growth in costs has been slower, as prices decline 5 percent a year. Today, electronic mail accounts for only 6 percent of electronic business-to-business information exchange. Most surveys forecast it will reach 10 to 12 percent by 2000. There will be a shift in the type of mail, from "unstructured" messages to structured forms that can be directly input to the recipient's computer systems without their having to be read and translated to those systems' formats. Whereas today only 2 percent of all information exchanges are structured e-mail messages, they are likely to reach 5 percent in 2000.

Because electronic mail systems were designed to make it easy to communicate with anyone, anywhere, security was a minor concern. In general, e-mail messages are no more protected from interception, fraud, and misuse than phone calls and faxes. That's not much of a problem for conversations between friends and colleagues, but it's a massive impediment to electronic commerce. On the Internet, electronic mail has created almost as many concerns as benefits: "spoofing" (messages that claim to come from someone else), "spamming" (flooding the Net with broadcast mass mailings), and "flaming," impulsive abuse and angry responses.

Naturally, the problems are being rapidly solved. Electronic mail software is now very easy to use. America Online, Netscape, and Microsoft's and Lotus's e-mail software, to list just a few, guide their users through the process of creating, sending, storing, and retrieving messages. More and more systems and services encrypt—code—messages. There are features for dealing with junk mail and organizing correspondence. The U.S. Postal Service is now offering an electronic stamp that establishes proof of transmission and receipt.

One large international firm took action in 1997 to stop its staff from wasting time logging onto its network to check their e-mail messages. Now, they are restricted to set periods in the morning, at lunch time, and at the end of the work day. This company is not an anti-technology bastion of conservatism— it is Computer Associates, one of the world's largest software companies. In another high-tech firm in Silicon Valley, the CEO once found over two thousand e-mail messages waiting for him when he returned from a one-week trip; in despair, he deleted the lot, unread. . . . (World Press Review, June 1997, 34)

Newspapers have assets new entrants into news services can't match. "We're small in technological name recognition, but the 800-pound gorilla in terms of content. It's hard, if you're not in the business, to appreciate the size and depth of local news staffs. . . . Even in a 500,000 person market, the staff may be 25 to 30. You're not going to see that duplicated by new entrants." (The manager of the San Jose Mercury's *Internet edition, one of the earliest newspapers to go onto the Web, in* NetGuide, *January 1997, 83)*

Electronic Newspapers Electronic newspapers published on the World Wide Web are a major target of both opportunity and concern for publishers. The opportunity is a new source of subscribers who can be reached at low incremental distribution costs. Skeptics, on the other hand, predict that few people will pay a fee for news via the Internet, given that the basic ethos of the Internet has always been an open flow of free information and that users can get so much just by browsing.

The many experiments in electronic news offerings are thus being monitored closely. One is the *Wall Street Journal's* Interactive Edition, which can be accessed free via Microsoft's Internet Explorer browser or subscribed to up to $49 a year. The paper edition costs $164 a year. As of December 1996, the Interactive Edition had 30,000 subscribers. It needs 100,000 to break even. The most interesting lesson from the sales to date is that close to 40 percent of the customers who pay for it also receive the print version. Discussions of print versus electronic publishing too easily take an either/or view—either paper will win and electronic delivery lose or the reverse. The outcome is likely to be both/and. The challenge, though, is to make money. Above the break-even point of 100,000, Interactive Edition could be very profitable indeed, since there are almost no incremental costs. At 30,000 subscribers, the *Journal* is losing around $3 million a year. That's $100 per sale of a good that costs less than $50.

The main relevance of electronic newspapers to electronic commerce is that newspapers are where businesses place much of their advertising. To date, there's no evidence that on-line advertising matches the traditional medium even if there are 30 million potential customers surfing the Web.

Electronic Purse/Wallet The electronic purse or wallet is an application of the related prepaid card or stored-value cash card. The term was coined while marketing what is often called the "smart card." As well, the terms "purse" and "wallet" further define and segment the concepts of these electronic payment tools.

The generally accepted meaning of the term *electronic purse* tends to be the use of a prepaid card for paying small amounts (less than $10.00). This is in contrast to the use of an *electronic wallet,* which is intended to be used for larger values or more diverse purchasing situations. But both terms refer to a card bearing an electronic strip on which is recorded the value of money the user has input at an electronic station like an ATM machine. Once the card has been "loaded" with a cash value, the user decrements the card value through reader devices at the merchant or sales outlet. Both the electronic purse and the electronic wallet are intended largely as a retail use of electronic cash.

See also **Digital Cash; Mondex.**

Electronic Tax Payments   Electronic tax payments are an important target of opportunity for beleaguered national, state, and local governments seeking revenues and looking to cut costs. Collecting taxes faster and with less administration and staffing will thus become more and more of a priority for them. The U.S. Internal Revenue Service notified over 1 million companies in July 1996, that they must begin to pay their taxes electronically by the end of the year. The penalty for noncompliance is 10 percent. Fifteen hundred larger firms already use TaxLink.

In October 1996, the State of Pennsylvania's Department of Revenue sent EDI software free of charge to 4,000 business tax-payers. This will save the state from $2 to $3 per return on Sales and Use tax filings. In addition, since the software has many built-in error checks and simplifies calculations and filling out of forms, there should be a substantial increase in timely filing and reduction of errors. The main problem the state agency has faced is providing incentives to taxpayers to file electronically. Pennsylvania has not yet decided to make this mandatory, although many states require payment by EFT. A manager for Tax Connect, a set of electronic commerce services provided by the nonprofit TaxNet Governmental Communications Agency (TGCA) points out that many states use electronic funds transfer (EFT) for han-

As late as September 1996, over 70 percent of businesses were unaware of the IRS regulation that requires any company with more than $50,000 in employment taxes in 1995 to switch to electronic payment of its federal taxes in January 1997.

dling business tax payments, but "it is the tax information, the data component of the return, that is really the next evolution of getting revenue agencies involved in electronic commerce."

There can be no doubt that within the next five years, all businesses above a certain size will be required to pay taxes electronically. Given that fact, it makes sense for them to plan ahead now and look at how they, not just the government, can benefit from their doing so, in terms of streamlining processes, reducing administrative costs, and ensuring a smooth transition to the environment of electronic taxes.

Electronic Tokens   A form of currency, rather like a traveler's check, electronic tokens can be used as if they are cash or cashier's checks. They don't yet exist except in pilot schemes. They are essential for mass marketing on the Internet and for handling purchases that are too small to cover the costs of processing as a credit card transaction.

See also **Electronic Cash.**

The logic of electronic commerce may be summarized as "NOW!"—now transactions, just-in-time logistics, and now information. It also rests on principles of control. EC is out of control in the sense that it moves too fast for the transaction to be checked, involves too many parties—including the Internet communities—to be boxed in, and offers too

Embedded Audit Modules   Embedded audit modules are examples of what is termed event-driven EDI, where a series of events are identified and have preprogrammed responses and reporting processes. The nature of auditing in electronic commerce differs substantially from traditional auditing in paper-based forms of commerce, where the audit process is largely focused on reviewing historical records and reports, comparing the supposed event to the expected outcome, and evaluating the process involved. As electronic commerce becomes more pervasive, there is obviously no physical paper created, save some final computer printout reports. Traditional audit review thus becomes virtually impossible.

In electronic commerce, there will be no more auditing at the computer, and audit professionals will have to become more involved with the development of new auditing techniques. These techniques focus on the processes and the controls that are environmental to the business, as well as the actual event management. The velocity of electronic commerce means that the audit may not be able to wait until the next review occurs. This suggests that reporting requirements and content evaluation must be done virtually on-line with the process itself, concurrently evaluating the system and the event as it happens.

For example, in traditional audit reviews, matching the paid and canceled check to the invoice provided satisfactory proof of a completed payment transaction. With electronic commerce, where there is neither paper invoice nor paper check, the proof of the event will be the record contained in the accounts receivable log and the inventory management/receipt system. Simply reviewing these system logs may provide a level of proof and control, but to meet reasonable control standards, an automated review, continuously and independently confirming the association of payment and product should be done. Embedded modules are the software that provides this audit-on-the-run rather than an audit-after-the-event.

The auditor now needs to be a part of the system design and development process, both to review the adequacy of the business and technical process, but also to provide requirements for the audit functions' own review needs. Does this mean the auditor loses independence and objectivity? Not at all. In fact, by defining the audit and control needs up front, the ability to ensure that the controls are consistent with both audit and management goals, can be assured with greater certainty.

See also **Auditing.**

many invitations for hackers to crack its security, and to suppliers and customers to make commercial transactions on-line that have minimal supporting documentation. The old audit mindset won't work and if efforts to impose it succeed then it blocks innovation. At the same time, audit and controls are essential in managing business risk. What is needed for both control and innovation is just-in-time auditing through software that is part of the transaction process.

ERS   See **Evaluated Receipt Settlement.**

Evaluated Receipt Settlement (ERS)   Evaluated receipt settlement is a payment method that eliminates invoices. To take advantage of the timeliness and accuracy of EDI, organizations do not wait for a paper invoice to pay vendors. Once the firm verifies receipt of materials against the advance shipment notice

(ASN), the electronic document that informs them when goods are shipped, and verifies the purchasing system's electronic order instruction, organizations can initiate payment immediately.

That simple description disguises one of the more radical innovations in electronic commerce: the ERS process is built on the exchanged price information by trading partners. It is crucial that the price information be accurate and timely since ERS payments are calculated on the basis of the number of units of goods received by the customer multiplied by the price on the electronic purchase order. Obviously, if the supplier has not provided up-to-date information on prices, there may be a dispute. Such disputes were quite frequent in the early days of ERS, since suppliers still sent price changes by paper. It's not enough in electronic commerce to substitute telecommunications for paper; the business processes must be synchronized to synchronize the needed information. One article on ERS stresses the "internal disciplines" it demands as being far more important than the technology it employs.

The savings the automotive industry has gained from ERS are immense. A 1992 *EDI Forum* survey reports the following:

- Cost to process an accounts receivable or payable: from $63 prior to ERS to effectively 0

- Average processing and administrative cost per shipment for truckers: from $61 to $6

- Average cost per shipment for prime (tier 1) large company suppliers: from $35 to $8

- Cost for tier 2 suppliers: from $41 to $9.

In 1987, Ford had 70 people working in its central accounts payable group. In 1989, it had just 5. This was obviously a major productivity gain for Ford. Its suppliers got comparable benefits. Prior to ERS, only 85 percent of invoices to Ford were paid on time; the figure rose to 98 percent using ERS. Tier 1 suppliers reported a reduction in their average accounts receivables balance of $60,000.

Ford's ERS was one of the two examples of the impact of business process reengineering (BPR) in Michael Hammer's July 1990 *Harvard Business Review* article that made BPR the hottest topic in management for several years. It's an example of how electronic commerce applied to fairly mundane everyday transactions can make a significant contribution to its performance.

Any problems entailed by ERS are problems of logistics, not technology—they are organizational rather than electronic, and electronics does not eliminate them. Just as if you yourself have a problem with an ATM transaction, you may have trouble finding someone in your bank who can resolve it, resolving discrepancies in an ERS transaction may be difficult because the supplier no longer needs a large accounts payable staff with a single location and thus a clear point of contact. Most discrepancies concern prices; from the customer's perspective, a price discrepancy should never occur, because it pays on the basis of the electronic information available to it at the time of the transaction. It's the supplier's responsibility—from the customer's perspective—to ensure accurate and updated information is *automatically* provided.

One of the greatest challenges in applying ERS principles in companies is overcoming the accounting and audit departments' reluctance to give up the paper invoice. It is not the simple elimination of the invoice that is the goal of ERS; rather it is the refinement of the material handling process that provides the information flow into the information systems and provides the certainty needed to generate a payment to the supplier.

The requirement for extremely accurate pricing and synchronization of pricing between the buyer and seller organizations is also critical to the long-term success of the concept. Using an electronic catalog, the supplier's sales or customer service department can send current prices directly to the customer's purchasing department. The receiver must update the appropriate files for future purchases—and be clear about dates price changes will be effective.

The principle called *pay as built* (PAB) or *paid on production* (POP), which has been introduced by a number of automobile manufacturers, carries the ERS principle even further. Instead of paying a supplier on the receipt of goods at the delivery point, several car manufacturers are now providing their suppliers with their build schedules on a daily, and even hourly, basis. It is the supplier's obligation to ensure that the correct parts are in place at the right time—or they could face a stiff penalty. When the vehicle rolls off the assembly line, a trigger is sent to the accounts payable system to generate the payment to the supplier.

Event-Driven EDI   EDI transactions that are automatically triggered by some event are referred to as event-driven EDI to distinguish them from those that are processed at given times under prespecified conditions.

When EDI processing is triggered by predetermined criteria, such as receipt of a purchase order from a specific trading partner, it creates an "event." This event is the signal for a response that is programmed into the computer systems of the recipient trading partner. For example, when an activity such as the production of raw steel is initiated, the output of the first stage of steel production needs to be moved to the next stage, the rolling mill. Event-driven EDI is employed here when the steel production system initiates a notification to the rolling mill that the output of the production process is cooling and can be expected within a preestablished period of time. Within minutes, the rolling mill begins to prepare for this material, determining what characteristics the metal has, its final thickness and shape, and so forth. Within the hour, the mill receives the material, acknowledges its arrival, and processes the steel. All these events are predetermined by the system and require virtually no human effort to manage.

It can also be extended and expanded to include triggers at the transaction set level, such as when, in Financial EDI, application acknowledgments are triggered by a limit check on quantity or amount. A positive or negative response is based on the system inquiry and not on a human intervention.

Expenditures on Electronic Commerce Expenditures on electronic commerce fall into two main categories: business-to-business EDI commerce, where there is a long base of experience, and Internet commerce, where there is not. Internet commerce is a blip on the scale as of early 1997. It's well under 1 percent total retail sales, banking transactions, and credit card transactions, and expenditures today give no real base for making predictions for even a year ahead. There is no reliable information on how much companies are investing in Internet consumer commerce; most banks, retailers, advertisers, automakers, and others have some sort of presence on the World Wide Web and almost all others are planning to have one, but the sites vary from small-scale pilots and simple information displays all the way up to electronic catalogs and full transaction systems. Given that two leading forecasts with well-established reputations and track records varied in their late-1996 predictions of the size of the Internet electronic commerce market in the year 2000 by a factor of 30—from the $6.5 billion predicted by Forrester Research and to the $150 billion predicted by IDC Research—figures on either expenditures or revenues today provide no reliable guides for tomorrow's planning.

The situation is very different for EDI. There's a base of solid historical survey data and predictions for EDI which is more grounded in experience than is the Internet where predictions are based on hopes and wishes as much as on extrapolation. One of the most reliable sources on expenditures and market growth in electronic commerce is The EDI Group, Ltd. of Oak Park, Illinois. The firm has by far the largest data base on EDI and its forecasts have been among the most accurate of any. Its focus is on business-to-business EDI and it does not address Internet consumer commerce. Below is a summary of The EDI Group's mid-1996 report. Its predictions for previous years were very accurate and its predictions for 1997 to 2000 are, in our own view, the best available.

- The growth for 1997 and 1998 is expected to be 23% and 18%.

- The overall five-year growth in the total EDI market is expected to average 16%, with a slowdown in 1999 and 2000 as companies face a continuing and growing need to upgrade telecommunications and computing infrastructures.

- The total market will grow from $2.4 billion in 1996 to $4.4 billion in 2000.

- Expenditures on Internet EDI transactions will grow from $1.8 million in 1996 to $42.6 million, an annual growth rate of 120%.

- Expenditures on non-Internet transactions will increase by 23% a year, from $785 million to $1.5 billion.

Note that The EDI Group reports Internet transaction expenditures increasing by 120% a year, but from such a small base that they will still amount to just $42.6 million in 2000. The rate of Internet commerce growth is the key uncertainty for electronic commerce. Analysts at IDC Research justify their prediction of a $150 billion market in 2000 by extrapolating from the rapid growth in the number of Internet users over the past few years. The analysts don't assume any massive spurt in the EC transactions per user but they do expect the continued massive increase in users to combine with growth in the fraction of them using the Internet for purchases, with total market growth as the result. Forrester Research, which sees a more modest $6.5 billion market, also extrapolates from the growth in the number of users but anticipates the increase in commerce per user to be much less. The EDI Group extrapolates from a longer data base of historical experience and does not assume that the Internet surge will mean an EDI surge. It even sees a slowing down of growth as the EDI market begins to mature.

Business managers simply can't use any forecast of Internet electronic commerce growth as the foundation for their firms' planning. We suggest another approach: simple conditional planning. There are four basic scenarios for Internet EC:

- *Explosion.* Internet electronic commerce continues its recent growth rates in numbers of users and more and more users make more and more EC transactions on it. That's the $150 billion scenario.

- *Acceleration.* The Internet grows and electronic commerce grows with it. That's a scenario for the year 2000 of anywhere from $2 to $30 billion, which leaves sales via the Internet still smaller than mail order catalog sales.

- *Expansion.* The growth follows the pattern of personal computers, corporate and international telecommunications, cellular phones, VCRs, and EDI—a long gestation period (PCs didn't take off in the mass market until their second decade and EDI dates from the 1970s), fast takeoff for a few years, then sustained growth of 20 to 40 percent a year sustained for 10 years or so, and eventually a flattening out of the curve.

- *Evolutionary.* Rapid early growth reflects only the early adoption by a demographically unrepresentative group of users which soon flattens out and further diffusion of the innovation takes a decade or more (electronic mail followed this path).

The issue for conditional planning is not to predict which of these scenarios will occur but what the consequences will be—considering each of the scenarios in turn—(1) if the firm bases its plans on a scenario that turns out to be the one that actually occurs or (2) if the firm bases its plans on that scenario and it doesn't happen.

Given the potential for boom or bust in electronic commerce even without the Internet, business managers need to ask themselves the following questions: (1) Are we ready to bet on one of these scenarios? (2) What are the issues we need to address if our choice turns out to be correct? incorrect? (3) Does that change what we should be doing now in such areas as digital cash, Internet transaction processing, security, electronic catalogs, etc?

Factoring Acceptance by a third party, known as a "factor," of a company's invoice to another firm is called factoring. The factor pays the company the value of the account receivable but at a discount that reflects the factor's risk and loss of the interest it would gain by investing the funds instead of waiting to collect from the firm that owes the money. Factoring has historically been a means for companies with limited liquid funds to get cash now instead of having to wait anywhere between 30 and 120 days. Banks have usually served as factors.

The origins of factoring are not entirely clear. However, factors have played a critical role in the development of international trade. The factor is a financial intermediary, originally a shipping agent, who focuses on the handling of incoming goods. In colonial times, the seller of the goods relied on a factor to collect the proceeds from the sale of the goods offered. In doing this, the factor often assumed the risk for loss due to a failure. This risk occurred because the factor would pay a ship's captain as he left port; accordingly he had plenty of incentive to be cautious about the buyer's creditworthiness and to arrange for some kind of collateral or security. For this service, factors often discounted the value they paid to the captain or seller's agent for the goods, or conversely charged a fee for their services. This role led to the development of other tools to mitigate the risk in a trade transaction, most commonly in the form of a letter of credit (LOC). The LOC is a guarantee of payment by the purchaser. When a bank provides that guarantee, the seller's agent can release the goods in secure knowledge that there is no risk in doing so.

In modern times, letters of credit are issued by commercial banks and have been a major tool in the development of trade. There are still factors and factoring services performed around the world; however, the fundamental concept of factoring is covered by the use of the LOC, which is now a largely electronic tool, sent via the SWIFT network between banks (SWIFT is the Society for Worldwide Interbank Financial Telecommunications).

Fax EDI Fax is still by far the most widely used vehicle for business-to-business electronic transactions. It constitutes 40 percent of total expenditures, with file transfers from computer to computer the next largest component of the total electronic commerce market. The volume of documents transferred by fax is twice that for electronic mail, but the volumes have been flat for several years now and are expected to decline by about 4 percent over the next five years. The cost of faxes is declining by 5 percent a year. They average just under 50 cents a document.

There has been a continuing debate in the electronic commerce community as to the value and appropriateness of the use of facsimile machines as part of the true electronic commerce matrix. Some commentators view them as a temporary and inefficient vehicle for communication that fails to take advantage of the EDI opportunity. It is unquestionable, however, that the fax machine has had a profound effect on the speed and method of business around the world. Linking the fax machine to the output of an EDI system has proven to be a popular and effective solution for many organizations to reach their trading partners, who would otherwise not participate. Many of the value added networks that specialize in EDI and other general-purpose network providers offer fax EDI services as well.

This approach is currently limited to a fax output from an EDI message originator. Some developers are working on software to convert to direct electronic input physical documents that are faxed; however, due to poor transmission quality and the fact that such transactions require extremely sophisticated and intelligent

CSX Railroad was unable to persuade most of its freight customers to adopt EDI. Only 20 percent of its transactions were electronic until it implemented a system that receives faxed bills of lading. The documents are electronically scanned through special-purpose software that converts the information to the inputs needed by CSX's processing systems. Now, over 80 percent of the railroad's customer orders are handled electronically.

optical character recognition (OCR), it is not yet fully practical to do this, except in special situations.

In providing fax EDI services, many firms not only convert the raw data into a format readable by humans and dispatch it to the appropriate fax number, but they add cosmetic touches such as additional names and references, logos, and even signatures. Whether fax EDI adheres to the true concept of EDI or not, it is an established and important part of the EDI and electronic commerce matrix. It is easy to use, requires minimal investment, is available worldwide, and works well for most small-scale communication needs.

"Daylight overdrafts" is a problem created by electronic payments systems. A bank, for instance, may send out funds for a transaction during the day, before a covering payment arrives. Banks routinely make end-of-day transfers to ensure that accounts are not overdrawn, but during the day there are around $50 billion in daylight overdrafts. When a firm cannot make its end-of-day payments, the results can be enormous. In 1985, for instance, a computer

FedWire   FedWire is the U.S. Federal Reserve Bank's domestic telecommunications system. It electronically links the 12 Federal Reserve District banks and a variety of other eligible financial organizations. The system is a series of network connections among these Federal Reserve banks, which links each bank with at least two others to provide backup communications in the case of problems.

A FedWire—the payment, not the organization—is an electronic funds transfer made through the communication system that links the 12 district branches and 25 additional branches of the Federal Reserve System. Every U.S. bank is assigned to one of the Federal Reserve branches. The key advantage of payment by a FedWire is that the recipient is paid with guaranteed funds from the transaction originator's bank. It is a real-time—that is, immediate—transfer of cash value from one bank to another. The payee's and the payer's reserve accounts are debited and credited immediately, on the same day. The FedWire system also may be used to send messages between banks, such as instructions to make a transfer or to inquire about the status of a transfer. It is also used to record the transfer of ownership of Treasury securities. Because the content of the messages is limited, information such as discounts for early payment cannot be included. This limitation can make it difficult to reconcile a transfer to a specific transaction, such as an invoice.

Companies can use FedWire without needing any telecommunications capability of their own, though more and more banks accept computer-initiated instructions. The sending bank immediately debits the payer company's account and sends a transfer request to the Federal Reserve. The Fed debits the sending bank's Reserve account and credits the receiving bank's account, notifying it of the transaction. The receiving bank then credits the payee company's account.

The transfers typically take just a few minutes to complete. The Federal Reserve guarantees all payments made through FedWire, eliminating the risks to each bank. The transfers are expensive, typically $10–20 each, because they are labor-intensive. They are thus used mostly for large value, nonroutine transfers, where immediate processing is required. Electronic commerce increasingly involves batching large volumes of transfers, such as daily payments to suppliers. For these, automated clearing houses (ACH) are a more cost-efficient alternative. ACH do not provide real-time processing, but store and forward the transfers. ACH systems allow for more complex instructions and message contents than FedWire. The Federal Reserve handles clearing—transfer of cash value—in both instances. The transfers will take one to two days to complete. The cost is between 5 cents and $1.50 per transfer.

Other bank-to-bank electronic payment systems include Clearing House Interbank Payments System (CHIPS), which handles over $500 billion a day of transfers, and Society for Worldwide Interbank Financial Telecommunications (SWIFT), the workhorse of international funds transfers. CHIPS links to around 140 financial institutions in New York City, the center of electronic money movements; other banks in turn link to CHIPS via FedWire. SWIFT is a telecommunications network operated on behalf of almost 2,000 banks in over 60 countries; it processes over $2 trillion a day in funds transfers.

failure at the Bank of New York prevented it from sending out payments by FedWire to balance its securities accounts. The Federal Reserve Bank was forced to give BONY an overnight loan of $22.6 billion, many times larger than BONY's entire capital. Interbank electronic transfers routinely represent billions of dollars a day for many banks, and trillions a day for the entire system. Problems are rare and quickly handled, and the Federal Reserve has tightened controls and regulations concerning daylight overdrafts. But, the movement of money from checks to digital bits has greatly increased systemic risk and also greatly reduced the balances of slow-moving cash that buffered banks from problems such as BONY's.

Each of these bank payment systems offers businesses different advantages and costs. The basic trade-off is between speed of processing—or rather, speed of crediting the payee account—and cost per transaction. The main disadvantage of FedWire is its high cost relative to other options; it is thus mainly used for important high-value payments. A fee is charged for the process, usually to the originator of the transaction.

See also **Automated Clearing Houses; Clearing House Interbank Payments System; Society for Worldwide Interbank Financial Telecommunications.**

The Chairman of J.P. Morgan told the 1994 Annual Symposium of the Bank and Financial Analysts Association, "There is no banking industry. Today, the label means nothing. Function is everything."

Financial EDI (FEDI)   Often referred to as EDI/EFT, FEDI has generally meant the transfer of substantial amounts of remittance detail along with funds, the value transfer. While EFT refers to the transaction that moves money and EDI refers to the movement of information that initiates a transaction, FEDI combines both.

Another definition of FEDI is emerging that includes transactions related to funds, such as reporting of balances and transactions. Essentially FEDI now means anything to do with the management of final transactions. Historically, the development of EDI was driven by businesses, not banks. Banks were the driving force in the development of electronic payment systems. Now, they are coming together.

Firewall   A firewall is a hardware and software barrier between the outside world and the entry point to a firm's communications and computing resources. Typically, for instance, a firewall is placed immediately behind the device called a server, into which Internet traffic flows as it accesses, say, a company's World Wide Web page. The firewall software checks whether the message seeking entry is authorized. It also handles other control and security operations, looks for evidence of any effort to break into systems or introduce viruses, malicious programming tricks intended to breed and spread across the network and cause damage.

Firewalls range widely in their features and functions. Some are little more than a traffic logging system that checks the address of the sending device and allows it through or blocks it; the particular application that the message accesses then handles security. Some check on the application request itself, allowing, say, a given user to access the employee phone directory but not the employee electronic mail system. Others are full-time security agents employing very sophisticated tools that include hiding names of files from potential hackers' scrutiny, looking for patterns that suggest efforts to misuse resources or intrude into unauthorized areas, blocking access to pornography on the Internet by curious or idle staff, and preventing overload of the network at given times of day. The cost per firewall may be thousands of dollars or even hundreds of thousands.

The issue of security in general and firewalls in particular is more a management policy issue than a technical one. How much security is desirable? How much is essential? Answering that question requires a detailed and ongoing assessment of business risk, which of course requires careful review of potential problems and their business consequences.

First Virtual Holdings An organization designed for the era of electronic commerce, First Virtual Holdings was unique at the time of its founding in two regards: (1) it is a "virtual" organization in that it has no physical offices, and (2) its sole activities are to provide financial services for Internet electronic commerce. It may or may not win out in the rapidly growing and aggressive market for electronic payments, digital cash, merchant systems, and the like, but its record and its managers' readiness to talk publicly about what they have learned since its startup makes First Virtual a striking, and perhaps soon to be typical, competitor in the world of electronic commerce.

Its staff work from their own home offices and meet by electronic mail and conference calls. That's what makes it a virtual organization. E-mail is the foundation of the firm; First Virtual has built its entire service base on it. Customers who wish to use the World Wide Web to buy goods and services must first open an account with First Virtual over the phone or Internet; they receive a unique and confidential personal identification number (PIN). To make a purchase, they do not use a credit card or send any form of payment directly to the merchant. Instead, they send an electronic mail message to the merchant which includes their PIN number. The merchant immediately forwards the number to First Virtual, which verifies the customer identification and also confirms with the customer—again by e-mail—that he or she did indeed initiate the transaction and wants to make the purchase.

The service uses the Internet *only* for messages. The sensitive part of the financial transaction is processed offline, using the banking system's automated clearing house network, computing services, and telecommunications provided by EDS to transfer information from purchaser to merchant, and credit card services through a rapidly growing company called First USA Merchant Services. Offline processing means that no hacker or cracker (the newer term for hackers with criminal intent) can use the telecommunications network to break into the system to steal information or try to enter fraudulent purchases.

First Virtual also offers its InfoHaus electronic mall for small businesses to sell information over the Internet. Merchants set up accounts for $10. First Virtual handles information storage, billing, and distribution, for an extra charge of 8 percent of the sale plus its regular transaction cost of 29 cents plus 2 percent of the transaction's value. That means that downloading a $20 piece of software over InfoHaus will cost the seller $2.29, a much more profitable deal than going through a retailer or a distributor or selling through 1-800 numbers and mail order.

Forgery Electronic commerce and forgery go together like shopping malls and pickpockets. One of the most far-reaching impacts of computer technology is in essence that we can no longer assume that anything we see in everyday life is real—photographs, films, documents, and sound can be copied, changed, and faked. Multimedia tools that are widely available on personal computers, combined with scanners and color printers, are low in price, high in quality, and very easy to use.

Electronic forgery and theft are massive potential problems, for the obvious reason that networks like the Internet, Compu-Serve, America Online, and the like are designed to encourage and simplify public access. They are intended to bring you in, not keep you out. There is a fundamental, not peripheral, conflict in electronic commerce between access and control. Recovering control is the main agenda for most developments in software and services now. It includes authentication of the message and the sender, digital signatures, encryption of messages, firewalls, electronic copyright techniques, and certification authorities, to name just a few security measures.

The success of many of these schemes is making the Internet and electronic commerce in general more secure than the use of documents, phones, cash, and checks, although most people are still wary of using their credit cards on the Internet. In a *well-designed* secure system, both buyer and seller, message sender and receiver, or merchant and bank, can be sure that the electronic transaction cannot be tampered with except through Herculean effort and that the electronic documents and payments cannot be forged.

Plenty of people are able and willing to make that effort, though. That's why the security has to be well designed and not handled as an add-on. Policies, procedures, audit, firewalls, choice of encryption, and so forth have to be made a management priority. They are often very abstruse and complex topics—a "basic" discussion of public and private key cryptography, for instance, may remind you of preparing for a math exam knowing that you really don't have a clue. It's easy then to dismiss the issue as something for "techies" to deal with, not business managers. The procedures and the policies and decisions about what level of risk the firm will accept (just as it accepts some risk whenever it gives credit) are all management issues, though.

In 1993, the number of detected forged copies of German banknotes was 17 times that of 1990. Sixty percent were produced by color photocopiers and color printers.

"U.S. currency is easy to copy. . . . and is made so sloppily that the best counterfeiters have to 'lower their quality' in order to duplicate it." (Business Week, *10 June 1996)*

The most immediate problems of forgery are offline rather than on-line. Wherever there is cash, a forger is working hard to produce copies. The same is true for documents. As cash and documents move from offline paper to on-line network equivalents, the forgers will move with them.

Government Agencies Involved in Electronic Commerce

A great many U.S. government agencies and committees will play a growing and often central role in the evolution of electronic commerce. The main ones are the following:

The General Services Administration's Federal Supply Service (GSA/FSS) has initiated an electronic catalog called GSA Advantage. Government shoppers may now shop on-line at GSA/FSS's site. They may use their government credit card (via a Netscape browser that enables credit card information encryption) or their password-protected GSA accounts to purchase merchandise. In November 1995, GSA's electronic catalog consisted of 13,000 items, and is projected to expand to about 4 million products represented by

- *National Telecommunications Information Administration.* NTIA is part of the U.S. Department of Commerce. It furthers the Administration's initiatives for a National Information Infrastructure but is peripheral to electronic commerce legislation, focusing mainly on policy recommendations and research.

- *The Federal Secure Infrastructure Program.* FSIP was set up to create an infrastructure that will enable all government agencies to carry out transactions to and communications with outside organizations and the general public. Its first initiative is the Paperless Federal Transaction for the Public (PFSIP). FSIP is supported by the General Services Administration, which oversees all government procurement, the National Security Agency, U.S. Postal Service, Department of Defense, and Department of the Treasury. It's likely to be a key player within the next five years.

- *National Institute of Standards and Technologies.* NIST plays a strong role in formulating technical standards for the export of encryption.

- *Department of the Treasury.* Within the U.S. Treasury, the Financial Crimes Enforcement Network (FinCEN) is actively exploring the role of electronic payments systems in money laundering and tax evasion and the ways to track and prevent them. The IRS is exploring all the tax ramifications of existing, emerging, and proposed electronic commerce applications, and extending electronic tax filing and collection.

- *Federal Trade Commission.* The main role of the FTC will be in consumer protection and informing consumers about electronic fraud.

- *The Federal Communications Commission.* The FCC regulates telecommunications and radio and TV broadcasting. The 1996 Telecommunications Act gives it some authority to regulate the Internet. It's unclear yet what that means and how far the FTC can intrude on the Internet's historical freedom from government supervision and interference.

- *U.S. Postal Service.* The USPS obviously has a strong interest in anything that affects the reduction in its volumes, such as electronic mail. It is actively planning to offer new services for electronic commerce, including electronic postmarks as proof of sending. The single greatest strength of the Postal Service as a major player in electronic commerce is its nationwide rights to investigate mail fraud. It argues very convincingly that the body of regulation supporting its efforts against crime, sabotage, harassment, and the like are the best protection in an area where most organizations and individuals lack comparable rights and capabilities.

- *Department of State.* The State Department plays a major role in the debates—fights is perhaps a more accurate word—about government restrictions on the use and export of cryptography. Its concerns are providing hostile foreign nations and terrorist organizations with advanced U.S. encryption technology.

- *Department of Justice.* The Justice Department is obviously strongly involved in preventing and punishing the

5,000–6,000 federal supply schedule contracts. GSA/FSS is beginning to require their vendors to provide their catalog electronically. This system is much easier and less time-consuming for agencies to use than a paper catalog system, and it allows agencies to download catalogs directly onto their own systems and order products from the site. In addition, it gives vendors access to all agencies, eliminating the need to target specific buyers within agencies.

growing range of criminal activities carried out over the Internet and on-line services.

- *Department of Defense.* DOD is a heavy user of all elements of electronic commerce, especially EDI for procurement, and a major funder of many initiatives. It originally funded the ARPANET, which generated the major telecommunications innovations that made the Internet practical and was as well the base for combining the government-sponsored networks that together became the Internet. CommerceNet, the organization dedicated to furthering consumer trust in the use of the Internet for electronic commerce, was funded by DOD's Technology Reinvestment Project.

One key agency's electronic commerce applications shows the likely long-term direction of the U.S. federal government's plans and implementations. The U.S. Treasury Department is a major user of EC tools. Its Treasury Communication System (TCS) network links to 7,500 sites in 4,100 geographic locations. It uses the international X.400 and X.500 protocols as the base for its messaging. Its Electronic Commerce Clearing House uses TCS for the Treasury EDI Procurement Gateway and the NAFTA Prototype (NAFTAP). The Gateway is used by all Treasury bureaus and provides services for translation of EDI messages from one transaction set format to another and for managing the message flow. It receives and sends requests for quotations of prices and terms, purchase orders, and award notices. It connects to the Department of Defense's networks via the TCP/IP telecommunications protocol that is the foundation base for the Internet, as well as X.400. NAFTAP is designed to coordinate trade among the three NAFTA countries: the United States, Canada, and Mexico. It includes the data elements—software dictionaries and translators—to convert messages from one nation's customs agencies, air, truck, and rail manifests, and other import/export documentation. It also implements a standard numbering system for identifying importers, carriers, and other trading parties. The Trade Software Package (TSP) that provides for this is available on the World Wide Web, free of charge. It offers encryption and security keys and key management. It also converts messages to and from the EDIFACT standard that is the base for international electronic data interchange, passing messages via the Internet, using a Treasury server computer. The prototype offers several new applications that go well beyond just electronic substitution for paper documents. An example is Vehicle to Roadside Communications/Radio Frequency Identification, which uses radio tag devices to identify and register the export and arrival of goods.

There can be no question that the government, in all countries, will be a major driver of electronic commerce, for the simple reasons that it is such a large customer for goods and services and that it controls so much of the paperwork required in international trade. The standards government chooses to adopt in most instances become the standards companies have little choice but to adopt. What's most important for business about the Treasury and NAFTA initiatives in electronic commerce is its use of EDIFACT, X.400, and X.500 standards. Most U.S. firms have little experience with these international standards, relying instead on a combination of ANSI X12 and industry-specific ones. It's very likely that the U.S. Treasury will play a major role in facilitating international business-to-business EDI.

Government Applications of Electronic Commerce   The U.S. federal government as well as state governments and corresponding governments in other countries will be major forces in the evolution of electronic commerce, for three obvious reasons: their role in regulation, their size as purchasers of goods and services, and their taxation systems.

In North America and Europe, government increasingly is moving to make EDI, electronic payments of taxes, and electronic payments in general the core of their procurement operations, especially in such areas as defense, transfer payments such as

The Defense Logistics Department has been the U.S. military's primary purchasing agent for "consumable items" for over 30 years. Its Material Management (MM) operation maintains five inventory control points, three service centers, and two distribution regions, which must be able to respond to the military's needs 24 hours a day, worldwide. DLD has made very effective use of the World Wide Web to give its military customers and its suppliers the information that enables both fast and accurate service. The features on its Web page include: on-line shopping from electronic catalogs that contain visual images and product data on 130,000 electronic parts, 7,000 branded products ranging from food services to machine tools, and 5,000 articles of

social security and welfare, and, outside the United States, medical supplies for the public healthcare system. In addition, they are moving to facilitate or even require that businesses above a certain size link to them electronically for filing and paying taxes. Finally, they recognize that if the Internet becomes a sizable market for buying and selling goods electronically, they will want their share of the action: meaning, sales taxes, and value added taxes.

The main development in governments' own use of electronic commerce has been in electronic data interchange. EDI is mostly thought of as applying to purchase orders, invoices, and related documents. It can be used, however, for any type of business communication where the parties involved agree on how to interpret the form and content of the message. Agreeing on standards is the key to EDI, not the technology, which is relatively simple, well-proven, and reliable. An example of how EDI is being extended to more and more areas of business and government is the definition by the ANSI X12G (G stands for government) committee of a transaction set that will be invaluable to implement the executive order President Clinton signed in September 1996 on collecting delinquent child support obligations. This will require cross-checking information about the delinquent individuals against computer records of federal government payments to be made to them. Those payments will then be offset or garnished and the delinquents will be denied federal loans, guarantees, or other government financial aid except in special situations.

The ANSI Task Group assigned to define the needed EDI standards reached an agreement quickly. The X12 521 and 540 transaction sets were sent out to relevant members of ANSI for approval by ballot, the routine process for X12 standards. They were approved even more quickly. X12 521 is an electronic equivalent of a levy or garnishment order that an agency charged with collecting delinquent payments can send to such agencies as Health and Human Services, Treasury, and Social Security. The message instructs the recipient to withhold payment and may also have the money rerouted to the agency. X12 540 goes well beyond this. It is designed to support proposed legislation requiring that employers notify state government of any changes in employment. The state will forward the information to the Social Security Administration, which plans to add it to a data base that will be cross-referenced with information from many other agencies. The 540 will be used to inform them that XYZ has a job and that will trigger the sending of a 521 to garnish XYZ's wages for that job.

This example goes well beyond substituting electronic for paper documents. It's hard to see how the work could be done at all without EDI. Obviously, government-specific applications of EDI like this one won't affect the basics of business, but it's a sign that the federal government has woken up to the opportunities electronic commerce offers to improve its own efficiency, reduce its costs, and handle electronically the large volumes of paperwork routinely associated with its operations. Some government applications of EDI do affect businesses. Governments are insisting on businesses' adopting a particular standard by a given date, but in many instances, businesses may not even be aware of government initiatives. For example, as late as September 1996, over 70 percent of businesses were unaware of the IRS regulation that requires any company with more than $50,000 in employment taxes in 1995 to switch to electronic payment of their federal taxes in January 1997.

Managers need to factor government into their planning for electronic commerce. Scanning the *Congressional Daily* or watching *C-Span* is not sufficient. Instead managers need to make sure that someone in their organization keeps track of government uses of electronic commerce. Often no one in the technical staff involved in the firm's EDI operations and no one in the finance department or elsewhere has the responsibility for including ANSI X12G in their work. Government procurement, health care

clothing; public access to lists of surplus goods for sale; regulatory and policy information for procurement transactions; alerts on product recalls, change in application and quality issues; solicitations to vendors for assistance in solving specific logistical problems; and notices to customers and vendors about transfers of items to specific inventory control points. These offerings are simple, sensible, and just what the Internet is most useful for in interorganizational relationships.

insurance, taxation, and even regulatory reporting are certain to be high on the EC agenda in coming years, so that someone in the organization must put it high on their own agenda.

So, too, does someone inside state and local government agencies. More and more agencies are seizing the opportunity to use electronic commerce to streamline their own operations. The State of West Virginia, for example, has a law requiring all goods provided through the state government to be paid for before they are delivered. Another law makes the state the wholesale distributor of alcoholic beverages to licensed stores. Together, the two pieces of legislation seem likely to increase even more the bureaucratic, cumbersome, and slow processes that government is too often associated with.

In practice, West Virginia's Alcohol Beverage Control Commission (ABCC) is a model of efficiency through electronic commerce. Store managers place orders by phone; they are informed of the total cost and that their bank accounts will be debited two days later. The next day, the ABCC sends a file of transactions electronically to the State Board of Investments, which has responsibility for handling the state's money. It creates an automated clearing house transaction that debits the store's bank account the next day. Unless there is a notification of Not Sufficient Funds (NSF) within the following two days, the goods are shipped by the fifth day after the order. The next step, well under way, is to use FEDI (Financial EDI) for settlement of accounts between the distillery and the ABCC.

Obviously, the process could be streamlined even more if the law did not require strong control by the ABCC. But it's a tidy solution to the problem of balancing control and responsiveness. In many areas of information technology, some of the most imaginative applications have been in state and local government, for two reasons: (1) governments have faced budget crunches for many years and (2) citizens demand that they continue to provide the same services or provide more services without asking for more funds. A few examples of areas in which efficiencies have been achieved by states via electronic commerce are transactions, taxes, electronic document management, information access for individuals and organizations, and vendor relationships.

Much of electronic commerce is concerned with getting rid of paper and reducing the delays, costs, administration, and errors inherent in paper-based systems. EDI is the obvious case here along with electronic mail, on or via the Internet, as the base for sending messages, including buying and selling goods and services. But much of the paper chase relates to government requirements to fill out and file forms. In more and more instances, forms can be sent electronically. State and federal agencies are at last reasonably committed to EDI and use of the Internet for communication to and from them as in any private business. But that doesn't reduce the burden of filling out all the forms, which demand special-purpose software in most instances. An example is all the documentation for exporting high-technology goods, an area that the government monitors closely and where there are many restrictions (including on the export of chips for the encryption of electronic messages and transactions). This is a small set of niche markets and not one where companies can just browse the Internet to find tools.

Because it's a small set of niches, companies largely can't afford to develop their own systems. As a result, even in 1996, according to the *Washington Post* (16 December 1996), most still used typewriters and pens as the fastest and most efficient solution for government forms. Obviously, they will switch only if a third party provides a package that can be quickly and cheaply customized to their specific needs. An example is a package for handling high-tech export documentation; the package costs around $125,000 per customer and the small software company that developed it has sales of $4 million a year from it. The main problem it reports is marketing what the *Washington Post* calls "obscure" software. It's the customization that matters most; that facilitates electronic filing, electronic storage, process streamlining, and links between the customer's transaction systems and shippers',

"In April, the U.S. Courts Administrative Office kicked off a plan to automate bankruptcy notices, one of several U.S. government EC/EDI initiatives this year that were business processes, rather than procurement oriented. The highest priority for the agency was to send out bankruptcy notices electronically rather than via paper, since the office prints out and mails more than 50 million bankruptcy notices every year, at a cost of 40–45 cents per notice for the printing and mailing alone." (EC/EDI Insider, *May 1996, 5*)

insurers', and other trading parties' systems. The founder of the software firm states that "if the perception is that all it does is produce paper, it's hard to justify."

The allure of the Internet and the relative ease of adopting EDI can lead companies to overlook other opportunities to apply the principles of electronic commerce to paper-heavy operations where software is not so available. They need to seek them out. There are plenty of $4 million software firms with good products that can't easily get their message across to small potential customers.

Government's Likely Legislative Agenda for Electronic Commerce   To date, government in the United States has kept back from proposing any radical innovations in legislation for electronic commerce, preferring instead to rely on existing law, making adjustments within it, and waiting until the trends and impacts are clear, which will be within this century. To date, no country has launched any basic new laws for EC, except to limit what may be published and communicated over public on-line services, most obviously the Internet. The 1996 Decency In Communications Act, which tried to impose stringent censorship of pornography down to the level of restricting words that might point to sexually explicit material, looks like the first shot in the battle over "decency" versus "freedom of expression."

Of growing importance to legislators, citizens, and businesses, are the following five areas where we can expect major legislative moves: (1) electronic cash, (2) the Internet, (3) censorship, (4) copyright, and (5) consumer protection. In none of these areas are the issues yet fully clear, let alone the legislative needs and range of likely political choices. While it's impossible to predict the specifics of government legislation that will affect the nature, scale, and procedures for electronic commerce, the areas discussed below provide safe assumptions for business planning.

Electronic cash will require new regulations once the government sees it as moving toward mass adoption; at present there's little to regulate except some pilot projects. When electronic cash seems likely to take off, governments everywhere will start moving fast. They have a strong interest in the continued use of cash. The currency notes in your wallet are in effect an interest-free loan to the government. In the United States, the $400 billion in currency that is circulating or stuck away somewhere generates around $20 billion in what is termed "seignorage," the amount the Federal Reserve Bank hands over to the Treasury Department.

Government will certainly want to influence and be part of the transition from physical to digital cash. Some have suggested that once the market emerges, the government should issue its own electronic currency, thereby providing the same security, guarantees, and acceptability as for today's currency. In addition, many uncertainties and complexities surround the question of how existing regulations affect the use of nontraditional payment mechanisms. The Electronic Funds Transfer Act and the Federal Reserve Regulation E, for instance, which include rules for the use of electronic funds transfer systems, may or may not apply to limiting consumers' liabilities for payments made electronically through stored-value cards. The Federal Reserve has opposed efforts to exempt electronic commerce transactions over the Internet from these regulations. It does not have the authority to impose reserve restrictions on nondepository institutions, which means that it is possible that digital cash will be floating around the Internet with no real money in deposit to back it up. Nonbanks are also free from most of the reporting, monitoring, and supervisory requirements of the Fed.

The Federal Reserve, Treasury, and the Clinton administration as a whole have encouraged and facilitated the evolution of electronic commerce. The National Information Initiative (1993) is a broad and somewhat misty blueprint for ensuring a nation of electronic "haves" instead of haves and have nots among schools, households, and public sector agencies. Federal agencies have greatly increased their hitherto laggardly use of EDI. Only in the

"We have a lot of smart lawyers in the government, and if we locked them in a room and asked them to think of every way a person could get screwed on the Internet, they could promulgate thousands of regulations. . . . But the result would be a tangle of bad laws that would take decades to dig out from." (Ira Magaziner, White House aide, in "Feds Lean Toward Minimal Electronic Commerce Regulations," by Mitch Wagner, Computer World, *24 March 1997, 20)*

aggressive blocking of the diffusion and export of "strong" cryptography by the National Intelligence Agency has government interfered in any major element of electronic commerce infrastructures. In Congress, there has been far more blockage, not of electronic commerce in particular, but in what may be transmitted over the Internet. Censorship of pornography was the priority of the Decency in Communications Act, which passed the House in 1996 and was promptly stalled by challenges in court to its constitutionality.

The Internet is sure to become a focus for legislation. Many commentators and politicians feel it's been allowed to grow too fast and too large with minimal control by government. At the other extreme are people who say that the very reason that the Internet grew so fast and so large is that government kept out of the way, as it should continue to do. The Clinton administration's intent seems to be to encourage investments that ensure broad and free access to the Internet, and it will remain especially concerned with small schools and isolated communities. Congress will resist many of these efforts, arguing that the market should be the driver.

Censorship will be a major social and political battleground for years to come. As the Web gets raunchier, louder, more abusive, and easier to access, the balance between First Amendment Rights, privacy, freedom of speech, and openness of information on one side and protection of minors, protection of consumers, crime prevention, and straightforward politics on the other will be harder and harder to maintain. There will certainly be many legislative and legal battles, but most should not affect businesses outside the entertainment, publishing, and pornography industries. But business can expect some pretty bizarre restrictions to be placed by individual countries on the Internet, for reasons of religion, politics, and protection of markets and information. Much of the regulation will be made by people who don't have a clue about technology. An example is the proposal announced by the European Commission on March 1, 1996, that the Internet be treated as a broadcast service (communication from one to many) rather than as an interactive network. The same standards would apply to the Net as to TV and radio broadcasting in terms of "decency." In addition, 51 percent of the "transmissions" on the Internet would have to originate "from within the countries of the EC." Good luck, dear EC. But good luck, too, to U.S. businesses that operate in the EC. They will be affected by the spirit of such legislation, even though such shortsighted proposals as this one—which confuses on-line with broadcast and totally misunderstands the nature of the information on the Internet—are unlikely to be approved. They will need to think through very carefully the exact countries in which they locate Web sites, for instance, and which local laws will apply to the World Wide part of World Wide Web. They will need to establish the legal "server of record" for much of their information.

In China, businesses will need to be very careful about the information they make available and access. Whereas Singapore bans (and rigorously enforces the ban) "statements which tend to bring the government into hatred or contempt, or which excite dissatisfaction against the government," China bans anything on the Net that "hinders public order."

Copyright is an area of active concern to the U.S. government, which has taken the lead in producing the international treaty on copyright that was announced in December 1996. The draft treaty was endorsed by 160 countries and steers a narrower course than was expected between the principle of fair use that applies in the United States and the protection of data bases as an economic good. Fair use restricts copying of information to limited use that does not damage the commercial interests of the owner of the information.

Consumer protection is an area where to date there has been little legislative action. In general, the government has relied on existing laws (for credit cards, banking, informed consent, and so forth), but if electronic commerce builds a mass market on the Internet, there will surely need to be new rules specifically for electronic purchases and payments. Another area of government concern that affects electronic commerce is encryption. The administration has had no choice but to relax the stranglehold on exporting of encryption chips and software, because it is impossible to contain either cryptography knowledge or manufacturing abroad and because the restrictions were losing the United States its strong lead in a burgeoning market. In January 1997, a Federal Court judge ruled part of the proposals to continue controls as unconstitutional.

Processing a health insurance claim via EDI typically takes 2 to 4 working days, though receipt of final payment may take 14 to 20 days, since most companies make payment settlements at the end of a week or every two weeks. Paper settlement adds an estimated 8 to 12 days.

Health care EDI   Health care EDI is the cooperation among the many parties involved in the expensive and complex processes involved in the administration of health care, most obviously insurance verification and payments. In its first report in July 1992, the Workgroup on EDI (WEDI), established jointly by the American Hospital Association (AHA) and the American Medical Association (AMA), estimated that savings from standardized EDI-based transactions could save the industry between $4 billion and $10 billion annually within four years. WEDI also estimated in October 1993 that $42 billion could be saved annually if all health care transactions were converted to EDI by 1999. The estimated cost for these savings were from $5 billion to $17 billion. Since around 25 cents of every one of the close to 1 trillion dollars spent in the United States on health care goes to administration, these estimates of the payoff from applying EDI look conservative, rather than radical, if and only if the industry can get its management act together.

The concept of health care EDI has emerged as a discrete application of electronic commerce linking the health maintenance organizations (HMO) and preferred provider organizations (PPO)—along with the drug and pharmaceutical product providers and distributors. EDI and electronic commerce are crucial for providing the links between these organizations and helping reduce the cost of health care management. Some of the key issues are related to drug and medication management, better communication of diagnoses, and the efficient exchange of information between providers and insurers.

Elements of this initiative are as follows:

- *Electronic claims submission and processing.* Electronic transfer of information between the provider and the insurer will expedite payments.

- *Nonclaims information.* This area concerns communication of information such as eligibility, benefits, and utilization reviews.

- *Between physicians and other practitioners.* Building effective communication tools between individual practitioners and organizations will also facilitate the dissemination of medical literature and updating of pharmaceutical product data, as well as provide access to other medical-related databases and information sources.

Over the long term, these activities are focused on changing health care EDI from the payment of claims to assisting and coordinating the exchange of care-related information among all the providers and support organizations.

Hedging   Locking in the exchange rate for a foreign currency, mainly through a *forward contract*, in order to protect an exporter from sudden fluctuations is called hedging. A company selling, say, $50,000 of goods to a customer in Sweden, to be paid within 90 days in krone, can purchase a contract from a bank that fixes the dollar–krone conversion rate the exporter will receive 90 days from now. There are many variations on this basic forward contract, which in essence sets the rate on the basis of differences in interest rates, inflation, political risk, and market perceptions. *Options,* unlike forward contracts, do not lock the purchaser in to exchanging a given amount at a given rate on a given date but instead gives the purchaser the option to do so, for a fee that ranges from 1.5 percent to 4.5 percent. The exporter of the goods gives up the chance of making an extra profit if the dollar weakens against the krone but avoids the risk of a currency swing that may make a previously profitable sale a loss.

In a global environment marked by often highly fluctuating exchange rates, hedging is a basic tool of finance—or should be. The two most common ways businesses address currency exchange risk is either to require payment in their own currency or take their chances with currency fluctuations. Given the historical volatility of exchange rates, this can be an expensive strategy. On one day in late 1995, the Japanese yen fell 7 percent against the U.S. dollar in just 20 minutes. The Canadian dollar moved from $1.10 to the U.S. dollar to $1.40 in under five years. In 1994, the Mexican peso in essence collapsed in a day. In 1996, exchange rate volatility decreased dramatically, and some commentators believe that with the efficiency of computer systems that track rates and make exchanges, volatility is a thing of the past. Perhaps.

Large companies can afford the tools, skills, and computers needed to hedge currency risk via such financial instruments as options, forward contracts, and currency swaps. Smaller companies need these instruments, too, and more and more banks offer them as services. As electronic commerce grows in scale and includes countries with unstable economies and political regimes, any firm that depends on trade across international boundaries needs a risk management strategy. For the typical firm that doesn't (and shouldn't) get involved in playing the FX market, that means hedging via the expertise and products of its banks.

Home Banking   For decades home banking—the use of a personal computer to manage personal finances—has been a solution looking for a problem. In the late 1970s, major banks such as Citibank launched many home banking systems that offered free PC software through which individuals could manage their bank accounts, make payments, and get information electronically. None of them generated more than 20,000 customers. They lacked the single essential for banking: getting cash and depositing checks. Few people saw any value in balancing their check-books on a PC.

Today many signs point to home banking beginning to move up the growth curve. Quicken, the financial planning and management software marketed by Intuit, has gained a multimillion dollar market, mainly by making it easy for users to organize expenditures and income by category (travel, home maintenance, office supplies, etc.), make budgets and projections, analyze cash flows and the like, get bank account information, and also write electronic checks. The penetration of personal computers into an estimated 40 percent of U.S. households opens up a mass market. Only about 10 percent of those PCs have modems, without which home banking is impossible, but the Internet and on-line information services, most obviously America Online, are extending use from "stand-alone" PCs to participation in telecommunications networks. There are now many competing products entering the market for home banking, including a consortium of banks, IBM, and Microsoft called Integrion, whose mandate is to promote the development and growth of electronic home financial service delivery.

Banks want to exploit these trends. Home banking offers them the chance to strengthen customer loyalty, lower their cost of delivery of services to the consumer, bring to the customer a flood of new services, such as on-line loan applications, and reduce their own costs. Today, a bank is still a paper factory that spends far more per transaction than it would cost electronically. More and more of today's services are being handled by ATMs and by phone. Home banking continues the substitution of electronic service for physical branch operations and paper.

Many larger banks have begun to reduce the number of branches that are available to the consumer. Many experts see this retrenchment as a necessary trend for the future if banks are to improve their cost base. Furthermore, the cost of operating an ATM has now begun to be a significant issue for many banks. It's

One-quarter of all U.S. households do not have bank accounts; this number has increased through the 1990s. There are 6,000 check-cashing shops, up from 2,000 in 1985. New York City alone has 550. Nationally, they handle 200 million checks amounting to $60 billion. The Chairman of the National Check Clearers Association states that the major growth is in the suburbs: "A lot of people have opted out of traditional banking." Proponents of home banking and on-line consumer electronic commerce need to keep that in mind. (Martin Mayer, The Bankers, *1997, 452)* expensive to install on every corner an ATM that costs as much as $30,000 a year to operate, just so customers can draw out $50 or less at a time. Banks hope that they can begin to provide the essential, noncash-oriented banking services via a home computer.

*"Where the Interactive Generation leads, the rest of the population will follow not far behind."
(Chuck Martin,* The Digital Estate, *New York: McGraw Hill, 1997, 161) Oh really?*

The move to home banking is also supported by the fact that as more and more direct debit services are provided, the need for bank notes decreases. As the use of physical cash becomes less important in conducting the mundane tasks of everyday life, the use of home banking tools should become more relevant to the everyday user. The banking industry's focus on cost reduction means that there will undoubtedly be more and more focus on cutting overhead over the coming years, with the hope that the Internet will turn out to be the promised low-cost customer contact and information service point. Branches are becoming overhead for many banks. Though a primary selling vehicle for some of them, they are not the preferred transaction location for any of them.

That said, cash, credit cards, and checks meet the everyday needs of most people very well. Despite all the investments and promotions made by banks, people have continued to stick with these. Quicken was part of the PC software evolution rather than any banking revolution. Consumers, not banks, will drive home banking, though as yet they haven't driven it very far.

Home Shopping   Home shopping is currently associated with such cable TV channels as the Home Shopping Network, QVC, and the 30-minute-long advertisements known as infomercials. Retailers and manufacturers want to see home shopping extended to interactive TV and the Internet. They hope that the World Wide Web will open up a mass market. For this to happen, issues of security and currency must be resolved; that is why there has been a flood of innovations in and experiments with encryption tools and digital cash. It's far too early to tell if consumers will use the Web for more than a fraction of their shopping and which of the innovations will become widely accepted by both buyers and sellers on the Net. There's far more hype and hope than evidence so far. Only a small number of companies are making money on consumer electronic commerce on the Web; they tend to be small firms for whom even $100,000 extra annual revenues is a substantial boost or ones that have created a special niche. Mail order catalog sales, by contrast, have been gathering a bigger and bigger share of total retailing; over 10 billion catalogs were mailed to households in 1996, a 20 percent increase over 1995. In 1996, mail and phone orders of goods grew around 11 percent, twice the rate for the overall retailing industry.

No one knows what will happen—or when—in the growth of electronic shopping on the Internet. Among the many grandiose predictions afloat is one claim that sales will reach as high as $250 billion within seven years. There's simply no basis for extrapolating from today's home shopping via electronic services. Our own view, which flavors the discussion of the Internet throughout this Manager's Guide, is that the consumer side of electronic commerce will take many more years to develop than Internet enthusiasts believe; we'd be very surprised to see even $1 billion of consumer sales on the Net by 2001. We strongly believe, though, that business-to-business electronic commerce with and without the Internet will move very fast indeed, because it already has. Growth in EDI has been around 20 percent a year for a decade.

It's almost impossible to make recommendations to business managers about how to plan their firm's strategy for positioning to take advantage of whatever happens in consumer retailing. Obviously, the past few years have shown that anything to do with the Internet can become hugely popular at any time. That said, Wal-Mart is moving toward revenues of $100 billion a year and home shopping via TV is a tiny proportion of retail sales.

Mail order catalog sales amount to $70 billion a year, of which around $45 billion is spent by consumers. Sales through TV home shopping ads are $5 billion. Sales through the Internet and on-line services were less, around $0.5 billion in 1996. Computer goods and travel together amount to half the sales over the Internet and on-line services.

*In a 1994 survey of television home shoppers, almost half stated that price was the main factor in their purchases. A quarter said they had no specific reason for buying an item. Only 7 percent reported that convenience was a factor. Over 10 percent agreed that "TV shopping is for lazy people." (*Banking Today, *21 June 1996)*

HTML   See **Hypertext Markup Language.**

Hypertext Markup Language (HTML) Hypertext Markup Language (HTML) is a simple tool for designing World Wide Web pages on the Internet. It's easy to learn and is included with most Internet software browsers, as well as with word processing and multimedia software packages. HTML is the most basic tool for getting a presence on the Internet. It is being rapidly superseded by other, more powerful tools that add three-dimensional graphics and virtual reality to the more staid traditional Web pages that are increasingly hard to differentiate.

Integrion Integrion Financial Network is a consortium of corporate heavies that aims at heading off the Internet as the next generation platform for banking services and putting banks firmly in the forefront of electronic commerce, whatever direction it takes and at whatever pace. The consortium is coordinated by IBM and includes 15 major banks, including Banc One, the Royal Bank of Canada, and NationsBank, all of which are leaders in the use of information technology and first rate in terms of operating high-volume transaction systems.

In announcing Integrion, IBM's chairman, Lou Gerstner, stated that "it's a tremendous threat," without needing to say "it" meant the Internet. Integrion will operate as a secure intranet within IBM's massive value added network, IBM Global Network. Banking customers will access it via the Internet, using a standard software browser such as Netscape Navigator. The system is designed to provide access by touch-tone phone and through financial planning software packages such as Intuit's Quicken.

One of the goals for Integrion is to enable the participating banks to focus on the business services they are developing in such areas as screen phones, Internet commerce, and multimedia kiosks, rather than have to deal with a wide range of technologies and systems components. In addition, the banks are facing increasing erosion of their core business activities. Five of the top 10 credit card providers are not banks, for instance, and Ford and

General Motors' credit subsidiaries account for 60 percent of all U.S. consumer loans.

One concern Integrion addresses is the technology base for processing the payment of bills electronically. The majority of those are handled by third parties, with Quicken and Microsoft comprising a growing customer base of 400,000. When Integrion announced that its first service offerings would be telecommunications connectivity and electronic bill payment processing, a consultant commented: "Banks want to define the protocol for managing the electronic payment system. They are scared stiff that an outside third party like Intuit or Microsoft would define those standards, and managing payments is a big source of revenue" (*Information Week*, September 16, 1996).

Intelligent Tagging Systems   Intelligent tagging systems are basically computer chips with radio antennae that are an extension of bar coding. They are also called radio frequency identification tags or simply electronic tags. They provide a flexible and simple way to keep track of goods and equipment. The tags are activated by a radio beam from the tag reader, so that they can be kept hidden if desired. The reader operates at distances of up to several yards. The tags can be scanned and information transferred far more quickly than with ordinary bar codes. Most tags are read-only, like bar code labels, but tags that can be updated with new information are on the market.

Bar codes have mainly benefited retailers, but electronic tags offer advantages to all the parties along the supply chain, especially shippers and distributors. Their price is currently too high—between 50 cents and $1.50 each—for them to be attached to low-priced items, and hence their main use to date has been for tagging pallets and large containers. Supermarkets use them to track trolleys. There are scattered uses of electronic tags to keep information about equipment updated; the tag contains a history of the item's features and maintenance. Currently being tested are tagging systems for airport baggage handling, for inventorying books on shelves (via an invisible tag embedded in the spine of the book), and inhibiting shoplifting of clothing.

Use of electronic tags seems certain to soar once their cost falls to a few cents through volume demand and mass production. The reason is that electronic supply chain management relies on information moving with the goods. The more information, the more effective the integration of information, goods, and logistical flows.

Interactive Television   Interactive television combines the existing reach and capabilities of television with the interactive features of telephones. Your TV zapper becomes a limited PC keyboard. The box on top of the set that the zapper communicates with is literally a special-purpose PC.

Interactive TV has for almost 20 years been seen as a pot of gold at the end of a beautiful rainbow. Billions of dollars have been spent on pilots, most notably Time-Warner's lengthy trial of this product in Orlando, Florida. The main question the pilots address is what type of interaction should there be? There are plenty of electronic commerce candidates, most obviously interactive shopping for goods and financial services, gambling, on-demand entertainment, and access to information.

According to an old saying, Brazil is the country of the future—and always will be. A saying like that may also apply to interactive television, which has been a promise for well over 20 years of trials that begin with expansive hopes and claims about its potential and end with just a few hundred or few thousand subscribers making about as much use of it as people make of the advanced programming buttons on a VCR. Just as the VCR is a device that we use almost entirely for playing videotapes and occasionally recording TV programs, a TV set is something we switch on to watch TV. To date, nothing has changed that. It may be years before viewers start using it to control their own programming. Here are extracts from two articles in *Time* magazine about interactive TV, published just over one year apart:

> The brave new world that futurists have been predicting for decades is not years away but months. By this time next year, vast new video services will be available, at a price, to millions of Americans in all fifty states. (12 April 1993)

And "this time" the next year?

> The faith [about interactive TV] is being sorely tested. It is here that the rhetoric about the information highway comes face to face with the realities of engineering. (23 May 1994)

In other words, the state of interactive TV in 1994 was no further advanced than in 1993. It was no further advanced in 1995, either. But that could change, and quite quickly. The players in interactive television are routinely spending a billion dollars on their pilots and we are seeing many of the cable TV operators, especially in Europe, place billion dollar orders for set top boxes. Perhaps the trials are not really failures at all. The players are positioning for the long term. They are learning what works and what doesn't. They see the TV as the electronic commerce access point of tomorrow.

Microsoft and Intel see the PC as the TV of tomorrow. So far, they seem to be the winners, but who knows?

Internal Corporate "Banks"   No generally used term yet exists to describe the use of the technology of electronic commerce for internal financial operations. One early example was British Petroleum's use of its own cash management and funds transfer systems to set up BP Financial Institution (BPFI). This Financial Institution managed all the internal funding needs of the oil firm's operating units, moving money to and from local bank accounts, investing spare cash, and moving receipts to the internal or outside location that offered the best overall return to the corporation.

Obviously, companies cannot replicate all the many services of banks, especially regulated services, but they can manage the financial resource in the same way that they handle other business functions and other relationships. Thus more and more large companies reduce the numbers of banks they deal with, outsourcing such functions as management of financial accounts. The largest, like British Petroleum, use their multibillion cash flow as a source of funding for many operations. Numerous opportunities exist, including the following (Ian Orton, *Non-bank Banks: A Looming Menace,* Lafferty Publications, 1994):

- *Consumer finance.* Mail order houses, automobile companies, and department stores use their large customer base to offer credit cards, leasing, loans, and insurance. General Motors and Ford together account for 60 percent of all U.S. consumer debt, through their financial credit subsidiaries, which are not directly internal banks but still an integral part of the firms.

- *Corporate finance.* Companies bring in the financial expertise they would otherwise pay banks for. This includes project financing as well as securing short- and long-term credit.

- *Payments.* Firms use their own electronic commerce base for handling payments, often using the banks only to "net out" their end-of-day position with a single deposit to their bank.

- *Funding and insurance.* By using their corporate clout, firms obtain favorable terms and rates for individual business units.

The list of companies that have been active and successful in these areas reads like a Who's Who of corporate heavyweights. Just a few examples include:

- *Consumer finance.* GE Capital (General Electric); Marks and Spenser, the most profitable retailer in the world (the United Kingdom); Volkswagen; Seibu (Japan)

- *Corporate finance.* AT&T, Sony, Mitsubishi, Toyota, IBM Credit

- *Payments.* General Electric, American Express

- *Corporate funding.* British Telecom; ICI (the United Kingdom's largest manufacturer); Elf-Aquitaine (the French petrochemical firm)

- *Insurance.* Sears Roebuck.

International EDI   Important facts to know about international EDI concern its use in international trade and the standards that are being established to make such electronic trade possible. Today, a division is fairly clear between EDI in North America and international EDI. That's partly because the needs differ and main uses by individual industries have been in internal trade and in the trade between Canada and the United States, which constitutes the world's largest single cross-border market. In addition, differences in quality, regulation, and availability of telecommunications have inhibited firms from taking an international perspective on electronic commerce, except in international electronic payments, where there are many long-established mechanisms and institutions, including the Society for Worldwide Interbank Financial Telecommunications (SWIFT) and the Clearing House Interbank Payments System (CHIPS).

The main organization driving and coordinating international EDI is EDIFACT, the international equivalent of the ANSI X12 committee. EDIFACT's focus is on standardization of trade documentation, such as shipping, customs, and insurance documents. One difference between these transaction sets and the most widely implemented ANSI X12 transaction sets is that the main EDIFACT sets, to date, relate to relatively low-volume trans-

According to the United Nations, the cost of paper and associated delays, bureaucracy, and administration amounts to 10 percent of the value of total world trade. A typical international trade transaction may involve 30 parties and 60 original documents that grow to 360 copies. The United Nations estimates that transaction costs will grow to $400 billion a year by 2000. Paperless trading should reduce this amount by 25%.

In industrialized countries, only an estimated 7% of companies were using EDI in 1994 (a survey by the United Nations).

In 1995, global trade grew by 8% while global output of goods increased by just 3%. In 1996, U.S. exports grew by 9%, accounting for about 20% of total economic growth.

actions. In contrast, to choose just one of the ANSI X12 sets, X12 purchase orders, for example, constitute thousands of orders a day, whereas a retailer may have just a few daily international shipments. However, as EDIFACT has expanded the range of standards it has defined, the two worlds of EDIFACT and ANSI have converged in several areas where they both offer standards for a given type of transaction. In the 1980s, EDI experts differed in their opinions as to which would dominate and saw them as competitors, but increasingly the two organizations cooperate although they continue on their own separate paths. The pace of development is faster for ANSI than for EDIFACT largely because international differences in national regulations, practices, language, and other aspects, make the standard-setting process more complex, except for international finance.

International Standards Organization (ISO) The International Standards Organization (ISO) is a cooperative forum for the development and certification of standards in many areas including electronic equipment, product quality, telecommunications, textiles, photography, and information technology. It works closely with relevant international organizations such as the World Trade Organization, the International Telecommunications Union, the International Electrotechnical Commission, the American National Standards Institute, and United Nations agencies. It has 120 member countries, over 800 standard-setting committees, and 2,000 working groups. The European Union has made the ISO 9000 standard a requirement for certification of the quality of goods for import and export.

The ISO is fairly bureaucratic in style; a company must follow very complex procedures to earn its stamp of approval. But the ISO manages to define quality with no reference to the customer's measures of quality. It summarizes one of its major strengths as follows: "The ISO system has the strong capacity to resolve differences and, when successfully completed, ISO standards represent the best possible consensus among all affected parties, including customers and suppliers, on the technical requirements needed to facilitate exchange of goods, services, and ideas among people of all nations." (ISO World Wide Web page)

Internet Electronic Commerce   For many commentators and companies, electronic commerce means the Internet. That's where the long-term opportunities are perceived to be, in terms of size of sales, number of customers, new services, and profit margins. The challenges are many and to date there's more hype than substance in many forecasts and claims. The Internet is growing so fast that figures on its size and use are of very dubious accuracy. Its fragmentation, which is at the very basis of its openness, ease of market entry, and innovation, means minimal coordination and oversight—hence little coordinated information.

Rolling Stone's World Wide Web page gets over a hundred thousand hits a day—and just three orders for the many goods offered on it.

Extrapolations are thus being made on the basis of an immature and highly volatile, uncertain, and unmanaged phenomenon that has no direct parallels in human history. The fact that a given element of Internet use may be growing at a rate of, say, 80 percent a year, up from 40 percent last year, tells us little about future growth. Over time that growth will form the S-curve or sine wave characteristic of the diffusion of all large-scale social and technical innovations. The curve has four distinct phases, the boundaries of which can be hard to discern until several years or even decades later.

Shopping is ranked last in a 1995 survey of users of Web browsers like Netscape. Around 90 percent of respondents use their Web browsers for surfing the Web, 60 percent for entertainment, and 50 percent for work. Only 10 percent use them to shop. (Source: GVU WWW Survey Web page)

A. *Initiation.* Growth begins with pilots, announcements, dissimilar products, scattered successes—and overoptimistic predictions.

B. *Takeoff.* Momentum builds, with evidence of growing adoption, vendors offering similar products, and working toward common standards, a "critical mass" of users.

C. *Maturation.* Market growth slows, vendors offer the same features, prices drop, users embed the technology or application in their routine operations.

D. *Erosion.* The technology or application is displaced by newer developments.

At times, the curve may look more like an arc, as shown below. At time A, where growth has started to take off, it's very tempting to posit that it will reach points B and C within just a few years, soaring to D within five more years.

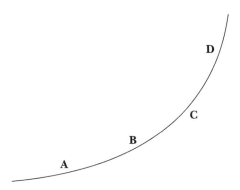

The start-up cost for a Web site is small. It cost General Motors' Saturn Division just $20,000 for initial development, according to Adweek *(1/15/96). GM's full Web site, which includes links to GM's many internal systems, cost the company an estimated $13 million, which is $2–3 million per division. Hitachi America's Web site cost $250,000 to develop and costs $45,000 a month for maintenance and upgrading.*

In fact, the growth may indeed match the arc from A to B to C over a few years. But at some point the curve will inevitably flatten out. *Inevitably.* In the early stages of growth, it makes little difference if the estimated rate of growth is overstated or understated. For example, in Table 3, from a base of 100, the third year growth goes to 274 at an annual rate of increase of 40% and 338 at 50%—or, a niche market on the Net that today amounts to $10 million in 1997 will be between $27 and $34 million in 2000. Extrapolating 10 years ahead, though, using the same rates, results in the forecast that this $10 million market will be between $2.9 and $5.8 billion. The 25% difference in forecast growth rate (50% versus 60%) results in a twofold difference in end point: make the forecasts 40% versus 100% and the forecasting gap is millions versus billions versus trillions.

Thousands of forecasters ignore the dips in the S-curve, boldly predicting massive markets within just a few years and refusing or failing to see any obstacles to the long-term sustaining of today's growth rates. They claim the only factor limiting PC diffusion,

Table 3   The projected size of a market that is $10 million in 1997 at different rates of growth (figures are in millions of dollars)

Annual growth (%)	1998	1999	2000	2001	2002	2007
10	110	121	133	146	161	259
20	120	144	173	207	249	619
30	130	169	220	286	371	1,379
40	140	196	274	384	538	2,893
50	150	225	338	506	759	5,767
60	160	256	410	655	1,049	10,995
70	170	289	491	835	1,420	20,160
80	180	324	583	1,050	1,890	35,705
90	190	361	686	1,303	2,476	61,311
100	200	400	800	1,600	3,200	102,400

Internet access, and hence electronic commerce is the size of the population of the earth.

Table 3 shows how sensitive the assumption of sustained growth rates is in such predictions. It shows the market size, starting at $10 million today, in each of the next 5 years and then 10 years from now, at varying rates of growth. So, if you're an Internet evangelist, your $10 million niche may explode to over $1 trillion in 2007. If you're a conservative optimist who sees 40% as a sustainable target, then you'll have to settle for just $29 billion. If you follow the historical norm of 20%, then you're looking at a market of less than $1 billion annually.

Of course, there *are* likely to be many $10 million markets that do grow 40, 60, 80, or even 100% and the astounding growth of the Web makes the wilder predictions not at all fantasies. They *could* happen—couldn't they? Who knows? Will electronic commerce be the $150 billion business several respected forecasters believe it will be in 2002?

According to Forrester Research, Internet commerce grew 46 percent between 1994 and 1995. But the total was still very small: $350 million. Advertising on the Net was around $37 million in 1995, a tiny fraction of the $60 billion total spent by companies.

The ethos of the Internet is exemplified by a widely quoted comment by the then chairman of Novell, Robert Franenberg, in a speech several years ago: "You're nobody if you're not somebody@somewhere.com." But somebody@some-where.com isn't yet buying many goods and services over the Net.

No one knows. The problem for business managers then is how to plan when you can't predict. Our own strong recommendation is to assume a 15–20% growth rate over the medium term of seven years *once a technology or application is well into the takeoff stage.* If the business case makes sense for that rate of growth, anything higher can be responded to as it occurs. That 20% figure holds well for most innovations in the use of technology in the past two decades: PC growth, EDI, international telecommunications, desktop publishing, and others.

Failures of many Internet electronic commerce ventures are inevitable, regardless of the size of the market. Many have already occurred. One was Shopping 2000, the first fully on-line shopping mall, which included JC Penney, Tower Records, Spiegel, and other catalog retailers. According to the business concept for Shopping 2000, consumers were expected to browse through on-line catalogs and then place orders by phone, using a credit card. It's still in business, but only as an offline CD-ROM. The on-line market didn't win interest.

The explanations for the failure of Shopping 2000 include the disjunction between looking at goods on a computer screen and ordering by phone; the shift dampens impulse buying, and even when customers do make the call, they rarely go back to the on-line catalog. Moreover, there was no advertising and promotion. At Thanksgiving 1993, Shopping 2000 had more content related to shopping than any other Internet site, with more than 60 well-known companies offering goods. It got plenty of media coverage, with Bell Atlantic featuring it as the shopping mall of the coming new century. But there was no investment in advertising on other Internet sites or in building consumer awareness. "The thinking was that if it was on the Internet, they will come" (Yesil, *Creating the Virtual Store,* p. 30). Customer support was also neglected. An early flood of customers "desperate for communication" sent opinions, suggestions, inquiries, and requests by e-mail but received little if any timely response.

A major concern of the founders of Shopping 2000 was that

many of the virtual stores on its mall would use it just to test the waters and then move on to set up their own on-line stores. And that's just what happened. Shopping 2000 did not add value to the individual stores or to their combination as an Internet *mall.* Once the large firms pulled out, all that was left were small retailers that could not afford to set up and maintain their own sites.

Internet Service Providers (ISPs)   Internet Service Providers (ISPs) are organizations that provide the link between an Internet user and the Net itself. An ISP can be a home business or a huge firm. An Internet address identifies 1) the user, and 2) the server computer to and from which Internet traffic is routed. This server is specified after the "@" sign that follows the user identifier. JJJones@erols.com is the user J.J. Jones at the ISP Erols, which has many customers in the mid-Atlantic states.

ISPs turn Internet access into a local phone call. They may offer many services, including help in setting up a Web site, feedback about accesses to the site, and options to use high-speed telecommunications links. When the World Wide Web took off, many new companies took advantage of the gaps in the marketplace to provide Internet access for small firms and individuals. They had technical expertise that was often lacking in the phone companies and they could get technically unskilled customers up on the Internet very quickly. Of course, AT&T, MCI, IBM, America Online, CompuServe, and other giants soon started to attack the ISP market, offering special deals and driving prices down. It is becoming harder and harder for small ISPs to compete. A shakeout is well underway and it is unlikely that many will survive. Even the leaders, such as UUNet, are marginally profitable.

Intranets   Intranets are mini-Internets in themselves. They employ Internet technology, plus links to their own systems, to create services that are accessible only to employees and specified outside parties. The Internet, of course, is open to anyone. Intranets can in themselves be massive. Hewlett-Packard's has 140,000 host

General Electric awarded over $1 billion in contracts in 1996 by using a link between the Internet and a special-

purpose in-house telecommunications network to routinely send Requests for Quotation (RFQs) to more than a thousand suppliers and allow them to respond electronically. The cycle time, from issuing the RFQ to choosing the supplier, has been cut from 15 to 7 days. GE has also benefited from opening up the RFQ process to new suppliers globally; this has cut prices of goods and services by up to 20 percent for GE Lighting. Costs of paperwork have also been slashed.

computers, 6,000 server computers, and 5 trillion bytes of data. It has 2,500 Internet Web servers as well. It is accessed by over 100,000 PCs and workstations. HP uses its intranet for many applications and projects.

- *Human resource management.* Distribution of personnel policies and guidelines
- *Product design.* Coordination of change orders, and design iterations
- *Software sharing.* Reduction of the number of copies of common PC applications such as word processing and presentation packages through access to a central server on the intranet
- *Electronic Sales Partner system.* ESP delivers sales and product information from the HP product divisions to the field, greatly enabling sales reps to spend their time responding to and talking with customers instead of hunting down documents. An internal HP survey shows that the 4,000 sales reps calculate that ESP saves them each five hours of wasted time a week. There are also substantial savings in mail and printing costs.

ISO   See **International Standards Organization.**

ISPs   See **Internet Service Providers.**

JEPI   See **Joint Electronic Payments Initiative.**

Joint Electronic Payments Initiative (JEPI)   JEPI is a specification for a universal electronic payments platform that will enable merchants and consumers to transact business over the Internet using many options for payment instead of being limited to specific ones. The venture has been undertaken by two leading consortia committed to advancing the use of the Internet, the World Wide Web Consortium (W3C) and CommerceNet. In late

1996, they jointly announced that the specifications were complete and ready for pilot implementation projects.

The JEPI specification includes procedures for negotiating the payment instrument between the parties and choosing the telecommunications transmission "protocol" for the two systems to communicate with each other. It's potentially a major development for electronic commerce on the World Wide Web, because W3C and CommerceNet have such strong credibility and influence that the specifications are almost sure to become a standard.

Kerberos Named after the three-headed watchdog of Greek mythology, this is a "private key" encryption routine that has become recognized as a potential solution for electronic commerce. By means of an encrypted packet of data, referred to as a "ticket," Kerberos identifies the user. In the case of a financial transaction, the user generates a ticket during the exchange of a series of coded messages with a Kerberos server. This server sits between the user and the receiving system and has a secret key that has been established with the receiving system. The server ensures that information has not been seen or altered during the exchange. A significant problem exists in that if there is a security breach, the system stops processing until it has been resolved.

When a client requests some service from a server, the server's first and immediate step is to check that the user is authorized to access it. Kerberos is a well-established software program for handling authentication, authorization, and security audit trails. It is stored on a secure server within the network and holds a data base of user passwords. A client system requesting a service first links to this server, which authenticates the user and electronically transmits an encrypted ticket to the client in response. The user then sends the ticket to the server that provides the service as proof that the user is permitted to access it.

Kerberos was created in a university and first used by the academic and research communities for securing electronic mail.

It is not designed for electronic commerce and is being gradually displaced by other, newer security tools.

Keys In electronic commerce, a *key* is a secret code consisting of a sequence of numerical values automatically combined in a computer either by means of hardware, such as an encryption board, or by means of software, such as an authentication program. Keys are created and applied via algorithms (a very large and complex calculation) and data (usually the message you are sending). The more numbers used—that is, the larger the key value—the more complex the key becomes and as a result, the more difficult the code is to break. The most widely used system is Data Encryption Standard (DES); though now obsolescent, it is still used to encrypt ATM transactions. In the DES cryptographic approach, keys were usually 16 digits long. This meant that to calculate against the DES algorithm, there were 10^{16}, or 10,000,000,000,000,000 possibilities—*per event or transaction!* Because modern computing power is increasing at a very rapid pace, security experts felt even this large number wasn't enough protection. Therefore, some systems have now implemented 10^{32} and even 10^{1024} keys. Breaking into systems with 1,024-long keys is generally thought to be beyond the power of most computing systems for the next several years, at least.

These keys are created in two ways. First, usually to begin a relationship, there is a manual key creation process, where software creates a key value. This key is often created by means of a random number generator device, which generates a mathematically random value. Some systems still use manual key generation, assigning a value such as a customer's account number. Some mathematicians argue that no matter how random one thinks such a tool is in creating a key value, it is still less "random" than a key generator. The result of this manual key creation process is often referred to as the MFK or Master File Key. It is used to generate a variety of automated keys.

The automated keys are created by the system itself, using either public key methodology or a private key methodology. Once a system has been started up, it creates numerous keys and usually is able to change these keys continually—often from one transaction to the next. Two common terms for automated keys in a DES or other "symmetrical" cryptographic system are:

- *Key Exchange Key (KEK)*. Used to protect either other key encryption keys or data keys during an exchange.

- *The Key Encryption Key (KPE)*. Also known as the data key or the working key. This is used exclusively to encrypt and decrypt keys.

Symmetrical means the same key is used to code and decode messages. The newer approach is to use a "private" key for encoding and a "public" key for decoding.

The person who creates and manages the key is referred to as the key custodian. There should always be at least two key custodians, to ensure that there is a reasonable separation of control and to prevent frauds. The process the custodians follow is called key management, and when they send a manual key part to another company, this transmission is called the key exchange.

Legal Issues Concerning Electronic Commerce   Since the introduction of electronic processes decades ago, there has been a continuing debate over the legal and control issues that surround the use of methodologies that replace the use of paper. Yet even before today's sophisticated technology, businesses conducted trade electronically—via telephone, with buyers placing orders with a simple phone call, and sellers completing the transaction with no proof beyond the word of the parties involved.

When the ATM first came into popular use, the concept of an electronic signature substitute was introduced, by way of the personal identification number (PIN). Since ATMs operated on a totally electronic basis, generating end-of-day logs and reports

Spamming—the sending of electronic junk mail— was the top complaint of America Online's members in 1996. When it tried to block messages from Wallace Sanford, the self-named Spam King, the fight generated lawsuits and a final compromise where AOL users can choose to have spams blocked. Sanford's company generates bulk electronic mail messages for its clients, and offers software for under $1,000 that lets users generate lists of e-mail addresses and disguise the bulk mail nature of communications they send. On many occasions, a flood of spams has "crashed" the networks of Internet service providers. For instance, Netcom, a California service, received a flood of 50,000 messages that so overloaded its systems that it had to close down for 4 hours. Wallace claims that no one has a

for reconciliation, their rapid adoption raised the question of whether or not computer-generated financial transactions were valid and whether these records could be introduced as evidence in the event of a dispute. Experience has shown that ATM transactions are valid and that courts in most jurisdictions support the legality of the technology and, more importantly, of the electronic evidence.

When EDI was first recognized as an emerging corporate electronic means of converting intercompany transactions from paper and signed orders, deliveries, and so on, to electronic messages, the general issues surrounding its legality focused on the question of whether or not an EDI order was valid in the case of a dispute. As with the ATM, debates ensued over the technical issues of a computer system's reliability and over the potential for disagreements and how to resolve them. Again the issue ultimately centered on the questions of proof of the action and response in a business transaction.

When Financial EDI came onto the scene, a number of business, technical, and legal experts raised the issue of the validity of transactions and the potential impact of fraud. It is interesting to note that, in the past nearly 25 years since electronic trading began, few if any legal cases have involved a dispute about the validity of electronic funds transfer transactions or EDI transactions. If the present trends continue, it is unlikely the legitimacy of EDI itself will be challenged; rather, any questions that arise are more likely to concern business issues surrounding transactions, rather than the mechanics of the process, whether electronic or paper.

Legal issues concerning Internet electronic commerce are unclear both within countries and internationally. In late 1996, two organizations in France brought a suit against a small Georgia Tech campus, also in France, because its Internet site is in English. They claim that's a violation of a 1994 French law that forbids the sale of goods and services in France in any language other than French. (Sony renamed its Walkman as Balladeur for this reason.) Georgia Tech points out that its courses are taught by American professors in English and most of the students are American.

The lawsuit reflects the widespread French fear of being "economically and culturally marginalized" (French President Chirac's phrase) by the dominance of the English language in entertainment, technology, and retailing. The French postal service was sued for naming its courier service Skypack. The Culture Minister asserted in 1994 that France "is menaced by a new form of colonialism"—the Internet. "If we do nothing, it will be too late. We will be colonized." The suit also raises important legal issues. Is the Internet a forum for private discussion or a public place? Where is it located? Does French national law apply to an organization whose site may be physically outside France? The answers will eventually affect the application of laws about pornography, consumer protection, commerce, freedom of expression, libel, and political statements in all nations.

Lockboxes A lockbox is a post office box opened in the name of the depositor but opened and accessed by the remittance processor, usually a bank. This lockbox receives checks sent from paying companies who are in reasonably close proximity to the lockbox location, thereby reducing the time it takes for the check to travel through the postal system. This postal delay, or float, can also incur a delay in value or "good funds" finding their way into the account, especially if the check is drawn on a bank across the country from the recipient; this is called "bank" float. The underlying purpose of a lockbox in electronic commerce is to provide a remote capture of the remittance detail and the funds in an expeditious manner. The capture of the funds occurs when the checks are deposited by the remittance processor in close proximity to the payer's bank. The remittance detail—details about what the payment is for—is captured by a human operator and converted into an electronic file. This file is then sent to the payee company to process into its accounts receivable system.

right to restrict free enterprise in the new medium of cyberspace. ISPs and others counterargue that unrestricted junk mail will bring the Internet and on-line services to a standstill. Lawsuits are in the works and legislation seems likely. Wallace previously built a business that specialized in junk mail fax transmission. Congress outlawed that in 1992.

Lockboxes are the main cash management system for handling paper-based checks. They save up to six days of lost float. A company that receives checks amounting to $500 million a year saves around $800,000 a year through lockboxes. Many firms have their own zip code for their lockboxes; their banks pick up checks several times a day and process *them immediately. Once checks disappear, so too will lockboxes, but this will take a long time. Lockboxes reflect one of the inefficiencies of the banking payments systems, one that banks profit from. Banks provide lockbox services for around 30 percent of the Fortune 500.*

The benefits of using a lockbox are:

- Faster availability of funds
- Reduced processing costs
- Greater reliability in deposit processing
- More flexibility in capturing remittance data
- Improved security over the remittance

There are two kinds of lockboxes—wholesale and retail. Both work in very much the same way, the main difference being in the type of payment data and payers that are involved. A wholesale lockbox is for the receipt and processing of corporate payments, usually of large value with significant amounts of remittance detail. A retail lockbox is focused on receiving consumer payments, generally of relatively low value and with only the remittance amount and the remitter's account number being recorded. A retail lockbox is ideal for a utility bill collection system, for example.

Until the early 1990s, used cars in Japan were sold at auction sites. Transporting unsold cars was expensive, but occurred with 45 percent of the vehicles brought to auction. Crowded urban areas and scarce parking space resulted in a cumbersome auction system. Now, Japan's ACUNET uses video images, on-line electronic data, and inspectors' ratings to auction cars without moving them.

Logistics   The business processes involved in the management of physical production and distribution of goods are collectively termed logistics. Much of the evolution of electronic commerce has centered on logistics, most obviously through EDI and its extensions, particularly in the handling of payments for goods. The leaders over the past 20 years have been in logistics-intensive industries, such as auto manufacturing, transportation, and retailing.

We recommend a broader view of logistics as the integration of the business processes that coordinate the delivery of the firm's services and products to its customers and its relationships with its trading partners. Total quality management, process investment, quick response, supply chain management, point-of-sale inventory management, EDI, and flexible production techniques have transformed logistics over the past decade. Many service companies have recognized that by applying the same manufacturing concepts and tools to their own supply chains, points of sale, and so on, they can achieve the same gains as manufacturers of products have.

For many commentators, electronic commerce means selling to consumers on the Internet. For us, electronic commerce is just as much, or even more, electronic logistics in business-to-business relationships and, increasingly, for coordination of internal information and logistics, via intranets. The business-to-business emphasis includes intranets and the Internet as key infrastructures for electronic commerce, but value added networks and companies' own networks are the platform for the enterprise logistics base. Logistics is intensely pragmatic, and the leaders in logistics—firms like Federal Express, Wal-Mart, Motorola, Toyota, and other much-admired names—are as adept in using the tools of electronic commerce as in managing their organizational process and human resources. Increasingly, they focus on interchange of information in their trading activities. Simply stated, without the main tools of EDI and electronic payments, firms can't get very far here; they certainly won't get within sight of the FedExes of this world.

Fifteen percent of logistics costs are for order processing, administration, and related overhead. The old rule of thumb was 11 days to process and acknowledge the order and 16 days for delivery. EDI cuts this to an average of 3 and 11. Leaders in integrated logistics have reduced this to as little as 1 day for order processing and 3 for delivery. (Kenneth Lyons, Purchasing, *Pitman, 1996)*

MAC   See **Message Authentication Code.**

Merchant Systems   The software, security, and communications components for handling information, orders, and payments at the seller's end in on-line commerce are called merchant systems. There are so many electronic commerce initiatives underway as the twentieth century draws to a close, involving so many consortia, that it is impossible for managers to keep track of them or to be able to guess which ones will win in the marketplace. Many initiatives address the needs of merchants to have not just a presence on the World Wide Web, but a comprehensive and reliable base for processing transactions, handling payments, maintaining records, and ensuring security and privacy.

If Microsoft or IBM is a leader in an initiative, the sponsoring consortium quickly signs up leading banks, telecommunications service providers, credit card firms, and retailers, and there's more than an even chance the initiative will take off. Two such ventures are Microsoft's Merchant Server and IBM's Integrion. Integrion is a consortium of banks plus IBM focused on the payment element of merchant systems, whereas Microsoft's initiative addresses the entire electronic base for selling. Merchant Server, announced at the end of October 1996, helps companies set up retail sites on the Internet. They can use a range of software to set up simple sites or create complex ones, with links to their existing transaction and accounting systems. Microsoft offers a set of what are called Application Programming Interfaces (APIs) from their own systems to order-processing routines included in the server. Merchant Server helps merchants handle promotions over the Net and develop sophisticated interactive catalogs.

Forty companies signed up before the announcement, to "support" Merchant Server. It is very unclear if this means only that they are hedging their bets to ensure the best position should the Microsoft juggernaut make Merchant Server a major force in electronic commerce; meanwhile they have committed no resources or effort in case it doesn't survive. The 40 include various Internet Service Providers (ISPs); American Express; Citibank Card Acceptance Corporation; Digital Equipment, the beleaguered computer maker that has made a close alliance with (or, in the opinion of some commentators, surrendered to) Microsoft; Verifone, the dominant force in credit card reading devices; and Sterling Commerce, the leader in EDI software.

Among companies implementing Merchant Server sites at the end of 1996 were Tower Records, 1-800-FLOWERS, and Microsoft itself. Tower's site allows shoppers to search through a data base of 150,000 titles by performer, title, album, or song. It also offers 100,000 30-second sound bite extracts from records. 1-800-FLOWERS, which already makes over $30 million a year from on-line orders, sees Merchant Server as its opportunity to reduce the costs of custom development needed to expand the volume of business and features it can offer, increase promotions, and add security.

Microsoft has used Merchant Server for its internal employee store, partly as a means of testing it in a fully operational environment. The first application is for placing purchase orders for office supplies. A Microsoft spokesperson claims (*EC/EDI Insider,* November 10, 1996) that Merchant Server will work with any vendor's electronic commerce software:

> We are payment agnostic, browser agnostic and database agnostic, so it makes it really easy either to connect our system either to third party software like Sterling Commerce or to existing legacy systems just by writing some kind of mapping [software] layer. We really do offer this end-to-end solution—everything from getting started easily to taking care of payment fulfillment, taxes, accounting systems—the whole shooting match—through some of our initial partners.

For many observers and competitors, Microsoft's announcement to support any type of software and vendor is like the fox announcing to the chickens that he's become a vegetarian. On the other hand, just as IBM had to abandon its highly successful strategy of offering mainly proprietary systems and adopt "open"—vendor-independent—ones, under pressure from business customers, Microsoft may see that the future of large-scale electronic commerce requires linking many existing "legacy" software systems and employing a mix of vendors' products. The approach is less "If you can't beat 'em, join 'em" than "Since you can't beat them, take the lead in bringing them together."

Regardless of the relative successes of these ventures, they send a clear signal to businesses everywhere. Electronic commerce on the Internet is shifting rapidly from being a matter of building a Web site to developing a complete retailing operation, with full transaction processing. It's the difference between a 1-800 number order-by-phone service and a full retail store.

See also **Integrion.**

Message   The common meaning of the term *message* is a complete communication of some sort. That sense applies to much but not all of electronic commerce. For electronic mail, a message is a complete unit of text plus any attachments, which is put into the electronic equivalent of an envelope and transmitted over a telecommunications network. However, in the telecommunications trade, a message is a discrete unit of data that is transmitted; an electronic mail message or electronic payments message may require many telecommunications messages.

Message is the term used for an EDI document as defined in the language of the EDIFACT standard, but the ANSI standard defines a document as either a *transaction set* or a *message*—the terms are interchangeable for ANSI. An EDI message is composed of data segments, which are themselves composed of data elements. Think of it as a document or paragraph that is commonly used in business, such as a purchase order, an invoice, or an instruction to make payment. A data segment is the same as a line of data in a document or a sentence in a paragraph. A data element is the same as a word or a term. There is a common data element dictionary for both the EDIFACT standard and the ANSI standard. However, segments and transaction sets and messages are constructed differently.

Most business managers will never need to know exactly what is a message, a transaction set, or a document. It's worth keeping in mind, though, that at times the commonsense and technical meanings of the term *message* may conflict. The business manager is interested in how many transactions a system can handle and what the cost per transaction is. That may be very different from the number of messages involved, and the cost per message may seem low, but that does not mean the cost per business transaction will be.

Managers have for a long time and with good reason been wary of, irritated by, or just plain fed up with the jargon of the information technology field, with terms like "NDMB-compliance" and ads that boast of a product with "the astounding NFS

Ops of 1,450." It's often the nonjargon words that cause miscommunication. Our recommendation for managers is that when they hear a commonsense word like "message" being used in a technical context they should ask directly and immediately if the meaning corresponds to its *business* meaning.

Message Authentication Code (MAC)   A message authentication code is a numeric value created electronically and inserted in a transaction to prevent repudiation and provide integrity. In essence, a MAC is a form of electronic signature and proof of nonrepudiation, which simply means the sender cannot claim not to have transmitted the message nor that it was transmitted by someone else or without authority. One practical way of creating a MAC is covered in the ANSI X12 standards under the X12.42 and X12.58 subsections. Also considered to be a form of digital signature, a MAC is created by adding up the entire contents of a transaction, within a prescribed set of parameters for starting and stopping, applying a mathematical algorithm and cryptographic key process to this sum, and then extracting a part of the

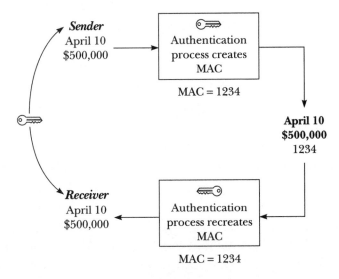

Figure 9

result and placing it into the message as a code or value. The recipient counts the same fields of data, as prescribed and then, using the same key and algorithm, calculates the same value. Should the value not recalculate, then the transaction is not valid as a result of tampering or some other problem.

The ongoing and long-established combination of the promise of smart cards and their results is well summarized by a merchant whose store in San Francisco is part of a test of smart cards: "We love Mondex sales. There's no cash, no paperwork involved." But, "It hasn't brought in much business." (Business Week, 19 May 1997, 122)

Mondex   The proprietary name for a particular type and brand of smart card used for holding and dispensing cash that was developed by the National Westminster Bank of England is Mondex. The card is based on the concept of "stored value" initially popularized by prepaid phone cards. The general principle of a stored-value card is that a user loads a certain cash value onto the card and this value can be sent electronically by inserting the card in a reader and having the amount deducted from the card. The recipient of the value then redeems the amount from its banker at a future date. Mondex specifically, and other similar schemes, use extremely sophisticated cryptographic techniques to prevent forgery and fraud. It is conceptually possible that a smart card could have its code broken and then be replicated. However, this is currently seen as well beyond the realm of probability.

The concept of stored-value cards has been around for a number of years, but Mondex offers a more generic, cross-service money card that can interact with a large and diverse number of vendors and individuals. Money value stored in Mondex can be transferred person to person, using a special device, and even over the phone. That means it bypasses both the banking and taxation systems, a concern of both banks and regulators. The Mondex approach was intended to be used for the relatively low-value transactions that are not appropriate for credit card or even debit card transactions. One might consider Mondex's ultimate goal as its card being seen as electronic pocket change.

In the early 1860s, the United States had no national paper currency. There were around 7,000 different notes issued by 1,600 state banks. Many, of course, were worthless.

There is also the potential for the use of Mondex in applications such as the Internet and other electronic media, where monetary value needs to be transferred via some form of electronic token or replacement. With an electronic reader in the home and an agreed upon procedure, it is quite viable that a Mondex card could be used to pay for a purchase over the Internet.

National Security Agency (NSA) The National Security Agency is believed to be the largest single purchaser of computer hardware in the world and to employ the largest number of mathematicians. We say "believed to be" because the Agency is very secretive and doesn't publish figures; even its existence wasn't made public for many years after its foundation in the 1940s. NSA's role is to monitor and decode foreign communications that may threaten U.S. national security.

NSA aggressively resists any outside development that may result in the dissemination of mathematical and technical tools that result in its being unable to crack a code. It used the full force of the law to prevent even the publication of the academic research that led to the creation of the most advanced cryptographic tools and is behind the long-established restrictions on the export of computer chips and software for encoding and decoding messages.

Nonbank Competition to Banks in Electronic Commerce

For any bank, the main competition now is more likely to be a nonbank company than another bank. Banking has been facing and largely losing business to firms from outside its previously well-bounded industry for decades now. Electronic commerce will surely accelerate that process, simply because fewer and fewer transactions legally require the banking system except as a payments processing vehicle. Customers look for convenience and service, which can as easily be provided by banks' competitors: automakers (General Motors and Ford together account for 60 percent of all consumer loans in the United States); retailers (credit cards); mutual fund companies (Fidelity, among many others, offers full-service banking with no bank branches); and

Table 4   Banking's market share

Annual percentage share of total U.S. household financial savings placed in bank deposits

	1977	1987	1990	1992*
	55	30	8	−2

Percentage of savings invested

Type of Investment	1952–1960	1960–1970	1970–1980	1980–1992
Bank deposits	42	52	56	31
Mutual funds	3	5	2	18
Pension funds	22	23	29	38

Percentage of Commercial Paper (short-term credit) issued by banks

1980	1991
21	5

*Note: A net imbalance between loans and deposits is shown in 1992.
Source: Lafferty Reports, "Banking and Nonbanking Competition," Dublin, Ireland, 1996.

even corporate customers (British Petroleum set up its own BP Financial Institution, which offers many wholesale banking services without having to buy deposits).

Table 4 shows just a few figures on the shift away from banks as the central vehicle for the handling of savings, deposits, loans, and payments. The banks' challenge is threefold: (1) to capture and retain customers, (2) to generate attractive new products, and (3) to transform their cost structures. Electronic commerce can contribute to all three, but of course it can also contribute to their competitors' efforts in these areas.

Nonrepudiation   The term nonrepudiation refers to the mechanisms or processes that are designed to prevent a sender from denying, or repudiating, the authenticity of a message or to prevent the receiver from disclaiming the receipt of a message. There are a number of ways that nonrepudiation can be established in electronic commerce:

- *Third-party network.* Maintenance of the log of a transaction by an unbiased party to the transaction is used widely for financial transactions that involve a bank debiting and crediting accounts. The third party's involvement provides clear and irrefutable proof the transaction was valid.

- *MAC with third-party network.* The application of a Message Authentication Code (MAC) or a digital signature also can assure nonrepudiation. As well, by itself a MAC or digital signature recorded in the message can be used to validate the transaction.

- *Management.* Finally, the management of the systems, carefully and regularly audited, can provide a level of adequacy that the system performed as it should and therefore validates the transaction. This has certainly been the case for many ATM systems that process large volumes of transactions successfully and regularly, so that saying that the system doesn't work, and therefore a transaction is invalid, is a poor defense.

NSA   See **National Security Agency.**

On-Line Services   On-line services (companies such as America Online, CompuServe, Prodigy, and Microsoft Network) first offered information and electronic mail services and now have added Internet access. In effect, they are now an integral part of the Internet in that millions of subscribers use them as their primary Internet "gateway." They are also proprietary services competing to differentiate themselves from both the Internet and each other, through such facilities as AOL's chat rooms, Compu-

Serve's library of business publications, and electronic commerce services including on-line shopping malls.

Prior to the emergence of the World Wide Web as the base for business and consumer access, a small number of firms were competing to build a business and/or consumer base with varied success. Many well-funded ones went out of business, including Apple's network and Genie. Others like Prodigy have struggled to build revenues and then profits. The most successful, AOL, has become a powerful brand with a huge base of customers. It faltered badly when it switched to a new pricing scheme that offered unlimited access for just $19.95 a month. The surge in usage badly overloaded its systems, preventing many subscribers from getting onto the system at peak hours for many months. AOL damaged both its reputation and its customer relationships. In addition, it was forced to change how it accounted for revenues and restate its earnings; the adjustments showed that it was not, as claimed, profitable.

Profits are the issue. The on-line services were building an expensive base for future growth but the Internet has taken away much of that growth opportunity and many observers doubt that the services can survive. AOL is betting on "content" by acquiring many providers of information in many different media. It sees the Internet as primarily an access vehicle to content. Microsoft set up its Microsoft Network with the same basic goal of building a wide range of content-rich services, including its own on-line magazine, *Slate*. Edited by Michael Kingsley, one of the best-known and most respected U.S. journalists, *Slate* has been widely touted and little read.

Outsourcing and Electronic Commerce   One of the opportunities electronic commerce opens up is what may be termed electronic outsourcing: using technology to send information to third parties who handle the outsourced function and return the information needed by the company. IBM outsourced its accounts receivable in this way, cutting the number of exception items that require special action and some degree of manual processing by almost half, to 21 percent, still a large fraction of the 28,000 checks totaling over $500 million it receives each month in its Northeast operation.

Up to 1990, IBM processed its receivables manually. The payments were sent to seven IBM locations, using 11 banks. After rationalizing this system, IBM was using just one bank and two electronic lockbox locations by 1995. The EC extension of this involves electronically sending a weekly file of open accounts receivable to the bank. As payments arrive to the lockbox, they are matched to the file, which contains the customer number, invoice number, date, and amount. Those that exactly match the data are entered into the file. Bank operators try to resolve the ones that are rejected. These may simply be an incorrect invoice number or incomplete payment. A daily report of exception items that the bank cannot resolve is sent to IBM. Prior to the new system, every single exception had to be handled by at least one person, these people often being at different IBM locations, with high costs for storing and accessing copies of documents. Now, IBM can get working on exceptions the day after they are discovered by the bank. The number of exceptions has dropped from 40 percent to 21 percent and cash collection has been speeded up substantially. A key element in the success of the outsourcing is the human touch. The bank's and IBM's staff hold a weekly scheduled conference call to review any problems found in the previous week. In addition, the software that matches a scanned image of the check to the data file contains very precise rules, which the team constantly refines; the rules address such issues as acceptance of partial payment, discounts, and validity of signatures.

This is a simple solution to a minor but cumbersome administrative burden. It's the business thinking plus the collaboration that makes the solution work, with the technology simply the tool.

Paid on Production (PoP)   The principle known as *paid on production* is based on the rule that no payment is generated until the actual product is pulled out of inventory or consumed by the buyer. That is different from traditional payment, which is due when goods arrive at the buyer's site and are put into inventory. It is an extension of the approach to inventory management known as vendor-managed inventory (VMI) where the supplier is responsible for scheduling, delivering, and maintaining the correct amount of product at the point of sale, or in the case of a manufacturer, at the point of use.

Several automobile manufacturers are using the paid on production method. For example, when they install seats, which have been preassembled and delivered by the seat manufacturer, they pay the supplier. In many cases, normal terms have been shortened because the delay from the delivery of the good until the installation is slightly variable. This is in contrast to the VMI model, which operates on the assumption that payment is generated upon receipt of the good at the loading dock, rather than upon installation or use.

The approach focuses on shortening the timeline for materials to the production point and is viewed as an incentive for the supplier to keep an adequate, but minimum, number of supplies in the supply chain. Some applications with high variability of consumption are not well suited to PoP. It fits the needs of the automotive industry particularly well because automakers have highly detailed production schedules, which they share with their suppliers. That way, the right color seats are available for the right car—at the right time.

Payables Management Disbursement Payables management disbursement is a service offered by banks to manage the entire accounts payable system for clients. This outsourcing of a corporate activity makes the assumption that a bank provides an economy of scale beyond that which most businesses can achieve, and that by combining EFT, EDI, and various other methods including the printing of checks if necessary, it can provide an over-

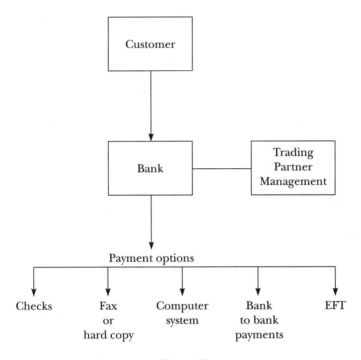

Figure 10

all lower cost payment to the customer than the customer can achieve on its own.

A key element in this approach is the paying organization's commitment to requiring electronic payment methods by their receivers. Persuading their trading partners to comply with this requirement is not always easy to accomplish. In many cases, the bank will provide a pricing incentive to the paying company, making the cost of a check much higher than an equivalent EFT or EDI transaction, and therefore more desirable.

The linkage between the corporate payer and the bank is almost always electronic. The entire payables file is sent to the bank, which then is responsible for sorting it and distributing the payments to the correct recipients. Recently, an additional service component has become prevalent at banks offering this kind of service, generically called trading partner management (TPM).

TPM checks a copy of all the valid suppliers in the accounts payable system of the paying organization and is administered independently of the delivery of transaction data. TPM ensures that parties who are being paid are in fact valid trading partners of the payer. This verification is designed to prevent any fraud in accounts payable, where numerous scams have been widely reported that involved false invoices being sent to companies. Figure 10 exemplifies the flows of this approach.

Payment Systems   The literal definition of a payment system is a set of instruments, banking procedures, and, typically, interbank funds transfer systems that ensure the circulation of money. The instruments involved can be paper based, such as cash, money orders, bank drafts, or checks. Or they can be electronic, such as electronic funds transfer, EDI, ATM, or any other mechanism that conveys instructions to pay. The banking procedures for payment mechanisms vary internationally. They are established in each country based on their specific geographic and social needs. These procedures can vary significantly and are often not transferable between countries.

For example, in the mid-1980s when the worldwide expansion of ATM networks began, it was discovered that in Japan, unlike North America, there were no electronic security measures taken to protect the personal identification number (PIN). A basic premise of Japanese society is that crime is dishonorable. Therefore, tapping into a data line is unthinkable, and as a consequence PIN protection was unnecessary. In North America, great effort and cost had been invested in high-grade security systems inside the ATMs to prevent illegal access to personal ID information. In order to participate in the ATM network expansion, the Japan Credit Bureau (JCB), one of the main ATM providers in Japan, had to install special secure ATMs at strategic locations for international access. This same problem had never occurred in connecting to systems in Canada or Europe.

Every country in the developed world has interbank transfer

Payments are at the core of electronic commerce innovation. They are also the area of most uncertainty, with 2 possible and parallel paths: (1) adapting established mechanisms such as credit cards, electronic funds transfers, and electronic data interchange to meet the demands of an electronic, rather than paper, transaction environment, and (2) inventing new mechanisms, including digital cash, smart wallets, and electronic tokens. Obviously, consumer confidence will determine which, if any, of the new systems will take off and when. Banker and regulator systems. Some of these are quite sophisticated, like the automated clearing houses in the United States and Europe. However, they can be as basic as the old fashioned approach used over a century ago by bankers who would sit down at a large table and present each item, such as a check, for acceptance or refusal. Many countries still follow such a practice today. The world of electronic commerce payment has system tools such as CHIPS and CHAPS, along with other domestic systems discussed elsewhere in this book. An international exchange system, based on SWIFT, facilitates the intercountry exchange of payments.

confidence and commitment will determine how much of an investment will be made by the institutions that currently manage existing payments systems.

PEM   See **Privacy Enhanced Mail Standard.**

PGP   See **Pretty Good Privacy.**

Point of Sale (POS)   Point of sale basically refers to the cash register, although the term has broadened to include its common-sense meaning of the exact location where a customer makes a transaction. The logic of electronic logistics is to use the point of sale to capture information that can then be routed back through the supply chain. The cash register becomes a computer and the store part of a network. The most obvious use of POS technology has been to update store inventory; as an item is scanned, its bar-coded product number is read into the system and stock records are updated. The extension of this record-keeping is to send information back to a central office where it can be combined with data from other stores to track sales patterns and trigger ordering of goods on a daily rather than weekly basis. The more advanced firms use POS as the base for integrating the entire supply chain. Vendor-managed inventory lets suppliers access POS data to stock directly to the shelf with no purchase orders. Quick Response and Efficient Consumer Response use the point of sale as the trigger for streamlining the entire supply chain.

PoP See **Paid on Production.**

POS See **Point of Sale.**

Pretty Good Privacy (PGP) Pretty Good Privacy is a free software package that has become a de facto standard for ensuring privacy and security of messages transmitted over the Internet. It was designed by one of the inventors of the most widely used cryptography technique, called RSA. It is simple even for PC users to implement.

See also **Public Key Cryptography.**

Privacy Enhanced Mail (PEM) Standard To ensure the security of electronic mail over the Net, the Internet Activities Board designed the standard called Privacy Enhanced Mail. It is a comprehensive specification of how messages must be created by different cryptographic systems. It adds many features needed for electronic mail to be a vehicle for electronic commerce transactions that have legal and contractual implications. One such feature is nonrepudiation, the legally provable evidence that the message was sent from a specific person who cannot now claim not to have done so.

PEM has not yet been widely adopted, but several companies are including it in their electronic mail services. The issue it addresses is fundamental to the future of electronic commerce over the Internet.

Private Key A private key is a tool used in cryptography. In contrast to a public key, a private key is known only to its owner and is used to encode messages. A public key decodes them.

See also **Public Key Cryptography.**

Proxy Servers Protecting a network against unauthorized access is done in either of two basic ways: (1) by packet filtering and (2) by using proxy servers. Packet filtering is fast but risky and proxy servers are safe but slow. Internet messages arrive at a server in packets that are reassembled to form the complete transmission. The packet indicates the sender's Internet address. Packet filtering checks the address and rejects any messages from unauthorized sites. Unfortunately, it's easy for a skilled hacker to falsify what is the equivalent of the return address on an envelope. Proxy servers guard against such fraud by building up the entire message in a firewall system that stands between the Internet and the company's own network and computers. If the message is valid, the server passes on a copy—a *proxy*. The process of examining, copying, and passing on the proxy slows down the flow of traffic. For Internet sites that receive millions of "hits" a day and for the mass marketing retailing and credit card transactions that many companies are aiming for, proxy servers are too slow but packet filtering too insecure. Currently many developers are working to combine the strengths of the two approaches. Check Point, which has been adopted by leading server providers such as Hewlett Packard and Sun Microsystems, examines each incoming packet and shoots it on very quickly, adding alerting information if needed, encryption, and virus scanning.

Given that many surveys show that around 40 percent of companies report attempts by hackers to break into their networks, firewalls are essential if secure electronic commerce is not to be an oxymoron like jumbo shrimp.

Public Key Cryptography Public key cryptography is the generally accepted base for guarding the security of information transmitted electronically. It employs complex mathematical theory and algorithms to generate two electronic values called keys. The private key is kept secret and must be highly guarded. It is used to encode messages—that is, to convert ordinary language, known as "plaintext," to an apparently random stream of electronic bits. Trading partners, via software applications and computer hardware chips, apply the public key, which can decode messages but cannot encode them.

Much referred to in the media, and in any article written about Internet security, public key cryptography is bandied about as the panacea for the concerns we all have about privacy and message integrity in the electronic universe. However, there is more to this than is first apparent. Any form of electronic security will involve the elements of technology, such as software and computers; technique, such as the calculations or algorithms; and administration, which includes the procedures and policies on how to apply the technology and techniques. Whether one uses electronic means to secure things, or a lock on the door to prevent unexpected visitors, one needs to understand the reasons for using these facilities in the first place. In a small town often people don't even lock their doors, let alone use high-grade deadbolts. In high-crime urban neighborhoods, people do have good locks, but many also use an alarm system and other security measures.

Electronic security processes may seem more complex than a deadbolt or house alarm, but ultimately their use, too, is defined by their relevance to the situation. Public key has certain features and attributes that make it more suitable to the Internet and certain other, relatively open environments but that may not be needed for all applications of security.

Public key cryptography, which is also known as *asymmetric security*, relates to the practical use of the techniques of combining a public key and a private key, assisted by an entity known as a certification authority (CA), to secure transactions through en-cryption and/or digital signature.

The main advantage of public key technology is its anony-mous or blind application—two parties interacting electronically need not actually be known to one another. This concept has proven to be extremely difficult to put into practice, however. The difficulty arises because, although the use of a common third party such as a CA is reasonable in theory, the actual rules, standards, participants, and fees have yet to be resolved. Manag-

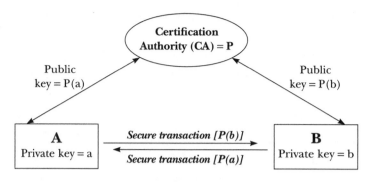

Figure 11

ing a public key system requires a significant amount of coordination, technology, and skill, all of which has not yet evolved into a stable situation or agreement.

The process for applying public key cryptography is as follows (see Figure 11):

1. Party A wishes to receive a confidential message from Party B.

2. Party A publishes a public key with a CA. Party B identifies that it wishes to send an encrypted message to Party A and obtains the public key from the CA and then uses the key to encrypt the data through suitable devices or software.

3. Party B sends the message to Party A, which uses its public key, combined privately with its private key, to decrypt and translate the message.

A similar process would be involved for a digital signature, which is a value created from the sum of all the data and the cryptography process (including the keys) which the receiving party uses to confirm that the message has arrived intact and is from the correct sending party.

Public key cryptography faces a number of challenges that must be resolved before it achieves widespread success:

- *Difficulty managing keys.* Both the public and the private keys require a process and a discipline to ensure they are created and managed correctly, as well as changed periodically. Of even greater concern is the compatibility and lack of definition of common algorithms for the cryptographic process.

- *Insufficient definition of the certification authority.* Many different communities of electronic data interchange are not certain as to which third parties would be appropriate certification authorities. Some agencies, such as the U.S. Postal Service, see themselves as providing this function, but industry groups and associations may be commissioned to perform this function instead. Requirements for a CA are impartiality in the transaction process as well as a clearly defined and managed operation with a high security ethic.

- *A question of need.* As in any business process, there should be a clear business need for the application of security, especially if it generates a significant cost to the users. While cost is not the only factor, internal management and coordination for security are not trivial issues and can become a major overhead. Providing a clear business mandate for security processes, whether managed by public or private key, can be a challenge.

- *Costs.* Not only is there a cost to the management of the process, but it is unlikely that CAs will provide their services without remuneration. As well, cryptographic technologies and consulting can be both expensive and time consuming. Just gaining consensus within an industry or interest group will require a significant cost for the effort.

QR See **Quick Response**

Quick Response (QR)   Quick Response is the term applied to the concept of just-in-time inventory management in the retail, generally clothing, industry. As in all JIT applications, QR is getting the right product to the right place at the right time in the right amount. As a result, implementing a QR system requires reengineering the underlying business processes, as well as the technical systems, in order for the process to be effective. The typical order cycle in the past was related to seasonal trends. Winter clothes were ordered and delivered all at once in advance of the coming season, often arriving together in late summer. If one winter was unseasonably warm, and purchases by consumers were down, then the buyer had excess and costly inventory to dispose of. The same was true of fashion goods.

Buyers are highly motivated to change their relationship with suppliers to mitigate this risk while at the same time ensuring that the popular products are continuously replenished and the shelves kept full to meet demand—this is the underlying philosophy of Quick Response supply. Many of the larger retail chains have been active users and advocates of electronic data interchange for years. But QR is not simply an application of an electronic trading relationship. Rather, QR fundamentally changes the way business is conducted and obligations are fulfilled between a buyer and a seller.

As a result, the most important component in a QR program is a friendly, long-term association between the buyer and the seller—to ensure fundamental trust. Because QR emphasizes the seller replacing sold inventory on a continuous and timely basis, the relationship is a critical component in the ongoing success of such a program. The relationship depends on maintaining a significant volume of business between the two parties. With volume, the supplier can gauge demand and replenishment based on actual consumption rather than on traditional seasonal order cycles.

Being able to identify and capture data about the individual product is a critical success factor for QR. All successful programs

Much of Wal-Mart's success in the 1980s was built on its half-billion dollar investment in Quick Response systems. This combination of point-of-sale terminals, scanners, telecommunications links, and computers cut inventory restocking time from the industry average of 6 weeks to 36 hours, a time that Wal-Mart has continued to cut. Kmart spent an estimated $2.4 billion on QR technology and store replenishment in an effort to recapture its number one position. Technology is not enough; Wal-Mart's lead was based on its business logistics processes plus the technology.

Benchmarking Consultants estimates that there is well over $700 billion in goods in the retailing supply pipeline. Experience in supply chain management suggests that this can be halved, resulting in huge savings in the cost of working capital. Wal-Mart and Warner-Lambert, for instance, cut the forecast to production to delivery cycle time from 12 to 6 weeks, using a new extension of Quick Response technology called Collaborative Forecasting and Replenishment (CFAR). In essence, CFAR focuses on using shared information for early forecasting, whereas QR focuses on EDI for ordering and delivery.

depend on accurate bar coding on products in order to eliminate rekeying of data along the deliver chain. Bar coding speeds up the data capture which goes to the supplier's order management system from the retailer's electronic cash register and inventory management system.

Ultimately, all these principles lead to the concept of vendor-managed inventory (VMI), a practice that gives the supplier the total responsibility for product management and replenishment to the buyer's shelf.

One of the newer tools used in QR is Demand Activated Manufacturing Architecture (DAMA). A DAMA system allows a shopper to select a garment, enter a fitting room, and be electronically scanned. The customer also can use an interactive merchandising computer to change the color, buttons, or pockets before placing the final order. The scanned measurements are sent electronically to the manufacturer, who then cuts and sews the product. Within 48 hours, the customer is wearing a custom-made garment.

The four key elements of a QR system approach are:

- Strategic business relationship
- Reengineering the existing process
- Bar coding
- Electronic commerce

One of the most successful users of QR in the retail industry is Wal-Mart. The megamerchandiser's success is often attributed to low prices, but it is in fact the highly refined application of QR that makes Wal-Mart so successful. It is a master in selling the right product at the right place, right time, right amount, and right price. Much of this success is related to the integration of the data flows between its suppliers and Wal-Mart—where the sharing of inventory status and sales data is a prerequisite to the relationship. Allowing a supplier to see its own product's consumption, both individually and in relation to other products, helps the supplier to refine its production and shipping schedules to be in line with the goals of the client. In a sense, Wal-Mart provides shelf space to its suppliers as if on consignment.

Real Estate Applications One of the fastest growing markets for electronic commerce is real estate. EC affords all parties involved in real estate trade an opportunity to make it more efficient. By using EC, banks, mortgage brokers, real estate agents, insurers, and such financing agencies as Fannie Mae (the largest source of home mortgage funds) can reduce the massive paper load and many delays that make a simple process unnecessarily cumbersome and expensive. Fidelity National Financial Inc., a California-based title insurance underwriter, launched its ExpressNet integrated software system, which provides an EDI facility for all parties in a real estate transaction. It integrates all the many subprocesses involved into a single process, that includes appraisal, credit, flood and title insurance, inspection, home warranty, status reports, commitments, closing documents, and policy production.

Fannie Mae began piloting an even more comprehensive system to streamline the mortgage origination process. The goal is to take $1,000 out of the cost of the paper and procedure chain for each mortgage origination. An executive at the government-supported agency commented that this will "create a $6 billion down payment assistance program because the consumer doesn't have to have as much money to go into the process because the origination costs less. . . . You could go to somebody's house and get a full loan decision on whether they qualified. . . . an eligibility and underwriting decision in under 30 minutes." The core of the system is the complex data base that collects all the pieces of the transaction needed by the insurer of the mortgage, plus an artificial intelligence system that scores an applicant's creditworthiness on the basis of prior behaviors. Fannie Mae has provided loan processors and brokers with EDI tools since 1994. Its new system, MortgageLinks, links these separate systems and "suddenly you've got this wealth of information that can be shared for other business transactions. . . . This is about having a secure, authenticated environment [where] multiple trading partners can rely on the data as being authentic."

One early user of the system comments that his company took just three weeks to implement it.

> We've done 138 percent more business this year than last year and we've got only 10 percent more back office staff. . . . For years and years we put together all these cumbersome files. All we really need to know is the value of the property, whether the people have good credit, whether they have the down payments and whether they have the wherewithal in their jobs to pay us back. What Fannie Mae has done [is] they've focused in on all those elements and through their mortgage and credit scoring systems they've been able to take those elements and eliminate a ton of paperwork and the hassle on behalf of the customer. (*EC/EDI Insider,* October 27, 1996)

The industry average for settlement in secondary loan markets is 60 days. With MortgageLinks, this is cut to 30–45 days. The sooner a mortgage company can deliver a loan to the investor, the better the price it can obtain.

An obvious extension of MortgageLinks is to access customers' bank accounts and tax records to verify down payment and income information, instead of requiring copies of tax records and pay stubs, and to handle all payments electronically. The core of the system is just-in-time loan origination, but the evolution is just-in-time processing end-to-end—that is, toward the integration of the entire logistical chain. The payoff is in the process integration, not the technology. The Fannie Mae innovation is typical of the development of electronic commerce. It begins with simple EDI, with either a consortium of industry allies or a power player taking the lead in the standard-setting process. (Fannie Mae coordinated the development of ANSI X12 transaction sets and the software systems.) The savings here are fairly immediate: reduction in paper, fax, FedEx, staff, time, and errors.

RSA Algorithm   The RSA algorithm is named after its creators, Rivest, Shamir, and Adelman, and is a patented technology in the United States. It is sublicensed to Public Key Partners by the Massachusetts Institute of Technology (MIT) and the Board of Trustees of Leland Stanford Junior University (Stanford).

RSA includes a mathematical algorithm to support the implementation of a public key cryptographic system in which each user is assigned a key pair consisting of a private key and a public key.

See also **Public Key Cryptography; RSA Encryption.**

RSA Encryption   RSA is a cryptographic system based on public keys for both encryption and authentication. It was invented in 1977 by Ron Rivest, Adi Shamir, and Leonard Adelman. Advantages of RSA over other public key cryptosystems include the fact that it can be used for both encryption and authentication, and that it has successfully withstood much scrutiny over many years. RSA has received far more attention, study, and actual use than any other public key cryptosystem, and thus RSA has more real-world evidence of its security than more recent systems. RSA Data Security, Inc., the corporate provider of the RSA Algorithm, claims that more than 75 million copies of RSA encryption and authentication technologies are in use worldwide. The number is large because this encryption technology is embedded in Microsoft Windows, Netscape Navigator, Intuit's Quicken, Lotus Notes, as well as hundreds of other, less well-known, products.

Modern encryption and authentication technologies are a critical element in the growth of electronic commerce. Consumers and businesses will both depend on encryption and authentication technologies, such as those developed by RSA, to protect the privacy of purchases, personal medical information, sensitive corporate data, and electronic commerce, including funds trans-

RSA Data Security's Japanese subsidiary made an agreement in mid-1996 with Nippon Telephone and Telegraph, one of the largest telecommunications companies in the world, to sell "superstrong" 1,024-bit public key crypto chip sets. One of RSA's managers comments that the United States has ceded this market to Japanese companies and that it's virtually too late to get it back.

One expert in computer security has had an RSA file security encryption program tattooed along his arm. That makes him contraband according to the U.S. government rules that make the export of strong encryption a felony. He has done this to draw attention to the issue; like the majority of computer professionals working in the field of security, he strongly opposes the rules. So far, no government agency has tried to confiscate his arm, but he has not yet tried to travel on an international flight out of the country.

fers, as they travel through the EC infrastructure of value-added networks and the Internet.

To give any curious reader a sense of how the keys are generated and why they are unbreakable, we provide below a brief review of the RSA procedures. Skip it if you're not interested or if the math makes your eyes glaze over.

In the RSA public key cryptosystem used for securing electronic cash transactions, both encryption and decryption are done by raising the digital representation of a message by a power that is the appropriate key; a simple example would be 321^3, which of course is $321 \times 321 \times 321$ or 33,076,161. Here, the key is 3. Anyone trying to break the code would have no trouble here; after trying 2 and seeing that the data was not an integer number, he or she would then try 3 and decode the key immediately. The larger the key, the harder it is to break. That's why the RSA key is 1,024 bits long. That can represent a number as large as 2^{1024}, a number that won't fit on this page. The cryptosystem doesn't use the result of the exponentiation but divides it by a fixed number and then saves only the result of division before the decimal point, called the modulus. (If you divide 7 by 4, the result is 1.75. The modulus is 1.) The modulus for an RSA key needs to be quite large, usually at least 150 digits.

When a digital signature system is set up, the keymaker software generates two large prime numbers, for example, p and q. A prime number is a number that is not divisible by any other pair of numbers. For example, 2, 3, 5, 7, 9, and 11 are primes, whereas 8, which is divisible by 2 and 4, is not a prime number. The mathematical trick with RSA is to multiply together prime numbers so large that it would take even the fastest computers in the world longer than the world has existed to try out all the combinations of divisors.

The basis of the RSA system is the mathematical theorem that proves that $x^{\wedge(p-1)(q-1)} = 1 \pmod{pq}$. This means that the product of p times q will be the modulus of the exponentiations (provided x is divisible neither by p nor by q, which possibility can safely be ignored by the very fact that they are both prime numbers). Next, the keymaker software chooses two other numbers, e and d, where $ed = 1 \; [\text{mod} \; (p - 1)(q - 1)]$.

The number e becomes the public key and d the private key. Consequently, anything encrypted with d can be decrypted with e, through the theorem that $(x^d)^e = x \; (\text{mod} \; pq)$. The keymaker disseminates the public key e to all users, together with the modulus pq, while of course never revealing p, q, or the private key d.

Amid this mathematical complexity are hidden some of the most contentious issues in electronic commerce. The U.S. federal government has been concerned that keys not be so long that they cannot be broken by the U.S. intelligence agencies' massive computer systems. Accordingly, over a 30-year period, the government first tried to prevent even the publication of their procedures by the three individuals who created and named RSA; then it tried to limit the length of keys that computer hardware and software vendors could use in their products; then banned the exportation of the systems that used the longest keys; then demanded that private keys be placed in an escrow, where law and intelligence agencies could apply through the courts to be given them—the electronic commerce equivalent of a wire tap.

The computer science community has been just as concerned that the cryptosystems that could not be cracked by the most powerful computers of 10 years ago will be a simple problem for the machines of the near future and that the keys must be permitted to get longer and longer. There's also a highly acrimonious debate about freedom of speech and protection of privacy versus the public interest needs, for instance, to prevent organized (and, in this case, well-educated) criminals or, say, pedophile groups on the Internet, from being able to communicate unbreakable ciphered information.

See also **Public Key Cryptography.**

Secure Electronic Transactions (SET) Developed jointly by Visa and MasterCard, the SET protocol is designed to secure credit card transactions over the Internet. As well, both Microsoft and Netscape have participated in the design and development of the protocol and will enable users to use their credit card numbers while making transactions on the Internet with improved security protection. SET is based on the use of the RSA algorithm.

The first fully operational use of SET was by Wells Fargo, a leader in extending traditional banking services to the Internet. Wells Fargo began issuing digital certificates to businesses wishing to collect payments on the Net. Merchants transmit information about a sale to the bank, which uses its own telecommunications network to verify the credit card transaction. It passes back a validation. This is a one-way certification process, in that SET does not yet enable purchasers to authenticate a merchant's identity, only the other way round.

Secure Hypertext Transfer Protocol (S-HTTP)   S-HTTP is a fairly simple means for ensuring that the basic traffic of the Internet can be moved securely. It is somewhat outdated and is being overtaken by more complex and secure schemes and tools. The protocol is really intended for old Internet applications—the Net has grown so fast in size and scope that old here means less than four years. It's not strong enough to be the base for the scale of electronic commerce that most Internet advocates and enthusiasts are aiming for, but it provides a reasonable level of security for messages where privacy is a preference rather than an absolute necessity.

There's nothing really new in the Internet IPO boom and potential bust. Between 1980 and 1994, according to Morgan Stanley, 581 technology companies went public, for a total of

Securities   The first company to go public on the Internet, in early 1996, was Spring Street Brewing, which raised $1.6 million from 3,500 investors, an average of $460 per person. It did not have to pay underwriters' fees or broker commissions. "Small capital" firms have historically found it difficult to persuade underwriters to help them go public, so that the use of the Internet opens up many possibilities. At least six firms were selling services for Independent Public Offerings. The SEC is carefully regulating what they may offer, to protect investors from fraud and their own ignorance.

Wall Street is obviously watching all this with a mixture of interest and fear. For the moment, though, it seems unlikely that the Web will be more than a very minor player. Small capital stocks that add up to just a few million of new equity lack liquidity and are thus hard to trade. An underwriter for a public offering guarantees that all the shares issued will be sold; it absorbs the risk. Even if all the 12,000 firms listed on NASDAQ and which have Web sites were to also trade their stocks via the Internet, the impact on the exchange would be small. Small capital firms amount to around 10 percent of NASDAQ's volumes. But, who knows? As a senior spokesperson for NASDAQ commented, "Anyone who says he knows where this is going is smoking something."

But how do investors tell the real offer from a fake one? There's a famous line by a much convicted bank robber, Willie Sutton. When asked why he chose to rob banks, he replied, "Because that's where the money is." Why would smart crooks rob the Internet?

$240 billion in market capitalization. Of these, 45 percent were trading below their initial IPO price at the end of 1994. Only 3 percent of them were dramatic successes—"ten baggers," in Morgan Stanley's phraseology. Of the top 100 PC-centered firms in 1981, just 17 remained on the list in 1995. Everyone investing in the high-premium, high-risk Internet market is looking for the next Microsoft and Cisco.

Securities Trading on the Internet Close to 30 discount brokerages today offer on-line self-service for buying and selling stocks, and a number of new firms provide stock information and trading facilities. Such firms are already changing the pricing structures of the securities and mutual funds industries and have attracted around 1.5 million customers, up from 600,000 in late 1995. Their pace of growth, albeit from a small base, is illustrated by e*Trade's 17 consecutive quarters of revenue growth, including more than doubling sales between 1995 and 1996. Its fiscal 1996 revenues were 121 percent higher than the previous year's; its customer base grew by 186 percent, to 91,400; but the year ended in a fiscal loss for the firm though, mostly because of its investments in new systems.

The commissions charged by the on-line services are as much as 80 percent below those charged by even the cheapest discount broker. Charles Schwab charges a flat $29.95 for any trade of up to 1,000 shares using its e.Schwab system, but it charges $55 for a telephone order for 100 shares. Apart from the savings in commissions, investors can make trades any time day or night and track their portfolio when and as they wish.

As always in electronic commerce, the main problems are network performance and customer safety. The Internet-based services suffer from the Net's overload at peak times, and the very popularity of on-line trading has led to the providers' processing systems being overloaded. Customers of e*Trade were unable to access their account data for $2\frac{1}{2}$ hours one day in mid-1996, for instance. The services that include telephone access frequently put customers on hold for up to 20 minutes.

The security issue is always a concern for on-line commerce, but to date there have been no reports of hackers breaking into the systems, and the services use the standard and effective tools for encrypting messages. Plenty of reports, though, tell of fraudulent efforts to manipulate investors, through "tips" and touting of small company stocks on Internet newsgroup discussions and on-line services' chat rooms. *U.S. News and World Report* (9 December 1996) describes a few of these scams. In May 1996, thousands of electronic mail messages were sent to on-line investment forums pushing a small firm whose shares were selling at pennies. The price jumped to $2 within a few days and then collapsed, eventually falling to around a cent a share. The Securities and Exchange Commission believes that this was the work of profiteers pushing the price up and dumping their holdings at the right moment. They can exploit the anonymity of electronic mail, where it's also easy to fake names and pretend to be a well-known investment advisory firm, broker, or knowledgeable insider.

In November 1996, the SEC brought its first lawsuit to halt securities manipulation on the Internet. A court order froze the assets of the chairman of a small company as well as those of the operators of an electronic newsletter touting his firm. The SEC claims that the group colluded to drive the price up from 25 cents at the start of 1996 to $4 in June. By the end of 1996, it was down to 20 cents. The case argues that the accused used electronic mail to build the hype and that investors then flooded the Internet with enthusiastic messages, building a bandwagon that soon collapsed. This is very likely to be the classic electronic scam, analogous to Ponzi schemes. As with Ponzi schemes and telemarketing fraud, it will be impossible to prevent them, although it might be possible to police the Internet to warn investors. Policing the Internet is, however, opposed by many proponents of freedom from censorship and government interference. Consequently the Internet remains a vast, open, and almost anarchic resource. The SEC branch chief in charge of investigation for the law suit mentioned earlier succinctly summarizes the danger: "Investors should be wary of biases of people who recommend securities, particularly when they are anonymous." The same combination of opportunities and concerns applies to another fast-growing area of stock selling: the raising of equity capital by small firms over the Internet instead of through venture capitalists and investment bankers. The opportunity is large; small companies are of little if any interest to underwriters, who charge what *The Economist* (23 November 1996) terms "astonishingly rapacious" fees. An offering of $5 million in stock may cost the company making the issue $700,000. One firm spent just $1,200 for a software package that automates the tedious process of compiling an offer document and then sold shares over the World Wide Web. The U.S. government estimates it takes 900 hours of work on average to prepare a share prospectus. The company that sells the software summarizes its views of venture capitalists in its phone number, which is 1-800-VC-GOAWAY. *The Economist* estimated in November 1996 that there were 30 companies in the process of going public via the Web. Fifteen on-line investment banks are offering help in doing so.

Security Security in electronic commerce is often equated with the use of highly technical and sophisticated techniques such as

". . . There is still a low level of awareness, particularly at a senior level, about controlling access into systems. Senior management is often too quick to jump on the bandwagon of new technology without allowing for the problems that come with it," says Chris Hook, an independent security expert. A survey of hackers in Britain found that three-quarters of them believe company safeguards are lax and getting more so. Fifty-five percent regard the growth of the use of Internet technology within firms as increasing their opportunity to hack. Most of the 136 people surveyed hack purely for the challenge, but over half commit some form of sabotage to the systems they break into and a third pass on confidential information they discover. Eighty-five percent have never been caught. (Jonathan

cryptography (encryption) and authentication, digital signatures, and other methods. While cryptographic methods can help secure both systems and transactions, it is more important to understand what needs to be protected, and why—before discussing the how.

Few companies have established clear policies related to the information contained within their systems. More often than not, they employ only simple methods such as password controls and log-on IDs to keep any intruder from directly accessing corporate data. Whether these are adequate or not depends on how much security matters—that is, what would be the impact of theft of data, corruption of data, misuse of data, or sabotage of software on the company and its trading partners?

The most cautious advisers believe that everything needs to be secured and call for high-grade security systems to be used for every matter—from information on products to the procurement of office supplies and from announcements to employees to the most sensitive personnel records. Others see this as mainly corporate paranoia and recommend sensible but not extreme levels of security, equivalent to the degree of security we use to safeguard our homes and cars.

Two very different types of security are required for electronic commerce: security of the contents of messages or transactions and security in the network that carries them. The four basic message security mechanisms—authentication, encryption, certification, and nonrepudiation—are increasingly effective and sophisticated. Most of the telecommunications networks that carry EDI and electronic funds transfer traffic are highly secure. The vulnerable element remains the Internet, for two reasons: (1) its accessibility, which is the essence of its basic design, and (2) the widespread in-depth knowledge of it among the hackers, persons likely to tamper with it just for the sake of the challenge.

Commerce over the Internet demands strong security because the Internet is basically not safe from intrusion and was not designed to be secure. Just about every element of electronic communications now requires security, however. A community of "hackers" and "crackers" skilled in and committed to breaking into systems, not necessarily for criminal purposes, roam the Internet looking for opportunities for malicious mischief. Even a prankster changing the announcement on the CIA's home page to "Criminal Idiocy Agency" shows how easy it would be for nonprankster criminals and saboteurs to find the same opening into that system or any other.

The Internet itself is the central problem. Designed for ease of communication and access, it lacks basic security features that companies have been building into their systems for decades. And even those secured systems are not attack-proof, as the case of a Russian hacker breaking into Citibank's international long-established cash management and electronic funds systems in 1996 showed. More important, the details of the technology of the Internet are well documented and computer scientists well trained in those details. The bad guys and pranksters know where to look to work their way around safeguards.

The telecommunications foundation of the Internet is the TCP/IP protocol developed in the 1970s for rapid and open communication, minimizing checks and controls that impede the flow of traffic. The original specifications did not provide for security; the protocol was used in the networks that became the Internet as a vehicle for collaboration among researchers and technical professionals who at the time had no concerns about protecting information. There remain many ways in which troublemakers can exploit features of the basic design and its limitations. In late 1996, for instance, customers of PANIX, a long-established Internet service provider, were unable to access their electronic mail and World Wide Web sites because a hacker had flooded PANIX's site with a nonstop series of "SYN" signals. These are the TCP/IP wake-up call; "SYN" (for synchronize) begins a message that basically states in computerese that an Internet address wishes to begin transmitting data to this address and is waiting for an "ACK" response (acknowledge). When the ACK

Lamberth, "Why hackers have no fear of security," Computer Weekly, *17 October 1996)*

The Financial Times *(13 December 1996) states that the percentage of U.S. businesses' computer systems that were affected by viruses rose from 6 percent to 14 percent between January and September 1996, with the growth in the linkages to the Internet being the main cause. The estimated cost of protecting against them and repairing the damage they produce is at least $1 billion a year. There are around 8,000 known viruses in circulation.*

signal is received, the flow begins. The SYN messages are received by the server computer in a queue—an electronic in-box—and processed one at a time.

The trick the unknown hacker used to overload the PANIX server was to flood its Web site with messages from nonexistent sites. The server sent back ACK messages to nonexistent addresses, added an entry to the connection queue, and waited for the flow of information to begin, which of course it never did. The connection queue grew longer and longer as the server spent all its time handling the false SYN messages and locked out legitimate users.

Once the attack was located, the Internet technical community raced to provide a "fix" to the specific problem, but the underlying problems remain: an Internet computer cannot immediately tell a genuine message from a fake one and in the words of an Internet expert, "there's always going to be an arms race between better security and hackers" (*Internet and Java Advisor,* January 1997).

There are plenty of skilled hackers roaming the Net. In 1996, one hacked into the Web sites of the U.S. Department of Justice and the CIA and changed their display to "Department of Injustice" and "Criminal Stupidity Agency." A survey carried out by *Information Week* magazine and Ernst and Young, the accounting firm (October 1996) reports that 54 percent of the 1,320 companies participating in the study had experienced losses due to security breaches within the preceding two years. The figure increases to 78 percent when virus attacks are added to the list. Twenty-five percent of the firms stated that in 1996 someone had used the Internet to try to break into their systems.

It isn't just the Internet that is vulnerable to people setting out to do damage. Thirty-two percent of companies reported that the attacks on their systems came from disgruntled employees or ex-employees. One well-known example of this occurred in Bloomberg, the on-line financial news service. A former employee returned to his office, logged on the system, and sent out a message insulting his former boss to all subscribers. Had it been an announcement of, say, a hike in German interest rates, the damage could have been substantial. Some insiders have been able to cause real damage by entering false data in computer systems and "corrupting" files.

There's no need for alarm here. The security risks of both electronic commerce and the more vulnerable Internet can be reduced in the same way as firms protect against financial fraud and break-ins to their physical offices. Companies can't, though, just rely on their network service providers, software vendors, and the Internet technical community for security. They need policies that determine what level of security is essential and what is "good enough" and investment in people, hardware and software, and procedures, and crisis response planning and teams.

But being secure isn't the same as feeling secure. Confidence about its security appears to be the key factor determining whether an on-line service gains customer acceptance. Chase Auto Finance began handling car loan applications entirely electronically in 1996, with around 400 contracts a month. The system uses a "gateway" to the Internet operated by IBM. (A gateway is rather like the metal detector at an airport security checkpoint, which you have to go through to get to the departure gates. For electronic commerce, the checks are for unauthorized intruders and "hackers" intent on mischief, malice, or malfeasance.) Chase charges dealers $700 a month for the service, which cuts the time for application and processing of a loan from days to minutes. It hopes to handle electronically by the end of 1997 between 15 percent and 20 percent of the 100,000 car loan applications it receives monthly, making this a potential $240 million a year business for the bank. But, as a banking consultant comments (*ComputerWorld,* October 21, 1996): "If people are uncomfortable about giving their credit card numbers over the 'net for incidental purchases, it would take another leap of faith to do a $15,000 car loan." The issue here, as so often in electronic commerce, is trust. Is Chase's name and reputation enough to offset the discomfort?

Will people trust an electronic service more than they trust car dealers? Will they trust the car dealer who offers them the link to Chase to get a car loan on the spot?

Security First Network Bank (SFNB)   Security First Network Bank has been bold in visualizing and implementing a secure system that offers banking services over the Internet. It is the first FDIC-insured Internet bank that has no bricks and mortar. Its strategy is to become both a wholesale provider to financial institutions worldwide and a retail provider to end-users.

This vision is backed by a Secure Web platform that allows the creation of financial software applications. This allows any financial institution worldwide to offer its customers the ability to display and transparently manipulate their bank, brokerage, insurance, loan, and other financial products over any device, such as computers, kiosks, interactive television—all connected to a public network such as the Internet or direct dial-up networks. The longer-term vision provides for the same financial institutions to offer and manage electronic bill payments systems supporting electronic commerce, full bill presentment, distributed payroll processing, and other services to corporate clients.

In developing its strategy, SFNB has developed a variety of strategic partnerships with systems integrators, hardware/software providers, Internet service providers, and financial products providers to assemble the necessary elements to deliver this full net worth solution. Some of the financial products providers (back-end processing) include Direct Deposit Accounts processing, bill payment services, credit card services, brokerage processing, insurance offerings, investment research, ATM card systems, and check ordering.

Servers   Servers are the hardware that links users to networks and that also stores information and communication resources. They are basically souped-up personal computers with specialized software and telecommunications features. They handle many general-purpose and special-purpose functions. Internet servers store World Wide Web home pages and store and forward electronic mail messages. File servers store data bases and handle user requests. Communication servers manage the flow of traffic from users to a wide range of networks. Merchant servers provide all the software and telecommunications needed for sellers of goods and services to have a presence on the Internet and other on-line services and to handle security, payments, and catalogs. Mail servers handle the entire process of electronic mail services, including accounting and archiving.

In many ways, servers *are* the network. They are increasingly complex and powerful "middleware" that sit between the community of PCs that access services and the many computers and networks that provide them. Historically, the evolution of computing has been to "distribute" more and more functions from centralized systems like mainframe computers to local area departmental networks and to PCs. The modern version of what used to be called distributed computing is now more generally termed client/server.

The more recent evolution of networked computing has moved from the PC inwards toward centralized and remote resources in contrast to the way distributed computing pushed from the center outwards. In both instances, the service is the core element in the linkage. In the era of the Internet, servers are the key determinant of performance and capabilities, especially in terms of managing the flow of traffic, providing security, and adding application features. In the next wave of innovation, electronic commerce will rely on servers to handle business functions.

SET   See **Secure Electronic Transactions.**

SFNB   See **Security First Network Bank.**

S-HTTP   See **Secure Hypertext Transfer Protocol.**

Simple Mail Transfer Protocol (SMTP)   Simple Mail Transfer Protocol is just that: the basic protocol—set of formats and procedures—for the transfer of electronic mail messages across and between networks. Designed for the Internet, it has been adopted by America Online. SMTP does not provide security features or handle multimedia, such as attaching images to an e-mail message. Those are offered by the follow-on Privacy Enhanced Mail (PEM) and Multimedia Internet Mail Extensions (MIME) standards. Many Internet users' electronic mail systems cannot interpret PEM and MIME messages, but SMTP is universal.

Skipjack   Skipjack is a complex set of algorithms, mathematical procedures, defined by the U.S. National Security Agency (and highly classified) to be included in its controversial Clipper Chip. The Clipper Chip was originally proposed and strongly opposed in the computer science community as the required chip to be used by U.S. firms as the base for encrypting data to be transmitted over telecommunications networks. The government wants to make sure that terrorists and criminals won't be able to make their communications untappable by law enforcement and intelligence agencies who have authorization from the courts. The Clipper Chip is intended as the base for a compromise between the personal and business right to privacy and security and the national interests as seen by the government.

See also **Clipper Chip.**

Small and Medium-Sized Enterprise (SME)   An SME is usually defined as a firm with fewer than 100 employees. It's a term that has crept into the electronic commerce vocabulary to describe what many companies and commentators see as a major growth opportunity: providing software, networks, and services such as EDI translation software, secure payment mechanisms, and access to their larger trading partner's EDI transaction services and information to small firms.

Historically, electronic commerce was almost entirely driven by large companies, and even now around 85 percent of firms cite their primary reason for adopting EC as being the demand of a key customer that they do so or lose its business. Big companies could afford the needed investment in what was then expensive telecommunications networks and computing capabilities, and had the clout, credit, and volumes to access banks' corporate services. They also could and did demand that suppliers adapt to their requirements and systems.

Personal computers, value added networks, and the Internet have opened up just about every area of electronic commerce or any other opportunity to SMEs now. The growth opportunity for providers of EC tools and services is thus also very large; most estimates are that only 150,000 of the more than 2 million firms in the United States are "EDI-enabled."

MacGregor Golf Company's experience with electronic commerce is typical for medium-sized firms. With sales of $40 million a year, MacGregor has been a leader in the golf equipment market for almost a century. Its computer systems were built on mainframes—sales reporting, accounting, customer billing, and so forth. They worked well enough, but did not link to each other. They were inflexible and drove business processes rather than the other way around. For example, inventory and sales information was updated only nightly, leaving sales reps always at least a day behind and having to play catchup after hours. Errors could be difficult to track down and repair. One manager described the situation as one of "information wars" and adds that MacGregor's staff "desperately needed to get out of the paper environment they were stuck in."

Getting out took eight months of development. Cutting over to the new system was fast, requiring just three days. MacGregor bought a general-purpose integrated software package, which a team of its own staff and outside consultants tailored to the company's specific needs and context. The main principle of the system is to capture information just once and update accounting, production, sales, and materials-planning information at the time of entry. The new work flows are triggered by a purchase order being automatically transmitted to the system over an EDI value added network (VAN). It sends back an acknowledgment message to the customer. Errors are automatically reported and tracked. Customers are billed nightly via EDI. Customers can change orders directly.

After two years of use, the benefits are substantial and range across just about every part of MacGregor's operations. As a direct result of the system, according to its MIS supervisor (*EDI World*, September 1996), sales volume has grown 25 percent and inventory costs have been reduced by $3 million. The article adds that MacGregor's relationships with large customers have improved and quotes a customer, who states, "We are seriously considering ending future relationships with vendors who haven't charted a path towards EDI."

MacGregor's movement to an EDI-enabled business is very typical of medium-sized companies in the following ways:

- Its existing computer systems were in the mainstream of business use of mainframe technology but have become more and more of a blockage to responsive service and timely decision making.

- The firm's medium size and relatively narrow range of products, customers, and organizational operations made it practical for the firm to purchase a comprehensive software package. Larger companies can rarely do this. Their systems have to be more customized and take many years of design and implementation.

- The growing availability of VANs meant the firm did not have to make heavy investments in telecommunications.

- The benefits were spread across its entire operation.

- "Power customers" will push a firm toward EDI if it does not move toward EDI on its own.

Cephalon Inc. is typical of medium-sized companies in terms of the disproportionate administrative costs in procurement of such items as office supplies and management of travel expenses. It issues around 7,000 purchase orders and processes about 21,000 vouchers a year. A 1995 analysis of its operations showed that a quarter of these amounted to 97 percent of the total dollar value. That means that 74 percent of the processing was for 3 percent of the dollar amounts. Each transaction cost $10. It cut the cost to $7 for travel and just 10 cents for procurement and also reduced purchase orders by 32 percent and vouchers by 13 percent in just three months, through the use of procurement cards and travel cards. The aim is to cut out the transaction middle man and eliminate low-volume vendors. Work teams and departments are issued a procurement card, with a merchant category code and transaction limits. They can use this seven days a week 24 hours a day. The user is responsible for documenting transactions and his or her supervisor must sign the monthly usage report. The travel card is used in similar ways.

Cephalon's simple innovation uses cards as an authorization mechanism to initiate transactions that previously required submitting a document to a central unit. Responsibility for verifying usage is similarly handled locally. The cards are specialized credit cards, with software ensuring that they are used only for specific types of transaction and within specified spending limits. They reflect the Reagan maxim for arms control: "Trust but verify." Users are trusted to make their own decisions.

Big companies' electronic commerce can create indirect benefits for SMEs. One of the most far-reaching impacts of the World Wide Web on EC has been for large firms to offer something to their small suppliers. Now, more and more larger firms make it easy for even the smallest customer or supplier to link to them over the Web and do business with them. They provide them with timely information and also attract nonsuppliers and noncustomers to look them up and become part of their supply chain.

Boeing's ongoing electronic commerce developments illustrate this. In late October 1996, it launched a Web site that gives its customer airlines fast access to information and electronic commerce transactions for over 410,000 different types of spare parts. It makes over 1 million shipments a year to its customers, which include 600 airlines. Prior to Boeing implementing the site, only its largest customers had access to its complex mainframe computer systems, via "private" leased-line telecommunications networks. They could make purchases via EDI. The others had to use mail, fax, and phone. That meant that Boeing had to key their orders into its systems manually, transcribing the customer's message into the EDI formats Boeing used to link its seven distribution centers worldwide. Boeing would then flood the customer with paper, such as order acknowledgments, shipping schedules, and airbills, whether or not the customer wanted the information. Now, customers simply fill in an electronic form on the Web site and state what information they want downloaded to them.

Not surprisingly, customer response has been highly enthusiastic. The only laggards have been those in the parts of the world where Internet access is either expensive, controlled, or badly limited by poor telecommunications.

Smart Card   A smart card is a credit-card-sized plastic card with a computer chip embedded in it. There are a number of different standards that determine where the chip is located on the card, the data size and storage methodology on the chip, and the way in which the chip can be loaded and unloaded with data—but they all have the common attribute of being capable of storing data and allowing it to be retrieved by a separate reader device. There have even been attempts to integrate the card with a built-in calculator and a magnetic strip. The result would be a "super card," usable by virtually anyone in almost any situation where identification and service entitlement are an issue.

Smart cards are widely used in France, where they have cut credit card and ATM fraud from 3 percent of all transactions to 1 percent.

The application of smart cards in business has been somewhat disjointed and unfocused since the cards came into commercial use in the late 1970s. The most prevalent and recognized early applications for smart cards were for applications of identification and security—often involving financial or telecommunications uses.

Other users have been healthcare organizations, which store personal information related to drug and pharmaceutical product usage—shared with doctors and healthcare providers—so that a portable record can be used by a patient. This is seen as an important development in the area of healthcare management and has the potential to reduce misapplication of drugs, as well as the reduction of insurance fraud.

Finally, there is the application of smart card technology in the concept called "stored-value" cards. This application has the highest probability for continuing use and success of the application of smart card technology in the near term.

The estimated number of smart cards in use around the world in 1994, the last for which reliable large-scale survey data is available, is 420 million. The breakdown of usage is: phone cards 70%, healthcare cards 19%, bank and supermarket loyalty cards 7%, pay TV 2%, use with cellular phones 2%, and access control to vending machines 1%. By far the largest penetration is in France, where there are 23 million cards in use, mostly for ATMs and debit transactions. They cost about 10 times as much to make as a credit card but can store 80 times as much information, and information also can be updated and added to, not just read from, the card.

In Belgium and the Netherlands, most adults have a Proton card that is used for small purchases and for paying parking meters. In Germany, there are close to 100 million cards used for managing health care information. Even so, the smart card remains a small part of payments systems and peoples' everyday lives. Logically, the smart card is an excellent complement to credit cards and is more secure than the card with a magnetic strip. Logically, it will be the base for very small payments called "microtransactions." And logically it is a base for digital cash.

SME See **Small and Medium-Sized Enterprise.**

SMTP See **Simple Mail Transfer Protocol.**

Society for Worldwide Interbank Financial Telecommunications (SWIFT) The Society for Worldwide Interbank Financial Telecommunications (SWIFT) was formed in Belgium in 1973 to provide banks with a global electronic messaging network and to facilitate the transfer of payment information between correspondent banks. The owners of SWIFT include over 2,000 banks and approved categories of financial institutions. SWIFT conveys financial messages between approximately 3,600 financial institutions in 88 countries. This concept, in its delivery, addressed the very issues that are currently envisaged in the application of Financial EDI.

In the early 1990s, there was a growing awareness in the international banking community that EDI and electronic commerce, particularly if based on EDIFACT standards and combined with a range of different telecommunications services, would be the basis for payments in the future. SWIFT took the initiative to identify the range of requirements for making payments with the intent of discovering the next generation of services that they would be developing. The discovery was that it was not simply a message-carrying capability that was inherent in the EDI process, but a complete rethinking of the business process and involvement banks using electronic technology would have.

The challenge posed by EDI to payments systems is greater than the challenge to any other type of data exchange. Although a substantial number of international payments are handled electronically, often using the SWIFT network and related clearing systems (CHAPS or CHIPS), the proprietary standards that these various systems use are deeply entrenched—both in the internal systems operated by banks and in their corporate customers.

Another factor was the realization that payments differ from most other EDI projects that had been undertaken. Clearly, EDI payments cross industries and cross borders. The design of financial transactions must satisfy the business needs of all sectors, both because payments need to operate across sectors and because the banking systems could not afford to support a multitude of different payments systems. Additionally, payments differ from other data exchanged in their security needs. Payments are generally perceived as requiring a greater level of security and systems reliability than other types of EDI.

Finally, there is the involvement of regulatory and government authorities. Because monetary policy is the keystone to modern economic planning, most payments systems are widely considered a utility that must be open to a larger community.

Sterling Commerce   The leader in electronic commerce software and network service is Sterling Commerce. It has around 17,000 business customers, and its electronic payment software, Verity, is used by 99 of the 100 largest U.S. banks. Sterling's 1991 sales were $71 million, with profits of over $8 million. The estimated figures for 1996 were $240 million in revenues and $53 million in profits. The firm has over 1,000 employees.

Store and Forward   Store and forward electronic communication allows a message to be sent at any time without regard to when the intended receiver will pick it up (i.e., read it off the computer screen). Rather than being delivered immediately, the message is stored until the intended recipient logs on to the relevant service. The main example of store and forward is electronic mail, which makes use of electronic "post office boxes," where you pick up your e-mail when and where you wish. This is in contrast to the transmission of fax messages over the phone; these are delivered immediately to the intended recipient's fax number, even if the intended recipient is not there to pick it up.

Many elements of electronic commerce use store and forward, which is by far the lowest cost way to handle the communication of occasional and intermittent messages from many originating points to many receiving points. For example, the U.S. Automated Clearing House system does not process corporate payments in real time—that is, it does not process them like faxes—but stores them and forwards them to the bank that they are addressed to at a prespecified time. That fits into the banks' end-of-day processing cycle. There's no point in adding the extra network capacity and complexity required for guaranteed real-time processing if the messages will simply be left sitting around until the end of the day. The same logic applies to many applications of EDI.

For some electronic commerce applications, though, transactions must be more carefully synchronized. Credit card purchases over the Internet, for instance, require that the authorization message be processed immediately; the *payment* request from the merchant to the purchaser's bank, however, could be stored and forwarded. Foreign exchange trades, high-value funds transfers, car manufacturer's tracking of inventory movements, and retailers' point-of-sales reports on each store's selling patterns more and more require direct transmission of messages, either in real time or at specified time intervals.

The technical community is positioning for real-time electronic commerce as the norm within a few years. Many of the banking systems that handle financial EDI and the value added networks that process EDI transactions for an industry or group of trading partners were built to handle relatively low volumes of traffic, with store and forward the most cost-effective option. The business network designs of today will not be able to handle the expected traffic of tomorrow. The frequent long and irritating delays that are now so commonplace on the Internet show how easily rapid increases in message flow can overload a network; as fast as the Internet is upgraded, traffic increases to soak up the extra capacity. In a network that is overloaded at peak times of day, store and forward eases the burden; the message can be processed later.

From the perspective of the business manager who wants to know only as much as he or she needs to know about electricity—that is, show me where the wall plug is and tell me if I need a voltage adapter (for international use)—the only questions about telecommunications to keep in mind and to ask technical planners to answer are (1) "What happens to network performance in terms of business performance—cost, reliability, and delays—if traffic becomes suddenly much heavier?" and (2) "If we're using store and forward today, should we still be using it two years from now?" The answers may trigger a need for an in-depth formal review of the business assumptions that must drive network planning.

Stored-Value Card   Employing a chip or "smart" card technology, a stored-value card is a specific application of the smart card concept. Data loaded onto the card is a specific value to be withdrawn at a later date. This is referred to as a "prepaid" card.

Stored-value cards are of two types: disposable or renewable. The disposable type of card is preloaded with a specific value and purchased as a stand-alone product. Many telephone companies have chosen to use the disposable stored-value card concept for prepaid telephone calls.

The renewable card requires the use of both a loading device and a personal security number or code. The Mondex system is one example of this approach where an individual can increase the value held in the card either by interacting with a commercial organization such as a bank or by means of a personal exchange method, using a small, portable device to accommodate the transfer.

In either case, if the card is lost or misplaced, the value is lost. In this way, the stored-value card is analogous to cash.

See also **Mondex; Smart Card.**

The European Commission proposes to ban the use of e-cash generated on the Internet by private parties. The U.S. Federal Reserve Bank is considering requiring companies who issue stored-value cards to register their activities with it and maintain reserves—in "real" money—to cover the value of the cards. (Martin Mayer, The Bankers, *1997, 43)*

Successes in Internet Electronic Commerce

There are few proven successes in electronic commerce on the Internet and the same small set of examples get written up and cited again and again. They include Virtual Vineyards and Amazon Books. So rather than detailing these cases, we highlight some managerial messages from the experiences of these two startup firms. Note that even though they are "successful," they still weren't making money at the start of 1997. One of the myths of Internet commerce is that because it's so cheap to create a home page or Web site on the World Wide Web that offers information and goods, it's easy to build a business on the Internet. It isn't.

The founder of Virtual Vineyards, Robert Olson, had a very clear business model for choosing the target for his startup company, which is now one of the most widely cited success stories about electronic commerce on the World Wide Web:

> The first thing is that information had to be crucial to the sale. I believe that most people on the Web today are information professionals. They're trained to be highly analytic, they like to make considered choices. The second thing is that it had to be a business that could hold its margins. . . . Also, whatever you're selling has to have a distribution problem, so you're not competing with Safeway. (Lynch and Lundquist, *Digital Money*, p. 135)

Wine fitted the description well. The most expensive wines are not stocked by large retailers. Small wineries may produce only 5,000 cases of a particular wine—100 cases per state, and therefore, carrying these wines is "not worth [a retailer's] time or their shelf space."

Olson adds:

> Most people think of the Internet as a low-cost option. In fact, it's a high-cost option. By the time we're cash-positive, we'll go through 1.5 to 2 million dollars. People going into this area today need to figure out how to leverage the characteristics of the medium to get (1) volume *and* (2) premium prices. It's possible to do the Internet inexpensively, but it usually looks it. To get a quality product, you have to spend the money. In the future that may change, since there will probably be a lot of off-the-shelf solutions, which will cut down the labor costs. But your personality always shows through. (*Digital Money*, p. 136)

The premise of the service that Olson's business, Virtual Vineyards, offers is that wine consumers need not have to choose between quality and price if they have expert advice. In the "discretionary" model that Virtual Vineyards represents, the seller is responsible for the choice you make, as an adviser and expert. One of the keys to Virtual Vineyard's success is that customers can access the company's expertise interactively. Olson's brother, Peter, provides spoken recommendations on the Web site and customers leave their comments about the wines they've bought. Virtual Vineyards seems to have been one of the earliest firms to recognize that success in electronic commerce on the Internet would require interaction, not passive electronic billboards or hyperactive multimedia.

Virtual Vineyards is one of the most successful and most widely publicized Internet electronic commerce companies. As such, it's one of the few Internet ventures where reliable estimates can be made about the costs and revenues needed for other startup firms to succeed. Virtual Vineyards spends about $80,000 per month on its Internet operation. Its goal is to maintain a 30 percent margin, so that it must generate around $250,000 per month, or $3 million per year to break even. Its founder stresses the need for high-speed telecommunications lines: "It's important to be snappy if you want repeat traffic, much more than being beautiful." The service uses the T1 communications link that has for decades been a standard for larger companies' data communications networks. This link is 50 to 100 times faster than the PC plus phone line connections its customers use in accessing it.

One of the most watched businesses whose commerce is entirely through the Internet is Amazon Books, another leading model for Internet EC startup companies. Founded in 1994 and operating literally out of a garage, it went on-line a year later, after the needed software had been designed and implemented by its five employees. It now employs 120 staff, including editors, marketers, and programmers. *Business Week* estimated its annualized 1996 sales rate as $17 million in late 1996. Amazon is attractive to book buyers because of both its convenience, its listing of around 1 million of the 1.5 million books in print, and its many interactive options, including automatic updates by e-mail about new books by specified authors or in specified categories. (Barnes and Noble's book superstores stock under 200,000 titles.)

Amazon may well have more impact on book publishers than

book buyers. Books are a weird business in that publishers must ship physical goods to stores, which must have far more stock on the shelf than they will ever sell; the publisher has to pay for the unsold items, which are returned to them by the store. Returns can amount to 50 percent of the printed edition of a book. It's an astonishingly inefficient and expensive process, but publishers have had no other choice. Amazon gives them a new option. First, it stocks in its warehouse only its own list of approximately 200 current best-sellers, so that publishers do not have *any* returns to pay for and none of the buffer inventories of the two to five copies of a slow-selling book that clutter the shelves of physical stores. Amazon orders everything else as a confirmed customer purchase. In addition, it presells forthcoming books via e-mail to its customers and provides publishers with advance information on demand for them. It welcomes links from other Web sites, magazines, and societies, paying them 8 percent of every sale they generate. An executive of Amazon comments: "We may not know what the best book on model rocketry or Labrador retrievers is, but there's already a Website out there run by a passionate person who does." (*The New Yorker,* 23 December 1996)

SWIFT   See **Society for Worldwide Interbank Financial Telecommunications.**

Trading Partner Agreement   A trading partner agreement is a formal contract between organizations that wish to use EDI in their business relationship. TPAs reflect the lack of clarity about the applicability to electronic trade of rules and laws that were designed in the age of documents. The question is whether existing contract law, rules of evidence, issues of liability, and the like will be applicable to the coming era of electronic messages. The American Banking Association, U.S. Defense Department, industry associations, and comparable organizations in other countries have defined model TPAs.

Developers of electronic commerce programs need to address

a number of key elements to ensure that appropriate controls are in place. Trading partner agreements are often viewed as a solution for preventing disagreements and misunderstandings between trading partners. But because each of many elements has to be reviewed, the number of discussions about individualized agreements could become unmanageably large if an organization has a lot of trading partners. Given that large corporations as well as governments tend to force their contracts and terms on smaller organizations, questions also arise about the value of preparing such an agreement in the first place.

What seems to be of value in negotiating agreements is redefining certain terms within existing agreements or contracts. Essentially, this means changing the face of traditional agreements to identify and accept that commerce may be done in an electronic fashion as well as on a paper basis, where applicable—and that both parties accept that fact as a valid process. Some key elements are as follows:

- *A statement of intent.* Trading partners outline their intentions to do business electronically and state that their EDI transactions shall not be held invalid or unenforceable.

- *Clarification of liability.* If third-party service providers are involved, such as VANs, the agreement needs to state some provision for the apportionment of liability and costs between the trading partners for the services the third parties will provide. This can simplify matters in the event of loss.

- *Security.* One purpose of security procedures is to improve or to ensure the ultimate reliability of electronic contracts. U.S. legislation, Uniform Commercial Code 4(a), states that "commercially reasonable" levels of security are necessary in the application of EDI in a financial transaction to ensure that the corporate consumer is protected.

*Here are some extracts
from a research paper on
collaborative electronic
commerce projects that
surveyed many
companies' experiences:
"Trust rather than
contracts" . . . "clan
relationships of trust and
honor" . . . "confidence
and mutual trust that
participants will abide
by the intention of
agreements" . . .
"representatives of an
insurance and a
financial services
organization and a
services provider shook
hands to seal the
alliance—a decision
based on mutual trust
and support by one
another's organizations'
cultures. The chief
executive fully supported
the alliance and made it
clear that management
would not put up with*

- *Signatures.* As was the case with the PIN in the ATM example, organizations should adopt symbol(s) or code(s) as their signatures. This could be in the form of a Message Authentication Code (MAC) or other means of corroboration of the identity of the transaction, such as digital signature. If this is combined with appropriate security procedures, a MAC can provide an electronic substitute for conventional signatures.

- *Receipt.* A message receipt can occur when:
  - the transaction arrives at the recipient's mailbox
  - a message arrives at a VAN or third-party mailbox;
  - the message arrives at the recipient's computer system; or
  - after the recipient communicates a valid acknowledgment to the originator.

  Some agreements also consider time limits by which trading partners must have checked their electronic mailboxes and responded—either negatively or positively—to the status of a transaction.

- *Confidentiality.* Trading partners should review their anticipated data exchanges and decide whether they should be considered confidential. Even though many business transactions may not be considered confidential in the world of traditional paper documents, the power of computers to integrate data and make it available in more accessible and intelligent forms may be a key factor in reevaluating the value and impact of data exchanges.

- *Arbitration.* A clause on arbitration should require that an EDI legal expert hear any dispute.

- *Miscellaneous.* Additional necessities include an agreed-upon attachment or list of the transaction standards; implementation guidelines; approved third-party service providers; and allocation of costs and efforts.

Finally, there is the matter of common sense. The partners in any business relationship must share a desire to build and sustain the relationship and to try and resolve problems and disputes amicably. Sellers tend not to sue or litigate against their clients. It just isn't good business practice. At the same time most reasonable buyers prefer to avoid doing business with difficult or litigious suppliers, and the market is usually too competitive to support nonconforming organizations. With electronic commerce, the key to success is cooperation.

There is no simple solution to the legal question, and no definitive laws governing electronic commerce. In the event of a dispute, trading partners can attach each party's terms and conditions covering the underlying business transaction to the TPA and allow the law to determine which of the attached terms and conditions pertains. Or, they can do nothing and leave these matters for the courts or arbitrators to resolve.

Although EDI doesn't have a legal track record yet, clearly the fact that it has been around for over two decades with no recorded dispute questioning its validity speaks strongly for its future. The absence of major court cases establishing precedent and the paucity of formal statute law are evidence that the technology and applications of EDI do work and have been gaining acceptance in the general market.

roadblocks to new developments." (Swatman et al., ed., Electronic Commerce for Trade Efficiency and Effectiveness, *1996) This type of relationship is very hard to build and sustain but appears to be one of the single most important factors for the success of business-to-business electronic commerce.*

Transaction Set A transaction set is the term used for an EDI document, as defined in the ANSI X12 language or standard. The term *message* is the same thing, as defined in the EDIFACT Standard. A transaction set is composed of data segments, which are themselves composed of data elements. Think of the transaction set as a document or paragraph commonly used in business, such as a purchase order or an invoice. A data segment is the same as

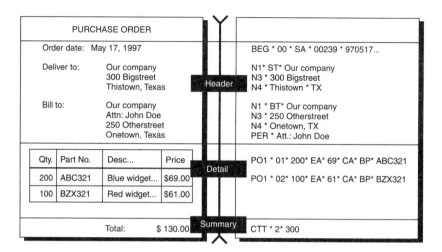

Figure 12

a line of data in a document or a sentence in a paragraph. A data element is the same as a word or a term. There is a common data element dictionary for both the EDIFACT standard and the ANSI standard; however, segments and transaction sets/messages are constructed differently.

Figure 12 shows a purchase order represented as an ANSI X12.850 transaction set. You can see the correlation between the physical data and the structure of the electronic message.

UCC See **Uniform Commercial Code.**

UCS See **Uniform Communication Standard.**

UNCID See **Uniform Rules of Conduct for Interchange of Trade Data by Teletransmission.**

Uniform Commercial Code (UCC) The UCC is a uniform statute that may be adopted in whole or in part by each State legislature in the United States. The Code focuses on specific fields of commerce, such as the sale of goods rather than services.

It has, however, been viewed as a reference to the application of electronic commerce and articles are being written in the code to deal with electronic commerce. For instance, the article on electronic banking, UCC 4(a), states that a bank must offer "commercially reasonable" levels of security for electronic payments—specifically EDI payments. Otherwise, the liability for the payment's completion (or lack thereof) rests with the bank. This has had the effect of increasing the care and caution that financial institutions place on such transactions.

Uniform Communication Standard (UCS) This is an EDI message structure standard, primarily used in the grocery industry in the United States and Canada. Much of the functionality of the UCS Standard has migrated to the ANSI X12 standard; however there is still significant use of the transaction sets in the industry, particularly in purchasing.

Uniform Rules of Conduct for Interchange of Trade Data by Teletransmission (UNCID) These rules were developed by the International Chamber of Commerce to provide guidelines for international EDI. They are less widely used in the United States than in other countries that have well-established EDI capabilities. A distinctive feature of UNCID is its recognition that to meet the existing legal rules about the enforceability of sales contracts, EDI systems must provide a complete historical record of all the trade data interchanged. A trade data log is the equivalent of the paper records that courts, regulators, and auditors require. It's still very unclear where electronic EDI records fit into existing laws and rules. UNCID aims at providing a general code of practice for EDI. It includes definitions of terms to reduce ambiguity and misunderstanding, identifies acceptable EDI standards, specifies the responsibilities of each party in ensuring accuracy and privacy of information, and defines procedures for acknowledging and confirming messages. UNCID also addresses issues of protection of trade data, including encryption, storage of data, and interpretation of its rules.

VAB See **Value Added Bank.**

Value Added Bank (VAB) One phenomenon arising from the electronic commerce revolution is the value added bank (VAB). A VAB is a financial institution that has decided to offer a variety of nonfinancial services, effectively competing with a VAN. These services may include communications, software, connectivity, and transactional processing support, along with the traditional payment processing and electronic cash management services usually associated with banks. A VAB seeks to solidify its relationship with a customer by providing a series of value added services, to make the transition to the use of EDI and electronic commerce easier.

Banks are skilled at handling messages but less so in carrying out business transactions. EDI reduces payment messages. One bank reports—with alarm— that its EDI-smart customers generate just one payment transaction for 133 business transactions. Over time, banks can either lose volume or add value to customer logistics. It's their own choice.

Not all the products and services that the VAB provides are owned by or developed by the bank. In many cases, the bank provides a reselling or referral service to a business partner or associate. By providing this breadth of service, the bank seeks to retain and expand the client relationship beyond the normal "bank-only" competition's capability. As well, by selling and servicing existing clients, the VAB has the ability to increase sales per client without the effort needed to obtain new clients. And the bank can add additional transactions to its already significant processing might, keeping the actual cost per transaction down to an extremely competitive rate.

Value Added Network (VAN) The term value added network originated as a legal term designating telecommunications services that added some special value over and above basic transmission, which was the legal monopoly of the phone company in every country of the world and still is in many instances. Companies could get licenses to operate only if they could show that their services added some sort of value, such as transactions, electronic mail, message formatting, or security, hence the name value added network. Most of these services were for EDI, offering groups of trading partners or companies within an industry a vehicle to share resources, costs, and expertise. Today, VAN and EDI are almost synonymous.

Many companies now provide facilities for the transfer and management of electronic messages between trading partners, acting as a public data network. A value added network provides not only the message transfer capability but also a number of services to assist the trading parties in managing their data. Most VANs provide communications and mailbox facilities as their basic services. They also may provide a measure of security or control by ensuring that passwords and log-on ID's are correctly used. Some networks allow the movement of encrypted or authenticated data as well.

Beyond the basic levels of service, EDI-specific VANs provide a number of additional services which enable businesses to maintain their EDI programs, such as:

- Translation software
- Network interconnection
- Trading partner profiling
- Supplemental communications support and network monitoring
- Education

To some extent, the Internet is a very low-cost substitution for VANs, and as such there's the strong possibility of VAN growth eroding. However, VANs retain the advantage of high customer loyalty, mainly because of their proven reliability, industry-specific expertise, consulting and support, and security.

Some of the larger VANs are provided by GE Information Services, IBM, AT&T, MCI, and Sterling Commerce. Other, more market-focused VANs serve specific industry groups and excel in their respective niches. These include Kleinschmidt, RailLinc, SNS, and others.

IVANS, whose name stands for Insurance Value Added Network Service, is one of the most successful and well-established VANs. The company describes itself as a unified insurance industry pathway, used by over 500 firms with a million workstations in property, casualty, life, and health insurance. It is used by agents, brokers, managed-care organizations, industry groups, financial service firms, government agencies, and suppliers of services to the insurance industry. It was founded in 1983 to address the complexity of providing telecommunications links among such varied parties, by sharing the costs of technical development, providing economies of scale, and eliminating the many problems caused by organizations having different and "incompatible" systems using "proprietary" communication methods. IVANS is able to provide discounts of 25 percent to 50 percent on the costs of telecommunications, largely because of its giant buying power. In addition, it can hedge technical risk for participants; the cost for this center of expertise to monitor, pilot, and implement new technology is obviously far lower than for even a fraction of its members to do so by themselves.

The basic concept of a VAN is that it is a hub—a term widely used in the trade—into which many pathways link. It is a gateway—another common term—to other networks. For example, IVANS links to the worldwide Brussels-based Reinsurance and Insurance Network (RINET), the London Insurance Market's LIMNET, and others. When IVANS implements a new EDI transaction set, such as the sets for First Report of Injury and Subsequent Reports for Workers Compensation Claims and for Glass Repair and Auto Collision Repair, participants do not have to make any change to their own systems.

VAN   See **Value Added Network.**

Vendor-Managed Inventory (VMI)   As a part of many of the schemes for just-in-time (JIT) production, the approach known as vendor-managed inventory is seen as the final step in efficient management of inventory logistics in the buyer/supplier relationship. In a VMI program, the supplier takes on the responsibility of keeping the buyer, in many cases a retail store operation, stocked with the goods the supplier sells. This means that a highly trusting relationship has been established between the two parties and is paramount to the ongoing success of the program.

VMI has two main features: (1) open and easily accessible status of the seller's inventory and (2) active monitoring and re-supply of material as it is depleted from the buyer's store shelves. Successful VMI relationships tend to be for items that are turned over in high enough volume to justify the supplier's effort and to produce measurable benefits to both parties.

The mechanics of a VMI system mandate that the supplier make an inquiry into the buyer's inventory data base daily. The accuracy of the inventory status at the retail level is managed by the capture of the data at the point of sale using bar coding and scanning technology. Without bar coding and scanning, the ac-curacy and speed of data capture can become cumbersome, even impossible. Throughout the day, the retailer updates the inven-tory data base and makes this data accessible to the vendor on demand. In many VMI applications, the entire data base is made available to the supplier, who is expected to scan the stocks and deduce the replenishment needed in its particular product.

Products are replenished by either a previously established set of parameters based on consumption, or at seasonally adjusted levels, based on the supplier's best estimates for sales. Excess or unpurchased products are usually shipped back to the supplier at no penalty to the buyer—creating a motivation to not overstock the shelves. At the same time, most VMI arrangements allow the supplier only a few stock outages, and apply severe penalties for nonperformance, the most severe being the loss of the client.

The goal of VMI is to remove the unnecessary and unproduc-tive steps of the buyer having to order on a frequent and recur-ring basis products that are going to be purchased on an ongoing and regular basis. The key variable is managing the volume and speed of replenishment. It is important to note that not all sup-pliers, or products, are suitable for VMI applications and not all should be considered as likely candidates.

Somerfield, a chain of stores in the intensely competitive and highly efficient U.K. supermarket industry, cut its inventory levels of individual goods by up to 25 percent through vendor-managed inventory in just two years. Somerfield provides its suppliers access to its sales data and the suppliers replenish stocks with no purchase orders from the supermarket. In effect, they become an extension of Somerfield's stock control and warehouse systems.

Vendor-managed inventory represents an entirely new style of supplier relationship, with two central components: mutual trust and first-rate technology. Trust removes procedures that slow down the continuous replenishment of stock. Why bother to issue a purchase order and get authorization? Keep the shelves full and we'll handle the paperwork later. Technology puts the supplier, in effect, in the store.

From a technical standpoint, a number of areas need to be considered:

- *Accuracy of the inventory data base.* At point of sale there must be an automated and accurate system to update inventory status. Inventory status depends on information recorded by the point-of-sale terminal (the cash register). This means that not only is the data replaced from bar coded and scanned products, but the linkage between the electronic cash register (ECR) and the data base should be updated throughout the day. This frequency is every two hours in some cases where consumption statistics during the day affect merchandising and stock replenishment.

- *Frequency and parameters of replenishment.* The VMI supplier needs to know the buyer's expectation of delivery of replacement goods. A key issue relates to ensuring the expected consumption and replenishment cycle activities are met. A greater issue concerns adjusting inventory according to seasonal variances or changing market conditions.

VMI See **Vendor-Managed Inventory.**

Warehouse Industry Network Standards (WINS) This is an EDI standard for the warehousing industry developed by the International Association of Refrigerated Warehouses and the American Warehouseman's Association. Although this standard is still used in the industry, much of its focus and functionality have been incorporated in the ANSI X12 standard, which has greater cross-industry functionality.

WEDI See **Working Group on [Health care] EDI.**

WINS See **Warehouse Industry Network Standards.**

Working Group on [Health care] EDI (WEDI) The Working Group on EDI (WEDI) was established jointly by the American Hospital Association (AHA) and the American Medical Association (AMA) and focuses on providing a framework and forum for addressing the business needs and the standards issues in the health care industry.

X12 Standards X12 is the comprehensive master framework for EDI standards in the United States discussed in detail in the entry for ANSI X12 in this Guide. There are many individual X12 standards, and their number grows annually. Here are some of the most widely used:

- X12.810. Invoice
- X12.811. Consolidated service invoice
- X12.820. Payment order/remittance advice
- X12.823. Lockbox
- X12.835. Health care claim payment/advice
- X12.850. Purchase order
- X12.855. PO Acknowledgment
- X12.856. Shipping notice/manifest
- X12.5. Interchange control structure. This standard defines the "envelope"—the message header and trailer—for interchanging an electronic message plus a structure for acknowledging receipt and processing of the envelope.

X.400 and X.500 X.400 is an international standard, created by the telecommunications agencies' CCITT association in cooperation with the International Standards Organization (ISO). X400 was expected to become the base for electronic messaging. It provides a comprehensive definition of the formats and procedures to transmit and receive electronic mail, EDI, and related documents. Up through the early 1990s, international telecommunications and EDI standards were largely defined by committees such as CCITT and ISO. It took years, even decades, to define, negotiate, and implement standards. One standard, the Open Systems Interconnection (OSI) was widely expected to overtake IBM's telecommunications protocols, then the dominant protocols in use.

Now OSI is rarely mentioned. Deregulation of telecommunications, market competition, the accelerating pace of change in technology, and the rise of the Internet have all made the cumbersome industry committee approach less and less practical or helpful. In the EDI world, few trading partners have connected using X.400 because of the cost, complexity, and overall lag in development of the standard. X.400 is actually a series of recommendations for message-handling systems, such as e-mail. It allows e-mail users to interchange mail between any mailboxes on any X.400-compatible network. With the emergence of the TCP/IP protocol for Internet applications, the long-term future of substantial use of X.400 is rather doubtful. This is even further accentuated by the emergence of intranets, the internal use within organizations of the TCP/IP protocol to facilitate privately accessible networks using the World Wide Web and Web browsers. X.400, while considered to be a technically superior methodology, is seen as cumbersome and expensive for this approach and purpose.

X.435 is a related international standard for sending EDI over X.400. Again, like X.400, this is primarily a communications layer issue and does not resolve the fundamental issues of application integration, trading partner agreements, and relationship development. X.435 provides a message envelope and tracking specifically designed for the highly structured nature of EDI transactions, so that the transaction can be more effectively tracked and managed as it passes along multiple value added networks through different telecommunications environments.

X.500 is a technical telecommunications standard for communicating across international networks. It was designed to meet the needs of European nations to link their networks for transmission of electronic messages. The equivalent of an ordinary telephone book in electronic data base format, the X.500 standard is typically employed by users of X.400 electronic message services. The X.500 standard was seen as a commercial, electronic "yellow pages" and would allow an EDI user to simply "look up" the addressing details of a trading partner in order to send an EDI business transaction. The reality is that few trading organizations would fulfill a purchase order or any other type of business document from a complete stranger, totally defeating this aspect of the X.500 approach. X.500 is still important to the operation of telecommunications agencies' data communications networks.

Index

Foundation term is indicated by boldface italic type.
Page number of primary glossary entry is indicated by boldface type.

About the Authors

Peter G.W. Keen is the author of sixteen books on the link between information technology and business strategy, an international adviser to top managers, named by *Information Week* as one of the top ten consultants in the world, and a professor who has held positions at leading U.S. and European universities, including Harvard, Stanford, MIT, and Stockholm University. Companies with which Keen has worked on an on-going, long-term basis include British Airways, Citibank, MCI Communications, Sweden Post, Cemex (Mexico), The Royal Bank of Canada, CTC (Chile), Unilever, and many others. All of his work focuses on bridging the worlds, cultures, and language of business and information technology.

Craigg Ballance is a globally recognized expert in the area of electronic commerce and financial EDI. During his twenty years with Royal Bank of Canada, he managed numerous progressive electronic product introductions, including the implementation of the bank's automated teller machine network (one of the largest in the world), and was largely responsible for the development of their EDI program. Ballance's work at Royal Bank culminated in the connection of their network to the PLUS System and Interac Networks in the mid 1980s.

Ballance was also the primary force in founding and chairing INTER*EDI, the creative force of financial EDI in Canada, and he has been a major contributor in the development of EDI and electronic payment systems in the United States. He is a member of the Bankers EDI Council of the National Automated Clearing House Association (NACHA), and was on the Chairing the Cross Border Payments Council from its inception in 1993 through 1995.

Ballance provides consulting and educational services to numerous corporations and financial institutions around the world, and is vice president and senior partner of Stratsys Consulting Services in Toronto, Canada.